4-27-00

ALSO BY CHARLES R. MORRIS

American Catholic

The AARP

Computer Wars: The Fall of IBM and the
Future of Global Technology
(with Charles H. Ferguson)

The Coming Global Boom

Iron Destinies, Lost Opportunities: The Postwar Arms Race

A Time of Passion: America 1960–1980

The Cost of Good Intentions:
New York City and the Liberal Experiment

MONEY, GREED, AND RISK

MONEY, GREED, AND RISK

Why Financial Crises and Crashes Happen

CHARLES R. MORRIS

A CENTURY FOUNDATION BOOK

TIMES BUSINESS

RANDOM HOUSE

Library of Congress Cataloging-in-Publication Data

Morris, Charles R.
   Money, greed, and risk : why financial crises and crashes happen / Charles R. Morris.
        p.   cm.
   Includes bibliographical references (p. 259).
   ISBN 0-8129-3173-4
   1. Financial crises—United States—History. 2. Stock exchanges—United States—History. 3. International finance. I. Title.
HB3722.M674   1999
332'.0973—dc21   98-32144

Random House website address: www.atrandom.com
Printed in the United States of America on acid-free paper

2   4   6   8   9   7   5   3

FIRST EDITION

Book design by Mina Greenstein

For Robin Elizabeth, who enriches us all

The Century Foundation, formerly the Twentieth Century Fund, sponsors and supervises timely analyses of economic policy, foreign affairs, and domestic political issues. Not-for-profit and nonpartisan, it was founded in 1919 and endowed by Edward A. Filene.

ACKNOWLEDGMENTS

My thanks to Dick Leone, Greg Anrig, and Beverly Goldberg at the Century Foundation for financing this book, and for their astute editorial and other advice during the writing of it. The original idea that I do such a book came, as usual, from Mike Bessie, and he was, again as usual, an invaluable reader and editor.

Writing a book is a license to impose, to a degree that is hardly captured by the short list of thank yous that follows. For some fifteen years, Doug Love, now of Investors Guaranty Fund, has been my mentor in the workings of capital markets, and I ransacked his store of knowledge shamelessly. Special thanks also to Dick Omohundro, Joe Coté, and John Frebota of Prospect Street Investment Management; Larry Fink and Charlie Hallac of Blackrock Investments; Tom Potts and Hance West of Dynex Financial Corporation; and Bob Corrigan of Merrill Lynch. Chris Waldman of Primeon, Inc., helped check my options math. I also greatly benefited from a detailed and thoughtful reading of the entire manuscript by Chris Reid of Fintec Corp., and from Robert Daymon's production assistance.

It is a pleasure to continue my association with John Mahaney, Nancy Inglis, and Naomi Osnos at Times Books. Last, but hardly least, my wife, Beverly, endured the production of yet another book with affection and good humor.

FOREWORD

Part of Communism's intellectual appeal may well have been its promise to resolve one of man's oldest quests—the search for a way to relieve the relentless tension produced by economic risk and uncertainty. In this sense, the Soviet Union's traditional five-year economic plans—with their detailed production targets, price controls, and promises of growth—represent an almost touching fairy tale, a dream based on the assumption that humans have the power to control their economic destiny. Now, with that illusion swept into the dustbin of history, societies everywhere are converging in a belief that high rates of economic growth and long-term prosperity are possible only with free markets. But they also are continuing to learn and relearn lessons about the risks that accompany free enterprise.

Charles Morris, public manager, investment banker, and author, has written on a wide range of topics from the social policy innovations of the sixties to arms control during the cold war, from the Catholic Church to international economics. In fact, only someone who combines his broad perspective with a sharp and restless intellect could have pulled together the story he tells in this volume. The historical development of finance in the United States has seldom been explained with more economy and good sense. And few authors could effectively use the example of boom and bust in early America to help illuminate the recent events in South Asia and Russia—in the process making us more realistic about what to expect during the early stages of capitalism and market development anywhere. Most of the names in this book are familiar—Carnegie, Morgan, Rockefeller—and so are some of the events, but in each case, Morris enlarges our comprehension. Even recent crises, such as the savings and loan debacle and the junk bond crash, are more sharply defined.

Tolstoy wrote that while happy families are all alike, every unhappy family is unhappy in its own way. Many have a parallel belief about markets: all booms and bull markets have a certain similarity, but each economic bust or bear market is triggered by a special set of events. Maybe. But one message of this book is that this observation is only superficially true. In fact, there seem to be significant common elements and historical resonance among most cases of boom and bust, excess and correction. Change, innovation, personality, and circumstance may shape the exact situations in which a Jay Gould or a Michael Milken operate, but as *Money, Greed, and Risk* makes clear, the reasons that financial crashes and crises happen most often derive from fundamental and recurring characteristics of any financial system.

Perhaps Morris's most valuable contribution is to help us understand the implications of the vast and ever-increasing array of exotic and new financial instruments, some of them forged out of such homely old standbys as simple fixed-rate, thirty-year, government-guaranteed mortgages. This complexity matters because it can hinder understanding and mask risk. Morris calls finance the plumbing that makes capitalism run, and in this metaphor he surely captures an essential truth about economics. As he puts it, "Therefore, [it is] with good reason that finance is among the most regulated of all businesses." And indeed, the framework that we have created is the most extensive in the world, going well beyond the federal and state government regulatory agencies. We depend, as well, on an expensive and elaborate legal system to help police contention among parties in the system; we rely on commercial credit guardians and an immense accounting profession; and we delegate important powers to self-regulatory private organizations such as exchanges. Paradoxically, America may have one of the world's freest financial markets only because it also has the world's most complex regulatory framework in place—a framework designed to keep the system from careening from one crash to another. And, we apparently have a never-ending need to update this extraordinary oversight apparatus.

Morris reminds us of an important reality: Fixed ideas about how to improve and modernize regulation are seldom decisively convincing or lasting. In the first place, given the pace of financial innovation, set regulatory regimes tend to be obsolescent by the time they are introduced because of the increased complexity of instruments, markets, and risks. This fact of financial life means that there are no easy—let alone permanent—answers. Here, as in many categories of democratic capitalism, the advantage of "muddling through" rather than seeking universal truths remains appealing. Indeed, the permanence of uncertainty and the prevalence of change in modern markets may make such an approach inevitable.

This necessity for ad hoc policy also means that the financial community and its regulators will be engaged in constant conflict about just how much rulemaking and oversight is enough. Of course, it is the American way to recognize the right of every business, including financial firms, to argue for special public policies or public dispensations, and to do so with a straight face. At the same time, it tests our tolerance when the same industry, in time of trouble, rushes to Congress or the White House or the Federal Reserve bank to plead for help to save, say, a "Long-Term Capital Management" or some other firm that's "too big to fail." But these contradictions, too, are inevitable. Public policy in this area must serve several, sometimes conflicting, missions: facilitating open and competitive markets, preventing fraud and other abuses, but also ensuring that we avoid financial panics because of short-term crises, especially those involving the overall liquidity of the system. Moreover, while the unforgiving "discipline of the market" makes great theory, it may be bad policy when there are potentially grave consequences for working people and communities.

Morris advocates a bias in regulation toward focusing more on types of financial instruments than on types of institutions, strengthening protections for the little guys, and emphasizing that risk takers must have the wherewithal (capital) to deal with inevitable crisis. The rub, as Morris stresses, is that the hard thing about this approach is staying the course—being willing to let the market be the market and allowing failures to occur that might even have negative short-term consequences for the system as a whole.

In the end, of course, there is no magic formula that will sweep away all the issues raised by the uncertainties of capitalism. Perhaps because so much chance is hard-wired into the human condition, most adults, despite the rush that may accompany high-stakes activity, understand that it is foolish to take unnecessary risks with regard to personal safety or economic well-being. In fact, economists have thoroughly documented the pervasiveness of risk-averse behavior: The average individual, according to this research, actually takes fewer risks than he or she should (should, that is, according to economists). Still, it seems true that Americans tolerate a greater degree of market risk than do many other wealthy societies. They do so not because they are exceptionally reckless, but rather because they place a high value on the positive results of a relatively unfettered free market. Given that reality about our nation, the importance of a better understanding of how financial crises happen is obvious.

Simply put, Charles Morris is a polymath. He is that rarest of all intellectuals—one who understands and can make us understand not simply one area, but many. Indeed, given the previous range of his writings and the frequently unexpected turns of his interest, one can know neither the limits of his curiosity nor the ultimate boundaries of his understanding of how things work. *Money, Greed, and Risk* is only the latest proof of how exceptional he is. On behalf of the Trustees of The Century Foundation/Twentieth Century Fund and of two decades of readers, I thank him for helping us to understand yet another part of our world.

—Richard C. Leone, president, The Century Foundation (formerly the Twentieth Century Fund)
January 1999

Contents

MONEY, GREED, AND RISK

Introduction

The world is awash in financial crises as this book is going to press. Japan's banking system is wallowing in $1 trillion of bad loans; the currencies of the erstwhile East Asian "Tiger" economies are barely worth their weight in wallpaper; Russia is disappearing down a black hole; and most of Latin America—Mexico, Brazil, Argentina, even straitlaced Chile—is teetering on the brink. The United States has so far escaped the worst of the crises, but fiascos like the collapse of Long Term Capital Management have kept its financial markets frazzled and jumpy.

It is usually easy to understand why a business gets in trouble—its cars or computers cost too much or aren't as good as the competition's. But financial crises seem to arise out of nowhere, driven by mysterious forces and agencies—"globalization," "derivatives," "junk bonds," "foreign speculators." In the 1960s, it was the "gnomes of Zurich," while in most other eras, and still today in the mind of the Prime Minister of Malaysia, it was always "the Jews."

Finance operates in the murky depths of the economy. Like a plumbing system, it is invisible when it is working well, but a broken pipe can be a disaster. Occasionally, a catchy name impels some aspect of finance into the public imagination. Jay Leno fans all knew there was a junk-bond crisis in the late 1980s, but few people heard of the CMO crash about five years later, although it was much bigger. Home buyers certainly knew that mortgage rates were rising sharply, but few would have understood why.

Although the jargon changes, one generation's financial crisis is often much like the next's. "Globalization" is the buzzword for the 1990s, but nineteenth-century investing was at least as global, and the currency crises in late-nineteenth-century America followed courses broadly similar to the recent ones in Mexico and East Asia. Investors also reacted about as quickly then as they do now, although it took longer to execute instructions—you couldn't ship bullion at the flick of a computer mouse. In both the 1870s and the 1890s, however, the reversal of capital flows from Europe to America was still brutally abrupt. The complexity of financing the railroads after the Civil War matches any that investment bankers solve today. Michael Milken didn't invent any financial instruments that Jay Gould hadn't already thought of, and Gould could also have given lessons to Indonesia's President Suharto in fleecing overseas investors. When J. P. Morgan stepped into the American crisis of the 1890s, his prescriptions were a lot like those of today's IMF.

Finance is a relatively late arrival in economic history. The Amsterdam Exchange of the early seventeenth century is probably the first recognizably modern financial market, with trading in company shares, government bonds, and a wide range of futures and options. Hard on the heels of proto-modern markets came John Law's Mississippi Company fiasco in Paris, and the South Sea Bubble in London, both of which cast shadows over national financial practice for a century or more. The link between financial innovation and crisis was there from the start.

Almost all primitive societies used some kind of money. The active trading culture of the Indians of the Great Plains and Rocky Mountains, for example, was mostly conducted by barter, but was often facilitated by the use of colored beads, or wampum, as an intertribal currency. In practice, taking beads for something as valuable as a steel ax would have been very risky, for as Lewis and Clark found to their chagrin, different tribes had quite different notions of the value of wampum, and many scorned it as a substitute for really valuable goods, like rifles and powder.

The path from money to finance is one of successive abstraction. The European analogue to bead wampum was gold and silver, the so-called precious metals, which were used to facilitate trade from the very earliest times. Over the course of several millennia, people became so accustomed to denominating traded goods in precious metals that the metal equivalent gradually became the measure of the value of the goods, rather than the other way around—which Indians would have found odd. Deciding that real wealth consists in inert metals, rather than in the goods they may temporarily represent, is an extremely useful trick, for then the metals can act as a long-term store of value in a way that perishable goods cannot. Money as a store of value is but a step away from the notion of money as capital, which is where finance begins.

Even in the high Middle Ages, the notion of money as finance capital was radical enough to earn the condemnation of the church. In the thirteenth century, Thomas Aquinas proved, citing Aristotle, that the natural purpose of money was as a medium of exchange, not as a store of value, from which it followed that the lending of money at interest, or usury, was unnatural and sinful. Aquinas was not a stupid man, and seen through his eyes, the conclusion is not so bizarre. The primary enterprises of medieval Europe were military adventure and religious display, and the primary forms of wealth were labor and land. The whole feudal system of vassal and liege was a vast machinery for putting manpower and land directly at the disposal of the nobility and the clergy to build castles and cathedrals and to wage war and stage ceremonies. Feudalism, in effect, was a comprehensive, but non-monetary, capital assemblage system. Money was needed mostly for the purposes of exchange in international trade, more or less as Aquinas said. Even in Augustan Rome, which was a much more sophisticated society, money seems similarly to have been used mostly for trade. The capital required to build aqueducts and roads was simply dragooned.

Modern finance capitalism is a creature of the vast expansion of trade in the fifteenth and sixteenth century. Trade was highly profitable, and a merchant could obviously get richer if he could put more ships to sea than his private means would allow. The logical step was to borrow the money to finance more cargoes. Usury laws were still in effect, so almost all lenders were Jews; and to assuage a Christian merchant's conscience, the loans were often couched as the purchase of a partnership, or as insurance. It was common for a lender to advance the funds for a cargo at a high rate of interest, but if the ship was lost, the loss fell on the lender. (The same classification cat-and-mouse game goes on today, but to minimize taxes rather than the risk of damnation.) Usury laws gradually fell into desuetude, and richer merchants went into the lending business themselves. As feudal obligations were replaced by monetary contracts, it was an easy step from financing cargoes to financing kings. Kings now often had to rely on foreign troops, and they insisted on being paid in cash.

Financing a cargo with a trade credit—paying with a mere promise instead of with hard money—was a conceptual leap almost as important as the original substitution of money for actual goods. The Italian city-states of the Renaissance, and later the burghers of Amsterdam, gradually transmuted the system of trade credits into a highly polished financial machine—certificates of credit were traded freely, as if it were the certificate that was the item of value. In principle, however, all credits were still a claim on some goods, or later, as credits were extended to sovereigns, on the king's taxing power.

The magic of credit is that a thought (*credere,* "to believe") creates wealth. Before the system of paper credits, trade was transacted in coin, which is heavy and easily stolen or clipped, or more frequently by barter. Barter voyages could stretch to ten years or more, as merchants plied from port to port, seeking just the right goods. The expansion of trade enabled by paper credit underpinned regional and national specialization, commodity agriculture, the growth of manufacturing centers, the industrial revolution.

Financing American railroads required another huge leap of abstraction. Instead of a claim on a cargo of cotton, investors received a vaguely defined share in the future success of a private enterprise. To wags, it looked like a repeat of the eighteenth-century South Sea Bubble fiasco. As enterprise became more complex, the nature of the claim, and the rights of various classes of claimants, became ever more problematic, the more so since the business corporation was itself a legal anomaly well into the nineteenth century.

Sorting through these myriad issues in America was largely accomplished in the three or four decades following the Civil War, when the financial industry assumed more or less the same contours and divisions of labor that define it today. Jay Gould, whose name has become synonymous with rapaciousness, gets too little credit for shaping it. But it was J. P. Morgan who set the stage for the vast American industrial expansion of the late nineteenth and early twentieth century when he took railroad financing into his own capable hands and created the rules that made private-company investing safe for the wealthy classes.

By the time of the Great War, the entire economy was monetizing. Hired labor on a family farm could be paid mostly in kind, but industrial workers received cash wages, and the monetary holdings of a new, broadly based middle class gradually became the primary source of finance capital. Transmuting millions of small pools of household savings into usable capital for commercial, industrial, and consumer finance became the primary task of financial services and opened boundless opportunities to fleece the unwary. Stock jobbers gleefully worked over the middle classes, until the New Deal reform government developed the regulatory, accounting, and disclosure apparatus to make investing safe for the proverbial prudent man or woman.

The story of finance is therefore one of innovation, crisis, and consolidation. Industrial, commercial, or technological change calls forth an innovation—paper trade credits, private-company stocks and bonds, retail stock markets, junk bonds, collateralized mortgage obligations, derivative instruments. In every case, the innovation solves an immediate problem—expanding trade, financing railroads, restructuring companies, stabilizing pension portfolios—and also triggers a period of greatly increased risk and instability, until institutions catch up. The cycles are as apparent today as they were two hundred years ago. Even many of the instruments are the same.

The first three chapters illustrate the cycle of innovation, crisis, and consolidation in America from the early nineteenth century through the market crash of 1929. The remainder of the book traces the operation of the same cycle in modern markets through six other crises—the S&L crisis of the 1980s; the junk-bond crisis; computerized trading and the crash of 1987; derivatives; the mortgage-backed crisis of 1994; and the Mexican and East Asian currency crises. As will be seen, events follow the same broad pattern today as always—currency crises are still currency crises—but move breathtakingly faster.

Chapter One

BOOM AND BUST IN EARLY AMERICA

The secret of successful banking, reported a New York practitioner of the banker's dark arts in 1836, was to issue notes with "a real furioso plate, one that will take with all creation—flaming with cupids, locomotives, rural scenery, and Hercules kicking the world over."

Mid-nineteenth-century America was desperate for capital, but the mistrust of banks and credit was so deep that many state legislatures outlawed banks altogether. Lending, however, turned out to be as hard to prohibit as liquor, and areas where banking was illegal drew legions of underground operators. Legislators sometimes leaped to the other extreme and passed "free banking" statutes that were usually worse than prohibition. In 1852, a banker described the broad road to riches in Indiana: Borrow some cash, buy up depreciated state bonds, deposit them with the Indiana state treasurer as banking capital at face value, and start printing banknotes. Pay off your loan with the banknotes and repeat the process. One group of promoters ran a $10,000 investment into $600,000 of circulating notes within just a couple of years, and collected $30,000-a-year interest on the bonds they had purchased, for an annual 300 percent return on equity. Leverage was not a 1980s invention.

Things could get awkward if noteholders tried to redeem their notes for real money, which in those days meant gold. Spectacular "furioso" notes helped minimize redemptions, but it was a good idea to keep your office as far away from civilization as possible, so noteholders had to hunt you in the woods, along with the wildcats—hence the term "wildcat" banking. The term may have originated in Michigan where wildcatters sprinkled gold coins on top of kegs of nails to display as their specie reserves. On the rare occasions when a state treasurer checked to see if banks had legal capital, the bankers would pass the same small specie reserve from hand to hand, staying one jump ahead of the inspectors. Thucydides reports that Sicilians used the same trick to fool Athenian ambassadors in the fifth century B.C.

The mid-century wildcat banking scandals were just one episode in America's century-long struggle to establish a credit and financial system that could support the soaring ambitions of an aggressively developing future superpower. The gross mismatch between America's overbrimming energies and her slender capital led to the jagged roller-coaster ride of boom and bust that characterized virtually the whole of the nineteenth-century American financial saga.

The Capital Scarcity in America

America's astonishing leap from the rural backwater of the 1820s to the industrial powerhouse of the 1890s is possibly the greatest development achievement in history, outstripping even the extraordinary growth in the Pacific Rim economies over the past thirty years. In 1820, American population was growing rapidly, almost doubling since the turn of the century to 10 million, counting almost 2 million slaves, but it was still thinly distributed along the Atlantic coast within the territories of the original thirteen colonies. Even in a long-settled state like Connecticut, there were only 275,000 people, only 10 percent of whom lived in cities. The vast territory of Illinois was home to only 55,000 settlers, with no cities at all. It would be the work of another two decades to extinguish Indian titles east of the Mississippi, and clashes between Indians and white settlers were still common. The "interior" branches of the Bank of the United States were offices scattered through Georgia, Alabama, Tennessee, and Ohio. Most rural people got along without any money at all—clothes were still home-spun; tools were made at home or bartered for from a local black-smith. Aside from the haphazard circulation of a potpourri of deeply depreciated banknotes, which were worthless in trade, a farm family's trove of hard money would typically consist of only a few copper coins.

The European travelers flocking to America to see for them-selves this fabled land of golden promise were more often repelled by what they found. Before Tocqueville's famous reports of the 1830s, travel narratives told of primitive cities with grasping and unlettered inhabitants; of an interior that was all impassable swamps, trackless forests, and terrifying Indians; of rural settle-ments that had attracted erstwhile Europeans of the lowest kind, who in manners and mores were themselves only a small step from savagery. The staple diet of the interior was salt pork and greasy baked dough, washed down by enormous quantities of hard liquor—even young children received their regular dram. An eighth-century Saxon farmer would have been at home with the farming techniques of the Appalachian settler, for American farm-ers were notoriously conservative about new technology. It took seventy years for a greatly improved plow invented early in the cen-tury to come into wide use. In a typical country inn, the guest sleeping space was a wooden floor over the pigsty, and frontier families lived in dark and smoky one-room cabins. In Henry Adams's words:

> The chance of being shot at or scalped by Indians was hardly worth considering when compared with the certainty of malarial fever, or the strange disease called milk-sickness, or the still more depressing home-sickness, or the misery of nervous prostration, which wore out generation after generation of women and children and left a tragedy in every log cabin. Not for love of ease did men plunge into the wilderness.

As an underdeveloped country, America's primary products were cotton, tobacco, timber, and furs from the interior. Its pri-mary economic challenge was to develop its interior businesses to the point where they could finance a national industrial takeoff. In the 1820s, regional barriers were still great enough to speak of interregional "trade balances" and "exports" and "imports," but the spread of post roads and improvements in river travel were slowly laying the basis for a national commercial infrastructure. The trip from Philadelphia to Pittsburgh had been cut from several weeks to less than a week, and a traveler could get from New York to Buffalo in what passed for reasonable comfort in only about four days. The trip from Virginia to Washington, D.C., no longer required the traveler to ford a horse through rivers, as Thomas Jefferson had to do on the way to his presidential inauguration.

Progress, however, would be slow until interior merchants and farmers had a ready source of capital for seed, tools, and equipment, and governments had the capital to build roads and canals. Interior merchants, for example, did not have the credit to buy British manufactures, so British merchant houses had fallen into the practice of shipping manufactured goods on consignment to their own agents. The goods selected for America naturally tended to be surplus items, often of the lowest quality, and poorly matched to market requirements.

The lack of a functioning credit system often had maddeningly perverse consequences. Effectively, it was the impecunious American planter who was forced to finance the British importer. With no way to be paid in advance for their crops, planters almost always shipped on consignment to agents of British merchants, and were paid only after their crop had been sold in England. It could take a year or more before planters got their money, duties ran as high as five times the value of the crop, there were hefty setoffs for handling and insurance, and fraud and sharp practices were rampant.

Nineteenth-century financial practices were still largely based on the system of trade credit perfected by Arab traders in the Levant around the end of the first millennium. In the ancient world, trade was conducted mostly through barter. A merchant either purchased a cargo of goods or took them on consignment, and then plied from port to port, trading them for other goods. Trading voyages stretched on for years, partly because a trader could never count on finding the kind or quality of goods he was looking to trade for. Barter was supplemented by purchases in gold and silver coin, but coins were scarce, heavy, easily stolen, and often so clipped or worn as to be worth far less than their face value. Arab traders therefore developed what became known as the "bill of exchange," an instrument which the historian Fernand Braudel has called "the key weapon in the armory of merchant capitalism in the West." A version of the bill of exchange occurs in almost all trading cultures, including the Indian and the Chinese. Its Western form was refined by the Italian trading states in the fifteenth century, and during the hegemony of the Dutch banking houses of the eighteenth century it became virtually a European-wide international paper currency.

A bill of exchange is essentially a check. When you write a check, you are drawing on your credit at a bank; if you have covered the check with deposits or a credit arrangement, your bank will honor it when it is eventually "presented" for payment by the holder. Similarly, a merchant wishing to purchase goods would pay with a bill drawn on a distant merchant banking house, and the merchant house would honor the bill when it was presented either on a specific date or upon delivery of the goods. Since the buyer issuing the bill is invoking the credit of the merchant house on which the bill is drawn, it was natural for trading companies to be based on families: if the buyer was part of the same family that the bill was drawn on, the seller was more likely to believe that the credit was good. The Italians generalized the system. Any merchant could draw upon an Italian banking house if he had a letter of credit authorizing him to do so, or if his bill was "accepted" by a local representative of the banking family. The acceptor would countersign the bill, confirming that his banking house would honor it at the due date, and listing the conditions that applied—the type of cargo, the method of shipping, whether insurance had to be purchased for the benefit of the accepting house.

By the fifteenth and sixteenth centuries, all the major trade routes had a network of bill brokers who readily bought and sold bills. Trade-based paper therefore moved from hand to hand in a converging stream flowing back to capital centers like Genoa or Venice, where they would be presented to the merchant houses for payment. The presenter could demand redemption in coin, but as the system professionalized, the accepting house would simply extend a like credit to the presenter or cancel an equivalent indebtedness. In the same way that one covers a check with funds in a checking account, the original drawer of the bill was supposed to have forwarded sufficient coin or other good bills to cover his bill before it was presented for payment. The merchant house's ultimate security was in the goods themselves, and most houses required the goods to be shipped and sold through their own networks. If the drawing party didn't cover the bill, the merchant house could sell the goods and keep the proceeds.

Traditional societies live close to the bone. A tiny percentage of the population may live in splendid luxury, but society as a whole generates only minimal surplus. The bill system was spectacularly successful in facilitating trade so long as merchant bankers limited credit to "real bills," or bills secured by specific shipments of goods. Sound bankers preached that banks provided *finance,* not *capital.* Real-bill doctrine simply recognized hard reality: while there might be sufficient surplus to support a season's production and shipment of a crop, society did not have the free capital to tie up in long-term projects, or ones with unpredictable returns. Whenever boom times tempted bankers to expand the credit system beyond real-bill–based trade finance into unsecured, implicitly longer-term lending, financial crises inevitably followed.

Excessive expansion of bills helped end the economic hegemony of the Dutch. A trade boom that followed a lull in the British-French wars was financed primarily by bills of exchange drawn on the Dutch banking houses. As fees and commissions came pouring into Amsterdam, new banking houses sprang into existence and financed new overseas merchants to keep the boom rolling. Given the day's cumbersome paperwork systems, the easiest way to expand bill issuance was to authorize merchants to draw "uncovered" bills, bills not linked to any specific cargo but secured merely by the general credit of the drawing merchant. As good times continued, that is what the Dutch did, until bills in circulation grew to five, ten, fifteen times the available specie. A contemporary observer remarked: "If ten or twelve Businessmen of Amsterdam of the first rank meet for a banking operation, they can in a moment send circulating throughout Europe over two hundred million florins in paper money, which is preferred to cash [specie]. There is no Sovereign who could do as much."

But as more and more Amsterdam houses extended lines of credit, and more and more entrepreneurs were drawn into trade and other business ventures, the flow of bills turned into such a deluge that it became harder and harder to know what an individual bill was worth. Who really knew who the drawers were? How many different lines of credit did they have? Would they ever cover? How far could the credit of the Amsterdam houses be stretched? The entire system finally collapsed amid the economic disruptions of the 1780s. By that time, the British, who had financed their own industrial takeoff with Dutch capital, were already moving to seize world financial leadership.

It required no special gifts to recognize the great economic promise of the American continent in the 1820s. The challenge was to devise a means of marshaling the slender capital available to put the exploitation of the country's resources on a commercial footing, then gradually bootstrap those profits into a self-sustaining program of investment and development. There were several distinct attempts to solve the conundrum in the first half of the nineteenth century, all of which in various ways came to grief. The most innovative, and the most intellectually advanced, was Nicholas Biddle's experiment in modern central banking at the Second Bank of the United States.

Nicholas Biddle and the Bank of the United States

Nicholas Biddle was Philadelphia nouveau-aristocrat, the son of a successful, but not extraordinarily wealthy, merchant. Although Biddle's economic ideas were remarkably advanced, his personal style conformed more to the eighteenth-century ideal of the Renaissance man than to the grasping commercialism of the nineteenth. Biddle matriculated at Princeton at age thirteen and became a patrician lawyer, a classicist, a gentleman farmer, a magazine editor, and essayist. He could toss off a witty sonnet at a moment's notice, he translated Greek and French poetry, and his edition of the journals of Lewis and Clark, which he undertook at Clark's request, remained the standard for more than a century. Just out of college, he served as secretary to the American minister in Paris from 1807 to 1809. As part of the deal for Louisiana, the United States had assumed a great mass of claims of American merchants against the French government; handling merchant claims was one of Biddle's primary responsibilities in Paris, and it gave him an eagle's-eye view of the ins and outs of trade finance.

Elected to the Pennsylvania Senate while still in his twenties, Biddle immersed himself in the study of economics and finance, and was one of the most effective defenders of the rechartering of the Bank of the United States. After serving as a government director of the Bank for four years, he was appointed president in 1823, at the age of thirty-seven. By taste and conviction, Biddle was a Hamiltonian: he believed that credit was the basic engine of the economy, and that prudent management of the credit environment was the primary duty of a central banker. His performance as a banker has been the subject of savage controversy among historians of the era, as it was in his own day, but he has a strong claim to being among the very first, and among the very greatest, practitioners of modern central banking.

The Bank of the United States was a public-private hybrid: 20 percent of its stock was owned by the government, and it operated under rules laid down by the Secretary of the Treasury. It was conservatively capitalized, with solid reserves of specie and U.S. government bonds, which were universally viewed as high-quality instruments. It was the depositary and paying agent of the federal government, and its notes were accepted at par in payment for the public lands. Prior to Biddle's tenure, in 1815, it had attempted to solve the interior capital scarcity by allowing its interior branches to issue bank notes. The experiment quickly became a major embarrassment that illustrates both the primitiveness of the early American financial system and the dangers of deviating from real-bill principles of finance.

Federal receipts from public land sales were mostly collected by the interior branches, and were usually left on deposit. Once the branches were authorized to issue notes, they were able to use growing federal deposits to expand their note issuance and their loans. Loans fueled further speculation in the public lands, and the new sales increased the federal deposits that much more. So the branches built a rapidly growing book of business secured mostly by long-term mortgages on raw land. The notes that didn't go to land sales tended to be spent on manufactured imports from the Eastern cities, exacerbating a persistent regional trade deficit. As the notes worked their way east, they were presented for redemption at the Eastern branches, draining away Eastern reserves.

To make matters worse, the national government, on good Jeffersonian principles, was aggressively paying off the national debt, adding to the cash demands on the Eastern branches, where foreign and domestic bondholders were most likely to present their bonds. The consequence was a persistent shortfall of Eastern reserves, to the point where, in 1818, the Bank had no choice but to engineer a major transfer of capital from West to East. The Bank therefore rescinded the interior branches' note-issuing powers, and ordered major shipments of specie eastward. Since the interior branches had so much of their assets tied up in illiquid mortgages, they had to to call in their lines of credit to the state banks to comply with the specie demand. The result was a massive credit crunch in the South and West that persisted for at least the next half decade.

Biddle took office determined to do better. Although he had supported the Bank's 1818 policy of contraction, and had warned against excessive note issuance in the West, he thought the contractionary policies had been carried much too far. While Biddle accepted the inevitability of financial cycles, he thought that intelligent credit management could make them much less destructive. And when he put his theories to the test, he solved the interior-seaboard capital mismatch with a speed and ease that was almost magical—altogether one of the signal feats of nineteenth-century central banking.

His first step was to reauthorize note issuance by his interior branches, but with the significant proviso that they could be issued only to purchase high-quality bills of exchange. The difference was crucial. Merchants' agents in the West drew bills on their principals in Eastern cities to pay farmers for their crops, and the farmers exchanged their bills for bank notes at the local branches of the Bank. As before, the farmers used their notes to buy Eastern manufactures, so the notes migrated eastward for eventual presentment at the Eastern branches, but the Bank's interior branches were accumulating highly liquid bills, which they also forwarded to the Eastern branches for collection. So now the notes and bills were moving eastward in a side-by-side stream with the exports of crops and other commodities. Merchants redeemed their bills with the proceeds from the crops, and the Bank redeemed its notes with the proceeds from the bills. In the earlier period, interior branch assets had been tied up in raw land; Biddle's policy of careful note expansion based on real bills linked the interior and the seaboard economies together via a smoothly flowing monetary pipeline.

The results were spectacular. Within six months, bills drawn in "interior" cities—like Charleston, which had typically traded at discounts of 10 to 20 percent or sometimes even more—were trading almost at par. Not even England, and certainly not France, could boast such a frictionless exchange system between its rural areas and major trading cities. The practical effect was a substantial infusion of capital to the interior, and interior merchants and farmers taking payment in bills of exchange were suddenly getting full value or close to it. Trade recovered immediately, helped along by Biddle's careful easing of credit availability. And since the Bank was in a far better position than interior bill brokers to assess the credit quality of the Eastern merchant houses, its willingness to buy a house's bills effectively certified to bill brokers that the bills could be traded near par. At a stroke, Biddle had created a reliable trading currency, consisting of the Bank's notes and high-quality bills of exchange. As the system took hold, people were less inclined to demand redemption of their notes, which reduced pressure on specie reserves that much further. The rest of the decade was to see very rapid growth and professionalization of interior–seaboard trading links. Within just a very few years, interior merchant houses were able to buy and sell British manufactures on their own credit, and could offer goods much better suited to local conditions than was possible under the old system of consignment sales through company agents.

One of the happy byproducts of Biddle's system was that it also gave him effective control over interior state bank notes. State banking charters rarely imposed any meaningful restraint on note issuance, and newly chartered banks often flooded their local market with notes. Since state bank notes were often useless in trade, people redeemed their state bank notes for the Bank's notes whenever they could, so the branches accumulated substantial holdings of local notes. The Bank's branch managers were instructed to monitor local note issuance closely and to refuse them or insist on redeeming them in specie whenever a local bank expanded unwisely. The Bank's willingness to purchase local bank notes therefore became a critical seal of approval on their creditworthiness, effectively imposing a ceiling on local note issuance. A number of the more important state banks, like those of New York, chose to stop issuing notes altogether, preferring to use the notes of the Bank of the United States. By the same processes of careful credit management, Biddle also stabilized Anglo-American exchange rates, greatly reducing the need for the export of specie—which, given the chronic American shortage of capital, was always extremely disruptive of the money markets.

Biddle worked an ingenious reverse wrinkle on his system in 1825 to finance American trade with the Far East: American merchants engaged in the Pacific trade were primarily importers at this time—the opium boom was still in the future—and Far Eastern merchants usually would not accept American bills because of the vast distances involved. American merchant ships bound for China therefore left with their holds laden with coin to finance their purchases. Specie withdrawals for the China voyages invariably unsettled the money markets, especially since wind patterns necessitated their leaving in the spring, precisely the time when planters were most in need of credit. Biddle, who had extensive credit lines with Baring Brothers, the leading London merchant banking house, solved the problem by selling bills of exchange drawn on the Barings to American merchants. Biddle would take his own bank notes for the bills—the merchants were effectively prepaying for their imports—and then six to nine months later, when the bills would start showing up in London, Biddle would cover the bills by remitting federal bonds or other good bills to the Barings. Since the Far Eastern traders were almost all of British origin, they were delighted to take bills on the Barings at par, or even at a premium. Once again, a reliable paper-based currency was substituted for a disruptive and risky system of shipping coin.

Biddle's conception of national banking was uniquely modern, and he was one of the first central bankers with a clear conception of countercyclical credit policies. In 1825, 1827–28, and 1830–31, he brilliantly eased the United States through severe credit contractions that originated, like most contractions of this period, with the Bank of England. Very much in the mercantilist tradition, the Bank of England tended to measure the country's financial health by the size of its specie reserves. It therefore concentrated single-mindedly on building reserves, which nearly always caused it to contract savagely at the first sign of stormy financial weather—a policy prejudice guaranteed to deepen and prolong almost any crisis at all. The financial historian Jacob Viner writes that "from about 1800 to 1860, the Bank of England almost continuously displayed . . . an inexcusable degree of incompetence." The cocksure Biddle would have heartily agreed, and he could not resist comparing the smoothness of his own credit interventions to the inveterate clumsiness of his British counterparts. "It is difficult and perhaps presumptuous," Biddle wrote in 1825,

> to say how far the disasters in England might have been prevented, but it may perhaps be safely asserted that the aid of £3,500,000 sterling to the sufferers which was extended in the month of May by the Bank of England might, had it been given in the month of December, have prevented some of the evils which it became necessary to remedy. A course of anticipation and prevention was pursued by the Bank of the United States in the autumn of last year by which there was no doubt that much inconvenience and distress was averted.

The Barings' close working relations with Biddle gave them a virtual lock on the lucrative American trade-finance and bond-underwriting business, but they were Bank of England stalwarts, and their avidity for Biddle's business was matched by a testy distaste for his policies and methods. In their case, moreover, disapproval was tinged by real grievances, for they often felt exploited. Biddle's new system of financing the Far Eastern trade, for example, they thought an outrage. From their point of view, Biddle was using *their* lines of credit to sell *their* bills to American merchants, effectively cutting them out from profitable commissions. And since Biddle usually covered the bills before they were presented in London, they didn't even earn any interest on the transactions. (The Barings occasionally argued that they should be paid interest as soon as they had been advised of the sale of a bill, but Biddle would pay only from the date a bill was actually presented.)

Even worse from the Barings' point of view, Biddle's counter-cyclical credit policies depended heavily on his lines of credit with the Barings. In effect, it was the Barings, not the Bank of the United States, who were acting as the bank of last resort for America, and Biddle usually accomplished his easings by overdrawing on his Baring lines at the worst possible times. As Thomas Baring complained to his American agent, Thomas Wren Ward, in 1831:

> Now just observe how this account works. . . . [W]e are entirely at the mercy of the Bank which views us in the light of a reserve fund to be used to any extent when the state of the internal circulation of the country requires it, and it always happens from a natural and intelligible sympathy between all money markets that it largely employs our cash at times when money is useful to us and overwhelms us with funds when money is a drug. This system is obviously very useful to the Bank as it answers all the purposes of an additional amount of specie.

The primacy that Biddle assigned to maintaining a high level of economic activity, as opposed to a high level of specie reserves, mystified the Barings, and they persisted in regarding him as a kind of frivolous financial grasshopper who "gets in all sorts of scrapes." Joshua Bates, an American national who was a senior Baring partner, humphed in 1831 that "a more straightforward man would be more suitable to that Institution."

Jackson Shuts Down the Bank

Biddle's experiment in central banking came to an abrupt end when Andrew Jackson, in a triumph of prejudice and ignorance, vetoed the recharter of the Bank of the United States in the summer of 1832, and the next year abruptly withdrew the federal deposits. (The recharter legislation had passed both houses of Congress by comfortable margins, but the Senate lacked the two-thirds majority necessary to override the veto.)

Jackson's motives were pure, if those of his friends and retainers who lobbied fiercely for the veto were not. The president reflected a rock-hard agrarian aversion to banks and paper money that could reach biblical intensity. The only money God made was gold. The spectacular "furioso" notes that so gulled the bumpkins were clearly the work of the devil, and the "Monster

Bank" was the seat of a conspiracy as far-reaching as popery. Paper money fueled the growth of urban centers, stockbroking, foppery, iniquity. James Fenimore Cooper's 1841 satire, *Autobiography of a Pocket Handkerchief,* chronicled the perfumed fripperies of Henry Halfacre and his set; Halfacre was a proto–Michael Milken who had built a leveraged fortune in New York town lots. William Gouge, the most prominent theorist of Jacksonian economics, wrote that banks were "the *principal* cause of social evil in the United States." John Calhoun said that the effect of banks was "to discourage industry and to convert the whole community into stock jobbers and speculators," with "fatal effects . . . on moral and intellectual development." Biddle had extolled the elasticity of a sound system of credit as its primary virtue, but in Gouge's view, the flexibility of bank credit "is not an excellence, but a defect," because the value of a circulating medium would always fall in precise proportion to the increase in its quantity. (It would be another half century before organized agrarians officially endorsed the pleasures of leverage and plumped for easy money.)

Jacksonian hard-money advocates were ignorant—they never conceived that judicious expansion of money might lead to a proportionate expansion in economic activity. But they were not foolish. The financial history of the previous couple of centuries had been marked by one debacle after another, destroying savings and laying waste to enterprise, almost always because of feckless debasement of money. Biddle's stewardship of the Bank of the United States pointed in new directions, but his grand experiment lasted only about seven years before it was summarily ended by Jackson, hardly enough time for his achievement to be appreciated, or even fully tested. If a Thomas Baring had trouble understanding what Biddle was up to, so must have a William Gouge.

But Jackson did not have the eyes to see that the real impetus for vetoing the Bank's recharter was not coming from hard-money ideologues like Gouge but from a rising new financial and commercial interest. They were the sansculottes of capitalism, a motley collection of stock jobbers, rural promoters, speculators, and money lenders "dressing up for the occasion in the rags of the poor and parading with outcries against oppression by Mr. Biddle's hydra of corruption, whose nest they aspired to occupy themselves." The order and stability that Biddle was imposing on the financial system was the enemy of them all, and if they were repellent in their seamy grabbiness, their iconclastic, ingenious energy was the fuel that eventually drove America to the top of the economic-league tables.

Jacob Barker was more colorful than most of his peers, but was otherwise typical of the blackbird flock of audacious quick-buck artists on the outer fringes of Jackson's "Kitchen Cabinet." Starting in 1825, Barker, a New York entrepreneur of modest means, engineered a series of what must be the first hostile leveraged takeovers in American history, at one point threatening to gain control of the Bank of the United States itself. He started by taking over a small bank, then used that bank's note issues to buy up, one by one, notes of several bigger banks. He used the threat of redeeming all of a target's notes at once as a lever to gain control of his prey, and quickly built a formidable pyramid of financial institutions. But when Barker ostentatiously began accumulating a position in Bank of United States notes, Biddle retaliated with a targeted squeeze that toppled his upstart empire. The patrician *sang-froid* with which Biddle crushed Barker must have been as maddening as the result. Barker was convicted of fraud, but avoided prison. With some justice, he always insisted he had done nothing wrong, but had been victimized by an "old boy" financial network.* He won a measure of revenge as a venomous foe of the Bank during the recharter fight, and capped a long and checkered career with a term as a carpetbagger post–Civil War congressman from New Orleans.

Over the next several years, Jacksonian fiscal management was

---

*Barker's assault on banking's aristocratic strongholds has parallels to Saul Steinberg's brash run at Chemical Bank in the late 1960s. Steinberg made the same claim of old-boy exclusionary tactics, also with some justice, when his attempt at Chemical was rebuffed by the coordinated efforts of the New York banking elite. He survived to become a key member of Michael Milken's junk-bond network in the 1980s, and a member of the country's cultural and financial establishment.

incompetent to the point of malignance. A forced-pace redistribu-
tion of federal deposits to the state banks touched off an explosion
of state banknote issues. Then, to dampen the speculative boom
that immediately followed, the administration ordered that only
specie would be accepted in payment for the public lands, hard on
the heels of a ruling that the federal government would no longer
accept notes of the Bank of the United States for taxes and other
payments. Inevitably, there was a violent curtailment: short-term
interest rates rose as high as 24 percent and merchant houses failed
all around the country. To top it off, with the national debt paid
off, the administration decided to distribute federal surpluses
among the states—which it accomplished by ordering large shipments of specie and other reserves from coastal banks to the interior in the fall of 1837, precisely when Eastern merchants were
most in need of credit to purchase crops and commodities. Specie
payments were suspended throughout the country, and even the
federal government—the presumed seat of fiscal rectitude—had
to resort to the humiliating expedient of issuing treasury scrip to
pay its bills.

Biddle's behavior in the years of the Bank's demise still shadows his reputation and is a source of endless controversy between
his supporters and his critics. Once he had determined that the
fight was lost, he engineered a harsh, years'-long credit contraction. Jacksonians accuse him of vindictiveness, but Biddle does not
seem to have had much choice; it was the Jacksonians, after all,
who were forcing the Bank out of business. Perversely, the administration and its supporters seized upon the subsequent financial
distress as proof of the evils of all banks. For several years, Biddle
attempted to keep the Bank going, restyled as "the United States
Bank" operating under a Pennsylvania charter. The new Bank collapsed in 1841, costing him both his credibility and much of his
fortune. The collapse was not entirely Biddle's fault, but a fatal
problem seems to have been his continued attempt to run the Bank
as if it were a national institution, rather than purely a profit-
making private venture. Before he ran afoul of Andrew Jackson,
however, Biddle's performance fully justifies the financial historian
Bray Hammond's judgment that "the central banking function was

apparently as clearly recognized and as successfully performed in the United States by the year 1825 as anywhere in the world—and more clearly and more successfully, I should say, than it was performed there a century later."

The Barings Try It Their Way

Thomas Wren Ward was an archetypal Boston Yankee, lean and hawk-nosed, dour and brusque to a fault. His official portrait radiates skepticism—the head is tilted slightly forward, eyebrows arched, the gaze utterly noncommittal. Ward's father, a successful merchant, sent Thomas to sea as a fledgling midshipman at the age of ten. He made first lieutenant by his mid-teens, brought a ship safely home from China when his captain fell ill, and had his own command at twenty. Having "amassed a competency," he retired from the sea and married the daughter of one of Boston's leading merchant bankers. Ward founded trading houses in New York and Boston, built one of Boston's finest private homes, and became rich enough to retire from business in 1825 before he was forty. Restless in retirement, he agreed, in 1830, to become the American agent for Baring Brothers; his diligence and acumen soon earned him virtually complete authority over the the Barings' American business dealings, making him arguably the most important businessman in the country.

The Barings' business was squarely in the Italian and Dutch tradition. They were *merchant* bankers—traders of goods who, as a business accommodation, extended credit to their customers. The house was founded by Johann Baring, who emigrated from Germany to Exeter in 1717, anglicized his name to John, and apprenticed himself to a maker of serge cloth. John quickly became the leading figure in his employer's business, expanded into the merchandising of cloth and a variety of other commodities, married into a wealthy mercantile family, and by his death, in 1748, was one of the richest men in his county. His descendants included a high proportion of men as shrewd and enterprising as he was, with the same knack for financially astute marriages. By the time London assumed first rank among Europe's capital centers, the Barings were already England's leading merchant banking house.

By the nineteenth century, in addition to traditional trade finance, a substantial portion of the Barings' business was dealing in government securities. They were the major underwriter of the bonds for the Louisiana Purchase, and in the 1820s rapidly expanded their underwritings of American state bonds to finance internal improvements. But the bookkeeping on their securities underwritings still followed trade-based forms. Issuers of bonds were authorized to draw bills of exchange on the Barings, which they would cover by forwarding the new securities to London, just as merchants would cover a trade bill by forwarding the documents on a cotton cargo. The Barings mingled American securities freely with trade-based bills in their "Bill Case," and would hold them for investment, resell them to investors, or use them as a form of paper money in settling accounts with other banking houses.

The combined trade and securities business made Barings the most important single conduit of foreign capital into America by a wide margin, and they were the only institution with the wherewithal to move into the financial vacuum created by Jackson's charter veto. By the mid-1830s, by dint of brilliant improvisation and extraordinary application, Ward had quintupled the firm's outstanding lines of credit in America to $50 million, or roughly a half billion dollars in today's currency, an enormous sum for the day. To put Ward's credit operations into perspective, the Bank of the United States at this time had about $80 million in assets, only about half of which were in loans, with the rest in government stock and specie. In effect, just as Biddle was being forced to curtail the Bank's operations, the Barings' extensions of credit were sufficient to supplant much of its lending activities.

The critical difference between Ward's and Biddle's systems is that Ward's was *personal.* Very much in the old, family-oriented tradition of merchant banking, his extensions of credit were based primarily on his own judgment of his correspondent's integrity.

The key to business, he continually reminded his principals, "is my knowing the character well here—*this is the great desideratum*—and I need not say that it is difficult to do it." Biddle, of course, also placed great stock in the character of his customers, but his primary goal was always to move the system to a higher level of generality. Even the very best bills carried some element of risk—for example, a merchant might not comply with some delivery specification. Biddle's system of monetizing high-quality bills by buying them for bank notes replaced a quirky, particularized instrument with a generic, legal-tender, circulating medium, with the ultimate result that financial transactions of all kinds were greatly facilitated.

Given the vast expansion of trade and commerce since the 1820s, for the Barings to supply the required trading liquidity with a financial instrument as highly customized as a bill of exchange entailed prodigious labor, but Ward was equal to the task. He was extremely well connected, a friend of Daniel Webster's (Webster was promptly put on a Barings retainer to ensure his loyal advice in the Senate), on first-name terms with most of the country's leading businessmen and traders, and able to call on presidents when he needed to. He was also extraordinarily diligent, maintaining an immense stream of correspondence with customers and informants throughout the country, which he sifted into detailed assessments of business conditions, trading opportunities, and customer creditworthiness for his masters in London. His credit assessments were minute and personal—"Heckscher is married to Miss Coster, who will have at least £50 m [£50,000]" and another credit applicant was "a man of prudence in his pecuniary concerns, and general good sense, but fond of sporting and fishing and good living." Keeping tabs on more than nine hundred correspondents entailed extensive travel, which Ward seems to have suffered without complaint, although traveling conditions were execrable everywhere. Although he was notably abstemious and taciturn, he willingly subjected himself to the fatty foods, the jovial pomposity, and the huge quantities of spiritous liquors that marked the era's rounds of business meetings and entertainments.

Like the Dutch a half century before, however, Ward was able to accomplish such a rapid expansion of credit only by shifting away from the normal practice of tying bills to specific transactions. The great majority of Ward's new credit lines were so-called uncovered, or clean, credits—tying each bill to a specific cargo would have overwhelmed his limited clerical capabilities. When Ward's clients drew bills on the Barings, they were effectively taking out unsecured loans, which is why Ward placed such stress on his customers' integrity. The bill of exchange, that is, was transmuting into generic checking account money. But for a few years, at least, it splendidly supplied the requirements of an international trading currency. Barings' partner Joshua Bates commented in some wonderment in 1835, "The system of credits is as great an improvement in the circulating medium of the world as Bank notes were for the currency of particular countries."

The test of the system came at the end of the 1830s, when the gross fiscal and monetary mismanagement of the Jackson administration had almost terminally destabilized the economy. From the perspective of the Barings' narrow self-interest, Ward's abilities were splendidly vindicated. He had been among the very first merchant bankers to institute regular credit evaluations of all his correspondents, he was vigilant in collecting overdue balances, and he did not hesitate to insist on greater security when a customer's circumstances changed. In 1843, after four years of continual crises, when the smoking ruins of once-proud American and British merchant banking houses were strewn all over the financial landscape, Ward's own credits had come through with flying colors. Of 250 accounts that Ward had deemed "undoubted" in 1835, only 16 had failed; of 245 "likely to continue good," only 22 had failed; and of the 280 accounts he ranked as his lowest credits, only 45 had failed. All in all, it was an impressive performance.

But to replicate the Barings' success, other merchant banking houses would need agents as prodigiously diligent as Ward, and he was a rare commodity. With no steadying hand like Biddle's on the credit balance wheel, the system of bill-based, checklike international money quickly ran out of control. At first, merchants were heartened when the Anglo-American trading economy managed to survive the demise of the Bank, partly because the Bank of England, quite unusually, temporarily adopted an easy-money, accommodationist posture. For a time, commerce continued almost unabated, even shrugging off suspensions of American specie payments in 1837, and again in 1839. As old-line merchant houses on both sides of the Atlantic expanded their businesses, new ones sprang into existence, extending great volumes of unsecured credit. But when the Bank of England began to tighten credit in 1839, great quantities of bills were suddenly thrown into question. The weeks'-long communications gap between England and America was a breeding ground for rumors that cast doubt on all financial transactions. If a London house accepted bills drawn by failing American houses, the London house itself might fail. But if it refused acceptance, and returned the bills, it could force its correspondents into bankruptcy. A Bank of England committee estimated that the cloud of doubtful bills hanging over London might be as high as £3 to 5 million, an enormous sum for the day. Barings may have been the only major trading house not to be seriously threatened.

The Bank of England eventually coordinated a rescue operation, providing the funds for a consortium of relatively healthy houses to buy up enough American paper to keep the system afloat—which also operated as a subsidy to the limping American economy. By no stretch of the imagination was the Bank practicing Biddle-style countercyclical central banking; instead, it was merely helping its friends, some of whom served on its board. The merchant houses that were the target of the rescue were old and established, run by the "best men" in London. It was simply unthinkable that the Bank would let them fail. Lesser houses were allowed to go down with little compunction.

When the crisis ended, British merchant houses, including the Barings, returned to a strict policy of tying their bills to specific cargoes of goods. Through the 1840s and 1850s, credit was very scarce, and there was substantial price deflation. As the economic historians Robert Fogel and Stanley Engerman have pointed out, the price deflation was accompanied by steady growth in America's specie reserves because of huge Western gold and silver finds. It is one of the rare instances of the money supply contracting, instead of expanding powerfully, as specie reserves grew, which is a measure of the damage Jackson had done to the banking system. American economic growth was still quite rapid, fueled by massive waves of immigrants from Europe, at this time primarily Irish and Germans. Interior state legislatures competed to attract settlers by pushing internal improvement schemes. Grandiose canal developments were being promoted everywhere, and more adventurous speculators were hawking the first opportunities in railroads. Reputable British houses would not touch railroad bonds, but they inevitably drew the attention of European yield chasers. On top of that, the flood of new state bond issues served as a capital base for state banks to spew out torrents of bank notes, leading to wild cycles of paper currency expansion and contraction. By the mid-1840s, about a third of all American states had defaulted on their bonds, including erstwhile blue-ribbon credits like Pennsylvania and Maryland.

The British investing public and financial press were thoroughly disgusted. Much of the blame was placed on the Barings, and from that point the house steadily reduced its exposure to America. The California gold strikes were a temporary stimulant to trans-Atlantic business, and for a few years Europeans plunged yet again into American investments, almost all of which came to grief. Arguably, the sudden flood of gold from the West exacerbated the cycles. When a packet ship carrying $2 million of gold from California sank in 1857, banks closed their doors up and down the East Coast. But by that time, all trade and financial arrangements had already been thrown into uncertainty by the looming shadow of the Civil War.

The Pattern of Innovation and Risk

Nicholas Biddle's brief experiment with a quasi-modern system of central banking may be unique in financial annals. Faced with an essentially new set of financial demands arising out of the rapid commercial development of the United States, he responded with a more or less comprehensive solution—an approach to credit and exchange-rate management that gave the country both a relatively stable currency and the means to expand or contract the circulating medium as circumstances dictated. Critics have pointed out that his creation never really stood the test of time before running afoul of Andrew Jackson, although that was hardly Biddle's fault.

The Barings-Ward adaptation of existing trade-based tools and practices in the 1830s is more typical of the financial system's response to new circumstances. Almost to the end of that decade, a bill-based international exchange system brilliantly served the need for a reliable circulating medium in international trade, to a degree that amazed even the most senior Barings partners, like Bates. But the adaptation was only a partial solution, that functioned as intended only when times were good. A transaction form that was cast purely as one between private parties could not supply the lack of a generic legal-tender instrument. And when the volume of bills overwhelmed the credit-monitoring capabilities of the merchant banking system, the whole system collapsed, just as the Dutch system had in the 1780s. The improvisation was inspired, but as soon as the system was stressed, it was revealed that risk had been greatly increased.

It is a pattern that was to be repeated many times. Demographic, industrial, technological, and commercial developments place new demands on the financial system, which appears to respond rapidly and splendidly, usually by working improvisations on existing forms and procedures. But the adaptations are almost always incomplete, and precipitate a period of greatly heightened risk. After the 1840s, the Anglo-American trading system careened from crisis to crisis for most of the next thirty years, an adjustment period that was greatly extended by the Civil War. Relative stability was achieved only after America's greenback, a new Civil War–era paper currency, was finally tied tightly to gold in 1878. From that point, gold-greenback-pound cross-rates were quite stable, and the stage was set for another vast expansion of international trade and finance.

The same pattern of brilliant adaptation and partial solution, followed by a long period of greatly heightened risk, marks the next major chapter in American financial history, the flowering of large-scale private business enterprise in the decades following the Civil War.

Chapter Two

FLEECING THE BRITISH

Jay Gould may have the worst reputation of any of America's Gilded Age industrial buccaneers. Matthew Josephson dubbed him an "inspired fiend." To Henry Adams, he was a "spider . . . [who] spun huge webs, in corners and in the dark." Even Daniel Drew, Gould's erstwhile partner, said of him that "his touch is of death." Criticism from the likes of Drew rings especially harsh, for Drew himself was one of the most unattractive figures in the history of Wall Street. A semiliterate former cattle drover, a coward and a sniveler, he was the very spirit of negativity, constant only in his disloyalties. It was from Drew that Gould learned the art of the "Bear Raid," attacking the stock of his own companies and reaping profit from the destruction of fellow shareholders.

Gould, the object of such contumely, was surely the most unprepossessing of nineteenth-century tycoons. He was a slight man—he weighed barely 120 pounds—with delicate hands, a nervous disposition, and an air of effeminacy in his gestures. He had a high domed forehead, a thick black beard, and deep-set eyes that crackled with extraordinary intelligence. Gould was a loner, famously poker-faced, a man of long silences, who betrayed the tensions of business by obsessively tearing small bits of paper. In constant ill health, he was also a faithful and loving husband who doted on his five children, who possessed a taste for literature, and who was in his later years a horticulturist of some distinction. It would be greatly stretching a point to call him honorable, but after his fashion, Gould could be relied upon to keep his word—provided that the relier parsed very precisely what Gould had promised, for he was master of the crucial ambiguity.

For all his flaws, Gould was a financial genius who transmuted the private corporation into a vehicle for raising massive amounts of private capital for large-scale enterprise. The period from the end of the Civil War until 1890 was the heroic age of American railroad building, and European investors poured tens of billions, in today's dollars, into privately owned railroad corporations. A great deal of that money passed through the hands of Gould, who in a very short space of time invented, or adapted, or worked variations on, virtually every conceivable form of corporate instrument. Even the creative financial structures of the computer-mediated takeover boom of the 1980s were almost all anticipated by Gould—payment-in-kind bonds, deeply subordinated convertibles, the rococo layering of junior securities. Although he gets little credit for it, Gould was also at least an adequate railroad manager, and as much as any other individual, shaped the map of American railroads that still prevails today. The Gould brand of private capitalism built thousands of miles of railroads and made him and his friends very rich; the problem was that even the canniest of investors were lucky to come away still owning their shirts. Sorting out how to make private enterprise safe for public investors was a work that took even longer than building railroads.

The Creation of the Private Corporation

Charles Dickens renders an on-the-ground account of the state of corporate law in the mid-nineteenth century. We meet Ralph Nickleby, one of Dickens's memorable scoundrels, on his way to a public meeting of the United Metropolitan Improved Hot Muffin and Crumpet Baking and Punctual Delivery Company. The purpose of the meeting is to petition Parliament to grant the company an exclusive franchise to supply muffins and crumpets to the people of London, and to pass legislation outlawing independent muffin vendors. The MPs who are present make rousing speeches extolling the great benefits to the poor from a uniform supply of muffins and crumpets, and the terrible evils, like child labor and alcoholism, that follow upon the existence of independent vendors. After "the meeting adjourned with acclamations," Dickens tells us, "Mr. Nickleby and the other directors went to the office for lunch, as they did every day at half past one o'clock; and to remunerate themselves for which trouble, (as the company was still in its infancy), they only charged three guineas for each man in attendance." *Plus ça change . . .* perhaps; for one could draw similar scenes from, say, today's scramble for FCC licenses. But the world *has* changed, and with the exception of the relatively few goods that remain at the disposal of government, like landing rights and telecommunications spectra, one no longer petitions the authorities for the right to start a business. Corporations must make the appropriate filings, of course, and muffin companies must comply with health regulations, but our jurisprudence requires neutral rule setting, favoring no competitor over any other.

A system of law organized around private property and private business enterprise is a recent development. Locke's insistence on rights of life, liberty, and property still had a revolutionary ring in the late eighteenth century, a hundred years after his *Two Treatises on Government*. The common-law tradition had been shaped by British feudalism—the crown, in theory, owned all the land in England, and rights to its use and produce descended via a complex web of duty and obligation through the vassals of the crown, down to the vassals of the vassals, all the way to the lowest rungs of society. American law was freer of feudal encrustations than Europe's, but still assumed that the right to do business was a privilege granted by government. Even the law of commercial property was relatively undeveloped until fairly late in the nineteenth century. The Barings frequently reminded Thomas Ward that if his correspondents defaulted, it was by no means clear what, if any, rights he would have against them. Lacking a consistent legal framework for organizing business enterprise, traditional societies, including America's, usually fell back on the family as the basic business unit, just as they did for farming.

The nineteenth-century mind had particular trouble with corporations. They were in wide use early in the century, but almost always for cooperative, nonprofit, purposes—schools, churches, public-improvement projects. Few states had general company laws, and courts relied mostly on common-law principles governing trusteeships and fiduciaries. The issuance of a business corporate charter was viewed as a potentially dangerous grant of power. Charters were almost always time-limited, usually for periods of five to thirty years, and most, like Ralph Nickleby's, had individually crafted terms. A bank charter in New Jersey in 1822, for example, required that it allocate capital to help the fisheries in Amboy, and it was common for charters to suspend limited liability for shareholders, or lay out detailed rules for shareholder voting. As often as not, the government was itself a partner and investor, as was usually the case in charters for banks, canals, or the early railroads. Issuing charters, of course, was a rich source of legislative graft, but it also betrayed a deep distrust of the very idea of a corporation. The old feudal tradition at least was concrete—at some level everything tracked back to *somebody*—but the corporation floated out in a metaphysical space that seemed all its own.

None of this was crazy. Great Britain's 1720 Bubble Act mandated one-off, special-purpose chartering for corporations with strict limits on transferring stock; the speculative frenzy of the South Sea Bubble had been sufficient lesson in the evils of widely held shares. But the sheer growth of enterprise overwhelmed the old chartering process, and by about 1870, almost all American states had adopted a recognizably modern system of company law: in most states anyone who registered and paid a modest fee could organize a perpetual corporation for any business purpose. Sophisticated observers still harbored misgivings. Charles Francis Adams, Jr., for example, brother of the historian Henry and John Quincy's grandson, was no academic naïf. He was a commissioner of railroads in Massachusetts, and later president of the Union Pacific, but Adams still worried that private railroad corporations portended an era of "corporate Caesarism." "Modern society," he wrote in 1869:

has created a class of artificial beings who bid fair soon to be masters of their creator. It is but a very few years since the existence of a corporation controlling a few millions of dollars was regarded as a subject of great apprehension, and now this country already contains single organizations which wield a power represented by hundreds of millions. . . . The system of corporate life and corporate power, as applied to industrial development, is yet in its infancy. It tends always to development—always to consolidation—it is ever grasping new powers or insidiously exercising covert influence.

What most disturbed Adams is that the giant new corporations had no soul—no *cestui que trust,* as he put it—no clearly defined beneficiary to whom it could be held accountable. With reason, he regarded public shareholders, with their poorly defined rights and diffuse interests, as no counterweight at all to a determined corporate chieftain in the mold of a Jay Gould. Gould's role in the riotous history of the Erie railroad amply justified Adams's fears.

Chapters of Erie

Cornelius Vanderbilt was the century's first great robber baron, a primary inspiration for Mark Twain's and Charles Dudley Warner's *The Gilded Age.* Vanderbilt made millions during the Civil War from government contracts for his steamboat business, which he had built from a family ferry service. As soon as the war ended, he began buying up and consolidating railroad lines, and proved a superbly efficient manager, although he was already in his seventies. In quick succession, he bought controlling interests in two failing systems running along both sides of the Hudson, which along with his steamship lines, gave him complete control over Hudson River shipping. When the lines became spectacularly profitable—their stock rose a hundredfold—the owners of another failing line, the New York Central, voted to give Vanderbilt a controlling position in their road. (There were no tax lawyers to complicate the transaction.) He immediately worked the same alchemy, forging the three systems into an efficient and highly profitable statewide network. A few years later, when he won legislative approval to consolidate all three lines into a single corporation, he awarded himself a fee of $26 million in cash and stock—more than a quarter billion dollars in today's prices, a handsome sum in any age—and became America's richest man.

There was one major line left in New York, the Erie, already known as "the scarlet woman of Wall Street," and controlled by Daniel Drew, known as the "Speculative Director." Drew's bear raid on the Erie in 1866 is a good example of his methods. He first made a substantial, but secret, loan to Erie, secured by a generous allocation of treasury stock and convertible bonds. Then, when the market rose later in the year, he began shorting the stock. (A trader goes short by selling stock which he does not yet own for future delivery. Since he must later cover his short position by buying stock in the market, he is betting that the stock price will fall.) As Drew's short position grew, Wall Street professionals, believing that he would be forced to buy huge quantities of Erie, gleefully bid up the price. At the crucial moment, of course, Drew dumped his huge trove of new stock and convertibles onto the market, the price of Erie collapsed, and he reaped millions in profits. Even in 1866, honest businessmen considered his behavior reprehensible.

The Erie was the missing piece in Vanderbilt's statewide network, and in 1868, he and Drew reached terms on a purchase agreement. Drew predictably reneged on the understanding, making a profit by quietly trading against the market's rumors. Vanderbilt was outraged, and tendered for Erie stock in the open market. Drew, worried about his own staying power, allied with Gould, then still a young trader, and Jim Fisk, a charismatic, Rabelaisian scoundrel, who was close to Tammany's Boss Tweed. The battle for Erie went its picaresque way for the rest of the year. All the protoganists had their pet judges, with as many as five at a time issuing injunctions and counterinjunctions. Vanderbilt temporarily got the upper hand in contempt citations, and Drew, Fisk, and Gould were forced to hole up in Jersey City for months. Both sides employed armies of thugs, and one right-of-way battle ended in a spectacular head-on crash of locomotives. Impeachment charges were later brought against two judges, George Barnard and Albert Cardozo, the father of the great jurist Benjamin Cardozo; Barnard was convicted, and Cardozo resigned rather than face trial. (It seems to have been only the openness and scale of their corruption that offended the organized bar.) On at least two separate occasions, Drew tried to sell out Fisk and Gould and ally with Vanderbilt but was incapable of keeping his word to anyone.

In the end, Drew, Fisk, and Gould brought Vanderbilt to his knees by what may have been the earliest "poison pill" defense. In anticipation of the takeover battle, the three had bought up and stockpiled small bankrupt lines around the state. Under state law, a railroad was allowed to issue new stock as payment for the 100 percent leasing of another line. Drew, Fisk, and Gould leased one line after the other to Erie, at wildly inflated values, taking payment in stock, which they immediately dumped on the market. Overall, they managed to pump out some $50 million in new stock (perhaps a half billion in today's dollars), tripling the number of shares outstanding, which had already been heavily watered by Drew's earlier bear manipulations. Apparently not realizing what was going on, Vanderbilt kept buying, but when the triumvirate's strategy became clear, the price of Erie collapsed, and Vanderbilt faced huge margin calls. (As with most big traders, his brokers supplied about 90 percent of the funds for his purchases, using the purchased stock as collateral. As the stock price nosedived, Vanderbilt had to stump up cash in order to maintain the value of the brokers' collateral.) Even with his great wealth, rumors swept the Street that Vanderbilt might fail.

Vanderbilt met his margin calls, but had the good sense to withdraw from the fray, admitting that he had learned "never to kick a skunk." As part of a truce, however, Gould and Fisk denuded the Erie treasury to make good most of the Commodore's losses. Shortly thereafter, tired of Drew's constant double crosses, they ganged up on the old bear and sent him packing as well. Fisk used the residue of Erie's funds to buy a palatial opera house. He installed Erie's offices on the top floor, took his nightly entertainment in the theater, and used the chorus as his harem. In 1872, still in his thirties, he was shot to death by a jealous lover.

Before Fisk was killed, however, he and Gould became even better known for a legendary attempt to corner the gold market in 1869. Later scholarship suggests that the attempt at a gold corner may indeed be only legend. It is true, however, that when Gould and Fisk found themselves with an excessively long position in gold, they bribed the president's brother-in-law in the hope of keeping the Treasury from entering the market as a seller. Characteristically, when Gould realized that the bribe had failed, he secretly sold out his position, leaving Fisk to take the losses. Fisk promptly produced forged documents to place the burden on *his* brokerage partner, and the losses were never made good. For its part, the Erie remained a capital-starved, third-rate operation that did not pay a dividend for another seventy years.

Bonfire of the Vanities

In the 1870s, Great Britain was brimming with cash. It had profited mightily from wars in Europe and America and was sole mistress of the seas, the imperial master of Asia, the unchallenged center of world trade. Yields on perpetual-term British government "consols" hovered in a trading range of only about 2 percent, and wealthy Englishmen were frantic for yield. The completion of the transcontinental railroad link in America in 1869 inspired financial imaginations, and London swarmed with a new breed of stockjobbers pushing American ventures of every description—the Santo Domingo loan, the Costa Rican loan, a trans-Honduran railroad, an immense variety of North American rail ventures—almost all of which came to grief. (There were rail ventures in Europe as well, but American rail mileage exceeded that in advanced European countries by a factor of ten or more.)

As Tom Wolfe did for 1980s New York, Anthony Trollope, in *The Way We Live Now,* paints an acid portrait of the vulgarity and monied social climbing of mid-1870s London. His Hamilton Fisker, who "had sprung out of some California gully, and had tumbled up in the world on the strength of his own audacity," is an American promoter flogging the stock of a mythical railroad, and is probably modeled on Jim Fisk. Augustus Melmotte, another of the novel's antiheroes, was born "in a gutter" in Europe. Trollope hints darkly that Melmotte may even be a Jew, but he proceeds to buy one of the grandest establishments in London, where royalty fawns upon him. "Were I to buy a little property," Trollope laments, "some humble cottage with a garden—or you, O reader, unless you were magnificent—the money to the last farthing would be wanted. . . . But money was the very breath of Melmotte's nostrils, and therefore his breath was taken for money." Melmotte is eventually exposed as a fraud, but not before riding his mystique all the way to Parliament:

> Of course there was a great amount of scolding and a loud clamour on the occasion [of Melmotte's election]. Some men said that Melmotte was not a citizen of London, others said that he was not a merchant, others again that he was not an Englishman. But no man could deny that he was able and willing to spend the necessary money; and as this combination of ability and will was the chief thing necessary, they who opposed the arrangement could only storm and scold.

With so many golden sheep almost pleading to be fleeced, it was inconceivable that a Jay Gould should not prosper. Shortly after Fisk's death, a shareholder rebellion forced him out of Erie, although the setback was cushioned by a lavish financial settlement. (Fisk's murder genuinely affected Gould and may have left him temporarily off his guard; he had few friends, and for all their differences in personality, he and Fisk had remained close even after the gold fiasco.) With ample capital, Gould contented himself for a while trading for his own account, and then, in the wake of the financial crash of 1873, suddenly emerged in a controlling position of the Union Pacific railroad, the transcontinental rail link from east of the Missouri to the Pacific Ocean. Contemporaries suspected Gould of having maneuvered his way into control through one of his patented bear raids. But he can hardly be blamed for the depressed value of the Union Pacific: It was widely viewed as a white elephant, and its shares had been battered by its link with the Credit Mobilier scandal, the Watergate of its era, a *cause célèbre* that forever clinched the image of the Grant years as ones of pervasive corruption.

The Union Pacific was chartered by the national government in 1862, which was about the earliest date that a transcontinental road was practicable. It was the last major railroad to have a direct government financial subvention other than land grants, for it was assumed that the venture was far too risky for private capital. Perversely, the government assistance was in a form that made private investment almost impossible. The aid was in the form of long-term loans that could be drawn down only after the completion of each twenty-mile length of track—at three different rates, according to the terrain crossed. The government had a first lien on the road, and a claim on a specified percentage of "net earnings." If the road was not completed on schedule, private investors would lose all their interest; even worse, after construction started, the Congress awarded a similar franchise on substantially the same terms to another railroad starting from the west, thereby diluting the profit opportunities of the original investors. Finally, Congress persisted in speaking of the loans as if they were outright subsidies, and interpreted the legislation in the harshest possible way. "Net earnings," for example, was taken to mean *operating* income—that is, before interest expense—an interpretation that was later upheld by the Supreme Court. No investor in his right mind would ante up cash on such terms.

The Union Pacific's promoters therefore fell back on the expedient of a construction company, which they dubbed the Credit Mobilier of America. To the confusion of generations of history students, the company had no connection with the French bank of the same name. The name was chosen only because one of the organizers liked its cachet. The confusion was compounded because the French *Crédit Mobilier* collapsed in 1867, so there was a

"Credit Mobilier scandal" in both countries at the same time. Inevitably, suspicious congressmen saw a sinister foreign hand at work.

Credit Mobilier was owned by the Union Pacific's promoters. It raised capital in its own name to finance the railroad's construction, and was repaid, at a healthy profit, as the Union Pacific drew down its federal loans. The construction company device became a favorite way for American railroad promoters to siphon money away from investors, and was frequently used by Gould. In Credit Mobilier's case, however, although there was certainly some skimming, the profits were not nearly as outrageous as contemporaries believed, given the enormous risks of the enterprise. The logistics of traversing unmapped mountains with tons of steel and rail were prodigious, to say nothing of the animal rustlers, hostile Indians, avalanches, blizzards, and grizzly bears that dogged the passage. From an investor's standpoint, such unpredictable costs made the government's fixed price per mile drawdown system even more unattractive.

Congressional investigations into Credit Mobilier came to an embarrassing, and hilarious, conclusion in 1873 when Oake Ames, a proper Bostonian who affected an air of stiff rectitude, conceded that large amounts of the company's stock had been distributed to congressmen—which, strictly speaking, was not illegal—but insisted that the names of the recipients were confidential. All congressmen thereupon denied having received any of the stock. Outraged, Ames released his account books listing the congressmen-beneficiaries. The investigating committee concluded that Ames was guilty of bribery, but that the congressmen were innocent of receiving bribes, since they did not understand his nefarious purpose. The notion that congressmen as a class were entitled to a defense of diminished responsibility delighted the nation's editorial writers.

Gould took over the Union Pacific just as the investigations were winding down, and during his five years as chief executive, turned in at least a creditable performance. Gould rode the length and breadth of the system every year, brought costs under control, and worked hard to exploit the line's collateral assets—

land sales, mining properties, and the like—with some real, if always mixed, successes. He was occasionally accused of skimping on maintenance, but the line was under terrible financial pressure—rate wars raged on every side—and his record was probably no worse than anyone else's. He manipulated the stock price shamelessly, although usually in the interest of the company, pushing it up in anticipation of bond flotations. (In this era, reputable houses would deal only in bonds and preferred stock. Theory held that the value of bonds and preferred stock should not exceed the value of a company's hard assets, while common equity represented intangibles like goodwill. Pushing up stock prices, however, usually improved the terms of a bond flotation.) During his entire tenure, Gould was a major creditor of the company, and he may well have invested more money than he ever got back.

Gould's reign at Union Pacific ultimately foundered on his inability to restructure the agreement with the government. He came within a congressional vote or two of a deal in 1878, but the lingering enmities of the Credit Mobilier scandal, and perhaps Gould's own reputation for sharp dealing, scuttled his hopes. He withdrew from active management of the company in 1879; rumors were that he was forced out, but that seems unlikely. He sold a good deal of his stock at a handsome profit but remained a major shareholder and kept his seat on the executive committee. Instead of retreating from railroad ventures, he was merely clearing his decks to fight on a much broader front.

The 1880s saw Gould at his most dazzling. Almost as soon as he stepped down from running the Union Pacific, he began to snap up a series of struggling, often bankrupt, rail lines—the Kansas Pacific, the Denver Pacific, the Katy, the Wabash, the Hannibal, the Bee Line, the Kansas City, the Missouri Pacific, the Kansas Central, the Rio Grande, the Texas Pacific. Since few people knew of his change of status, speculators assumed he was executing a mysterious strategy for the Union Pacific. On the contrary, he was surrounding it, and stitching together the skeleton of a vast, unified rail system with the potential of monopolizing traffic among the most important Western cities and agricultural centers. He eventually sold a substantial portion of his holdings back to the Union Pacific at a large profit. Muckrakers cried highway robbery, and the transaction severely strained the Union Pacific's balance sheet, but it gave the road the rate base and geographic reach to become a viable enterprise.

Gould leveraged his growing dominance in railroads into simultaneous control of the telegraph industry. The two industries were symbiotic: rail lines were logical routes for telegraph wires and were regularly patrolled by maintenance crews, while stationmasters conveniently doubled as telegraph operators. New federal legislation that prohibited exclusive contracts between railroad and telegraph companies—somewhat like 1990s "open-access" rules for telephone systems—allowed Gould to invade the Vanderbilt railroad empire, which was the base for the Vanderbilt-owned Western Union. After a classic bear raid on Western Union stock, coupled with an aggressive competitive assault by Gould's upstart telegraph companies, the Commodore's son, William H., who lacked his father's stomach for warfare, sold out on attractive terms. Within two years of stepping down from Union Pacific, Gould was the dominant figure in both the railroad and telecommunications industries.

Gould's path to the top was very rough on bondholders. Much like a Victor Posner in the 1980s, he was a master of bankruptcy proceedings, and he typically took a small piece of each class of security so he would always have a seat at the creditors' table. More than once he paid a defaulted interest payment out of his pocket, which bondholders gratefully accepted, only to find that Gould had thereby established a senior position. Or he would push a line into bankruptcy having first assured that a friendly judge would appoint him or his minions as receivers. Self-dealing contracts—for construction, real estate management, mineral exploitation—generated big profits for insiders, even while bondholders were wallowing in the coils of receivership. The markets for common stock were very thin, and prices very volatile, so it was easy to bull a stock, or drive it through the floor, as Gould chose. His weapons were paper. By simultaneously driving up the stock of Company A and driving down of that of Company B, he could force an acquisition on attractive terms. Even when B's management knew they were being paid in fictional coin, it was often better to join with Gould and benefit from his maneuvers than to stay outside and get battered.

The very secretiveness of Gould's operations added to his legend. As in the case of the famous 1869 "gold corner," when he was probably just trying to escape from an unwise position, his contemporaries perceived a Gould plot behind every market tremor. Instead of being associated with a single showcase line, like most railroad men, he seemed to pop up here, there, and everywhere. Serious people worried that he had bugged the telegraph wires and knew all of his rivals' moves in advance. In reality, he had his share of setbacks; in the late 1880s especially, when rivals turned his favorite bear raid technique against him, it took all of his genius to escape, but escape he did. The cap of his career may have been in 1890, two years before his death, when he wrested back control of the Union Pacific from Charles Francis Adams, who, he knew, despised him. When the two men finally met during the transfer of control, Gould, whose manners were always exquisite, was quiet and deferential, taking pains to spare Adams's feelings. Adams was too much the snob to be grateful to such as Gould and crowed in his diary that the little man had been cowed by his own evident class superiority.

The most recent serious scholarship on Gould suggests that behind all the financial razzle-dazzle, he was seriously interested in his railroads, that he did at least a decent job of maintaining them—he had to, for competition was fierce—and that he was driven more by the challenge of imposing order on a chaotic system than a lust for money. To be sure, he ran roughshod over investors, but in a Darwinian world, yield-crazed Europeans, lined up with open purses as far as the eye could see, surely invited running over.

The more interesting question, perhaps, is why did investors put up with it? By the early 1890s, perhaps a third of all railroads, measured by miles, were in bankruptcy; most of the other railroad companies were teetering on the edge, and a whole generation of European investors were at risk of losing everything. Part of the answer is undoubtedly the eternal vulnerability of the greedy. But part of it is also the romance of the railroads. They were a transformative industry, and besotted Gould as much as his investors. The Union Pacific that struggled its way across the Rockies in the 1860s was a venture from the era of mules and covered wagons. Just thirty years later, it was a modern industrial enterprise, with factory-sized central machine shops, modern logistics, engineered maintenance systems, far-flung contractual connections with the coal, steel, and timber industries. In the decade of the 1880s alone, America built more than 75,000 new miles of railroad and rebuilt many tens of thousands of miles of obsolete road. Railroads powered the country into the industrial era; in 1882, for example, the railroad industry consumed 75 percent of the nation's rolled-steel output. More important, railroads linked steel mills to their ore and coal supplies; tank cars were moving pipelines from oil fields to industrial cities; farms became food factories for urban masses. The face of the world changed forever.

The millennial promise of railroads that so transfixed investors, in short, came true. That so few people made money was partly because of the financial machinations of Gould and his ilk, but also because of the brutal, fixed-cost nature of the business. When Gould began surrounding the Union Pacific lines with his own network in 1879, he touched off an era of cutthroat competition. For most of the 1880s, the maneuverings of the railroad magnates looked like an intricate version of the Chinese game of Go—each line attempting to outflank every other, pick off the fattest rates, get fastest access to the preferred city. The economics of enormous sunk costs inexorably pushed toward filling cars at any price, so the industry careened from rate war to rate war. The DRAM (dynamic random access memory chip) industry is a modern analogue. DRAM factories cost a billion dollars or more, but the variable cost of making a chip is only pennies, so companies are willy-nilly forced into price wars to fill capacity. Similarly, the airline industry, an example even closer to railroads, has almost never made a profit in its half-century history. The logic of DRAMS, airlines, and railroads—massive fixed costs and low marginal costs—generates the cycle of huge upfront investment, price wars, bankruptcy, and, usually, a cartel, either by government intervention or by private agreement, as among the Japanese DRAM makers in the 1980s.

Speculation and the Economy

The years from the Civil War to the end of the century were mostly ones of financial chaos. A market crash in 1873 persisted for six years, and prices of all commodities sank like a stone. Gould himself was almost trapped in the financial turmoil of the late 1880s, and the crash of 1892–93 was particularly savage, with effects that persisted for years. The Grange movement, the campaign for "Free Silver," and William Jennings Bryan's famous "Cross of Gold" speech mark the strength of the popular distress at the continuing financial depression.

Part of the problem was the country's primitive financial system. During the war, the Union government had tried to float bonds for specie. The bond issue failed, but it sucked enough specie out of the banks to force a nationwide suspension of specie payments. The government tried to substitute paper "greenbacks," which depreciated rapidly, and midway through the war finally created a system of national banks. They were individually chartered, had higher reserve requirements than most state banks, and were authorized to issue notes backed by government bonds, but there was no central mechanism, like the Bank of the United States or the Federal Reserve System, to maintain order in the credit markets, and no protection for depositors when banks failed.

Market professionals like Gould readily exploited the disorder. For much of the postwar period, for example, the country effectively had a dual currency system—internal trade was denominated in greenbacks, but foreign transactions were in gold. So American exporters typically borrowed ("shorted") gold in the fall and sold it to finance the purchase of crops, and would then pay back the gold when they sold the crops in Europe. Shorting gold accomplished two objectives. Borrowing gold and selling it for greenbacks was, in the first place, a convenient way to finance crop purchases. Secondly, it protected merchants from a rise in the greenback while their goods were in transit— they owed gold at home and collected gold abroad. But since America was short enough of gold in normal times because of persistent trade deficits, the annual crop-related gold operations invariably meant a contraction in credit availability. So a Jay Gould routinely timed bear raids to coincide with the fall crop financings. With credit so tight—brokers' loan rates regularly went as high as 20 percent in September and October—it was very hard for a company to finance a defense against a determined bear.

But remarkably, and quite unlike the 1930s, the travails of the financial community seem to have had little to do with the real economy. At the very top of the economy, financiers decried falling prices, collapsing real estate ventures, unrefinanceable mortgages, bankrupt railroads, and savage contractions in the credit markets. But at precisely the same time, for more than forty years after the Civil War, the country enjoyed the fastest sustained rate of real economic growth in its history. The annual rate of real growth over the entire forty years was 4.3 percent. Only the 1960s saw a faster real growth rate, of 4.5 percent, but it was mostly concentrated in just the five years from 1964 through 1968. In part, the very rapid growth was fueled by immigration. In the first decade of the twentieth century, for example, when immigration was at its all-time high, new immigrants, mostly younger people of working age, swelled the population by more than 10 percent. But even on a per capita basis, growth was still very high, at 2.2 percent for the entire forty years. Per capita growth rates were slightly higher, at 2.3 percent, during the post–World War II years (1950–69) and were slightly higher again, at 2.4 percent, from 1982 through 1990, but in neither case was the growth sustained over so long a period. Even during the 1870s, a time of constant financial crisis, which historians like Allan Nevins reflexively dubbed a period of "long and merciless depression," real annual growth was between 5 and

6 percent. The best available historical reconstructions suggest that American per capita incomes actually passed those in Great Britain sometime in the 1870s. In the depths of that "merciless depression," that is, Americans somehow became the richest people in the world.

It would be too much to say that there was a disconnect between the financial sector and the real economy. From 1870 to 1900, the net inflow of capital from Europe—in the form of export credits, purchases of state and federal bonds, and direct investment in industry—was in the tens of billions of dollars, in today's currency. But at the ground level, the economy was still relatively unmonetized. The very rapid growth of the 1870s, for example, coincided with a pronounced fall in prices—the cost of living fell by about a fourth from the end of the war to 1880. During this entire period, the national Treasury, on "sound money" principles, despite an uproar in Congress, succeeded in keeping the growth of money to a pace much slower than the growth of the economy. Rapid economic growth and rising purchasing power, therefore, instead of showing up in the form of rising nominal incomes, as it would today, worked its way through as falling prices. It is inconceivable that a modern economy could adjust so flexibly.

The perception of great economic hardship during the 1870s and 1880s, to some substantial degree, therefore, reflects what economists call "money illusion." Farmers bewailed the persistent drop in farm prices, without noticing that the price of almost everything else was falling too. Falling prices favor creditors, of course; farm foreclosures were common, and the rate of tenantry in the West increased during this period. But farmers were actually quite cautious about taking on debt—according to one study, farm debt averaged only about 13 percent of assets during this period—and the picture of great numbers of cruelly dispossessed farm families may contain a good seasoning of mythmaking. Similarly, there were violent uprisings by railroad workers in 1877, after their wages had fallen by some 20 percent, but price levels fell at least as fast, so they may have actually been gaining ground. In a time of unceasing railroad rate wars and falling freight rates, rural-state legislatures were still besieged with complaints about the railroads' monopoly pricing power. Reform exposés of dreadful conditions in teeming slums added to an impression of great hardship, but huge investments were under way in sanitation, clean water supplies, transportation, police forces, paved streets, lighting, parks, and public schools. Life was hard for a European peasant landing in an American industrial city, but for an Irishman fleeing famine, or an Italian laborer escaping the grip of the *padrone* system, it was real economic progress.

The tendency of the financial press to treat the stock market as a proxy for the real economy was therefore even more of an error in the 1870s and 1880s than it is today. The value of the assets traded on public exchanges was only an infinitesimal fraction of the total business economy. Trading in all stocks was very thin, and some of the biggest and most successful companies, like Carnegie Steel and Standard Oil, were closely held corporations that financed themselves from their own earnings. Wall Street operated much like the stock markets in emerging economies today. Holdings were concentrated in the hands of a narrow class of professional investors and traders, price manipulation was standard practice, and market values often fluctuated wildly for no obvious economic reason. Unwary investors could get battered in the markets, even as the underlying economy charged from strength to strength.

The harum-scarum American markets probably did little damage in the 1870s, colorful as the escapades of a Gould or a Drew may have been, but they would not serve as the American economy approached maturity. To fulfill its burgeoning industrial ambitions, the country needed financial markets with transparent operations, predictable rules and procedures, and reasonably tight links with the real world. That program—effectively, making the world safe for public-company investors—was well under way in the 1890s, largely through the imposing agency of J. Pierpont Morgan.

Morgan Steps In

The market crash of 1892–93 was mostly about railroads, which accounted for almost 60 percent of all stock market issues. Even the endlessly masochistic Europeans had had enough. The railroads were grossly overcapitalized; their resources had been squandered in twenty years of price wars and overbuilding in pursuit of fleeting positional advantages; their profits, such as they were, had been drained away by insiders. If Jay Gould and Cornelius Vanderbilt symbolized the entrepreneurial, buccaneering stage of railroad development, J. P. Morgan personified the transition to a more mature stage of industrial capitalism. Morgan's early career had been shadowed by rumors of a swindle involving defective Civil War army rifles. But over the course of thirty years, he had built his father's business into the leading American investment bank and earned a reputation for absolute integrity and straight dealing. When unwise Argentinean investments brought down the house of Barings in 1890, Morgan's firm succeeded to the Barings' old position as the major financier for Anglo-American trade and securities underwriting. In contrast to the secretive and subtle Gould, Morgan was a great bull of a man who could cow his opponents with a roar, who announced his objectives openly and carried them by main force.

Although Morgan is sometimes credited with ending the railroads' rate wars, true rate stabilization was not achieved until the first decade of the next century, mostly through the agency of the Interstate Commerce Commission. (Reformers who had worked hard to legislate government rate setting believed that the new commission had been captured by the industry.) Morgan is better understood as a kind of proto–Securities and Exchange Commission for rich people. Almost single-handedly, he imposed order on public-company investing, clarified the rights of bondholders, and laid down the fiduciary obligations of management. As he once bellowed at a shocked railroad president, "The railroad belongs to *my clients!* Sir." It was a defining moment in the transition from a Gould regime to a new dispensation governed by Morgan.

Morgan's medicine was straightforward. The industry was desperate for new capital, and as one of the only American financiers Europeans trusted, he effectively controlled the pipeline for new money. His price for recapitalizing shaky lines was that they cede control of their finances. He then proceeded to simplify railroad debt structures, usually permitting only two or three layers of debt and preferred stock with an interest burden that could be readily managed. All the rest of the baroque capital structures that Gould so loved were converted to common stock at a price that effectively squeezed out all the water in company capital structures. (Today, we would call it "cramdown paper," for the junior security holders were given no choice in the matter.) A company's collateral assets, the mineral and real estate rights that had been routinely milked by promoters and other insiders, were tightly locked up for the benefit of investors. To keep management on the straight and narrow, a trust controlled by Morgan's nominees would typically vote the company's stock for a period of years—there would be no siphoning of cash flows into management-owned construction companies a la Credit Mobilier.

The course of the transition was hardly smooth, and there were many of the patented Morgan bellowing confrontations, but it was substantially completed by about 1896. Many banks besides Morgan's participated in the effort—Kuhn, Loeb was always right behind Morgan in the investment-banking league tables—but he was unquestionably the leading figure, and he well deserved the rich fees he extracted. Although Morgan also tried hard to broker industry-wide rate agreements, he never quite succeeded, although the enforced merger of many of the smaller lines undoubtedly eased competitive pressures.

Morgan's restructuring of the railroads can be understood as the last critical step in the transition to a system of private-enterprise industrial capitalism financed by public issuance of securities. The first stage was the adoption, in most states, of a sufficiently modern system of property and company law after the Civil War. Ingenious entrepreneurs like Cornelius Vanderbilt and Jay Gould then converted the private corporation into an unparalleled instrument for organizing large-scale enterprise. Their new creations mediated the huge inflows of capital that built America's infrastructure and powered it into world industrial leadership. But the formative years of large-scale private corporate enterprise were a time of greatly heightened risk, for the Goulds of the world proved as ingenious at exploiting investors as they were at building enterprise. Morgan completed the transition by clearly establishing, and personally enforcing, the rights of outside investors against managers and entrepreneurs.

It is no coincidence that within five years after the restructuring of the railroad industry, the country saw the biggest merger boom in its history. Between 1901 and 1907, the American industrial map took its modern form, with the organization of the steel, tobacco, chemicals, liquor, copper, soap, and oil companies that would dominate their industry for most of the next half-century. Almost all the mergers required enormous amounts of outside capital—U.S. Steel alone was capitalized at $1.4 billion—with many of the flotations managed by Morgan. Although muckrakers complained that the new securities were grossly "watered," most of them turned in decent performances, so valuations were probably fair. Despite some anxious moments on Morgan's part, even the purchasers of U.S. Steel's common realized respectable returns.

Morgan's system still had its holes. Like his father and like the Barings, Morgan grew up in an era of private merchant banking. Investing was properly a rich man's game; the obligations of integrity and straight dealing extended only to those of one's own class. All finance, in one way or another, is an information-brokering exercise, but it is remarkable how little information Morgan and the other white-shoe investment firms, like Kuhn, Loeb, passed along even within their own circle. In 1902, Kuhn, Loeb, for example, distributed a large Chilean bond issue in only two days, long before a prospectus even reached the Kuhn, Loeb office in New York. The fact that Kuhn, Loeb, who trusted their man on the site, had blessed the issue was information enough for investors.

Morgan could not have foreseen the eventual democratization of the financial system. But even amid the great inequalities of the

Gilded Age, the wealth machine he had helped create was putting money into the pockets of average men and women, who would shortly want their own turn at the investing table. And that phenomenon would in due course trigger yet another cycle of innovation and greatly heightened risk, followed by yet another process of rebuilding amid the wreckage.

Chapter Three

FLEECING THE MIDDLE CLASSES

Andrew Carnegie and J. P. Morgan represent the eternal dichotomy between the industrialist and the financier. Carnegie was the large-scale entrepreneur, driven restlessly on by his own private demons to improve technology, cut costs, expand his market share, and destroy his competitors. A characteristic Carnegie tale is that having just built a brand-new steel plant, he discovered more advanced open-hearth technology while traveling in Europe. He immediately returned home, tore down his new mill, and rebuilt it according to the more advanced model. Morgan would have been horrified. He thought like a bondholder, and liked rationality, stability, and order. He detested what Elbert Gary, the Morgan man who ran U.S. Steel, called "bitter, destructive competition" that always led to "demoralization and ruin." To Morgan, Carnegie was "what the Anabaptist was to Calvin, the fanatical enthusiast who in an excess of fervor would destroy God's and Calvin's orderly plan for the universe." Morgan's horror was much like that of American managers in the 1970s and 1980s when they awoke to the relentless Japanese quality- and price-based drive on their domestic markets.

Morgan's creation of U.S. Steel in 1901, the world's first billion-dollar corporation, held pride of place as the largest industrial merger in history until the merger boom of the late 1980s. It was almost purely a defensive move. In the late 1890s, Morgan had recapitalized much of the steel industry, just as he had recapitalized the railroads earlier in the decade, and his bondholders were being eaten alive by Carnegie's relentless drive for market share.

The precipitating incident may have been a tube plant that Carnegie was planning in the Great Lakes iron ore district. As the old Scotsman himself later explained to a congressional committee:

> [I]t did not require much consideration to let us see that if we . . . put a modern steel plant there, the ore would come there and be dumped from the boat right in the furnace yard. And Mr. [Charles] Schwab drew up plans. The mill was 1,100 feet long . . . with all new, modern machinery, no men hardly, all rolls conveying the masses without hand labor, and all that. . . . [A]nd I said: "Schwab, what difference can you make?" and he said, "Mr. Carnegie, not less than $10 a ton." Of course you must remember that the [competitive] tube works were very old, and had been running for a long time, and this project of ours was a total departure. . . .
>
> THE CHAIRMAN: Was anything ever said about this great steel plant that you were going to build and the tremendous advantages you had?
>
> MR. CARNEGIE: We bought the land and that was known.
>
> THE CHAIRMAN: And you knew what you were going to do.
>
> MR. CARNEGIE: Yes; indeed we did. *[Laughter.]*
>
> THE CHAIRMAN: There has been some intimation that, even with your sanguine temperament, and your long experience, that the Carnegie works, like Napoleon at Waterloo, were face to face with a combination so extensive, so manned by men so experienced, and sustained by resources so tremendous . . . to have made it no longer interesting for you to have continued in the steel business; and that perhaps you escaped destructive competition by retiring from the field. Was it possible for Carnegie Co. to have met these combined forces?
>
> MR. CARNEGIE: Nonsense. *[Laughter.]* Why did Morgan send word to me that he would like to buy me out?
>
> THE CHAIRMAN: I understand that he was uneasy about the condition of your health, and gave that as a reason.
>
> MR. CARNEGIE: I was still able to take sustenance. *[Laughter.]*

Morgan's offer, which was mediated by Schwab, came just as Carnegie had turned sixty-five and was thinking of turning to philanthropy. There was virtually no negotiation. Carnegie named a figure of $320 million, all in senior bonds, making him, roughly, the Bill Gates of his era. Morgan accepted instantly, and later told Carnegie he would have paid much more. Carnegie's committee testimony sounds a bit wistful: "I did not realize then so fully that it takes a great deal more anxious thought and labor to distribute money wisely than it ever did to me to make it. . . . You can do more harm distributing money unwisely, and do more to pauperize people than you can do good, almost, in trying to assist them."

Carnegie's business methods, like John D. Rockefeller's in the oil industry, inevitably led to the kind of monopoly actually achieved by Rockefeller's Standard Oil Company. But there was a profound difference between companies like Carnegie Steel and Standard Oil, and the combinations brokered by Morgan. Rockefeller and Carnegie were agents of what the economist Joseph Schumpeter called "creative destruction." Although Rockefeller's methods could be very rough, and he paid enormous bribes, he was the first, and possibly the greatest, genius of large-scale enterprise. An extraordinary combination of piratical entrepreneur and steady-handed corporate administrator, he achieved dominance primarily by being more farsighted, more technologically advanced, more ruthlessly focused on costs and efficiency than anyone else. When Rockefeller was consolidating the refining industry in the 1870s, for example, he simply invited competitors to his office and showed them his books. One refiner—who quickly sold out on favorable terms—was "astonished" that Rockefeller could profitably sell kerosene at a price far below his own cost of production. Rockefeller usually just razed the new properties and incorporated their production into his own plants, which were typically 10 to 50 times larger. He had little truck with bankers, and thought Morgan "was very much—well, like Mr. Morgan. . . . I have never been able to see why any man should have such a high and mighty feeling about himself." In a mid-1870s competitive battle with the Pennsylvania Railroad, which had decided to try its hand at the pipeline business, Rockefeller's huge cash trove, and the fact that he did not have to pay dividends, proved a decisive advantage over an opponent dependent on skittish public markets for its financing.

Morgan, in sharp contrast, was attempting to *freeze* technology. None of the motley collection of tube, wire, bridge, and other steel-product companies that he merged into U.S. Steel were technologically advanced, and all had been under threat from Carnegie. Elbert Gary, the man he put in charge of the new company, was a prototype of a 1970s American business school graduate. He was a financially astute lawyer who knew nothing about steel and had little interest in advancing industry technology. His job was to manage a "portfolio" of businesses, to allocate production among the various branches of the conglomerate, and at all costs to avoid cutthroat price competition. After the Sherman Act barred the most flagrant industry price-fixing agreements, Gary, whose U.S. Steel had a 50 percent market share, instituted his famous "Gary dinners" for steel industry executives. As he explained it with almost ingenuous candor:

> [W]e believed we had no moral or legal right to become involved in bitter and destructive competition, such as used to follow any kind of depression in business among the iron and steel manufacturers . . . for a competition of that kind meant a war of the survival of the fittest; it meant that a large percentage, as in old times, of the people engaged in the manufacture of steel would be forced into bankruptcy for many reasons—their facilities for manufacture were not so good, their cost of production was high, their equipment, their organization, their decreased ownership of some of the raw products and other things of that kind which enter into the cost of production would place them at a disadvantage. . . . Then it seemed to me that the only way we could lawfully prevent such demoralization and maintain a reasonable steadiness in business . . . was for the steel people to come together occasionally and tell each other exactly what his business was. . . .
>
> Now . . . if I should tell you what I was doing, both of us being perfectly neighborly and frank, and then I should leave and go to one of your customers and offer to sell him goods at a less price than you told me you were selling at, that would be most dishonorable conduct on my part.

Since the dinners exerted only moral pressure on the attendees, Gary insisted, and no binding agreements were entered into, there was no violation of the Sherman Act. The law, he said, "does not compel people to compete."

Charles Schwab, who had been Carnegie's right-hand man, and who had supported the merger, was disgusted. After several frustrating years under Gary, he resigned to take control of Bethlehem Steel, then a medium-sized Pennsylvania armor plate and ordnance maker. Within a decade, applying Carnegie's old methods, and with crucial financial help from his old mentor, he had powered Bethlehem to the number-two position, snapping at Gary's heels.* U.S. Steel's stock came under severe pressure until a bonanza of orders from a rearming Europe bailed out the entire industry. By the end of the war, Schwab was getting old himself. Semiretired, with a baronial chateau in the mountains of Pennsylvania, he inherited Gary's mantle as industry spokesman and chief overseer of the cozy system of market-sharing and administered pricing. With little competition from abroad—where competitors periodically blew each other up—the American steel industry slipped into a state of self-satisfied torpor that lasted for a half-century.

The Sherman Act notwithstanding, various refined forms of the Morgan/Gary "neighborly" competitive methods became the norm in large-scale industry, including oil after John D. passed from the scene. While big-company coziness probably slowed the rate of advance in industrial technology, it helped to make American equity investing respectable. After the merger movement of the first decade of the century, the number of companies trading on the exchanges was greatly reduced, but markets were deeper and more stable. Big issues—like U.S. Steel, DuPont, or American Tobacco—were much too widely held to be easily manipulated by a latter-day Gould. Even the white-shoe firms, like Morgan and

---

*One of Schwab's first actions at Bethlehem was to jettison the "scientific management" methods of Frederick W. Taylor, who had made the company his special laboratory. Taylor lamented that Schwab let a manager "use whatever methods of managing the men he sees fit," as long as he had good results. Schwab abhorred Taylor's micromanagement and piecework pay systems, preferring an elaborate system of production- and quality-based bonuses for all workers. The bankruptcy of Taylorism was demonstrated by the Japanese, whose methods were closer to those of Carnegie and Schwab.

Kuhn, Loeb, that had never dealt in equities were forced to reconsider their business. More fundamentally, the rapid accumulation of capital by American industry, the upsurge in military spending in Europe, and the newly acquired stability of American financial markets were gradually shifting world financial leadership away from England to the United States.

The "Money Trust"

Cold statistics track the growth of American financial power. Except for periods when credit was very scarce, as in the 1840s, the United States almost always ran a trade deficit with Europe—the wheat, cotton, and timber that Americans sold overseas typically had a market value of about 20 to 30 percent less than the consumer goods, the tools, and the industrial machinery that Americans bought from abroad. Most of the steel for American railroads had to be imported from England until well into the 1880s because of lack of capacity in American mills. New gold and silver from American and Mexican mines covered about 10 percent of the persistent merchandise trade deficit, but the rest had to be funded by capital inflows from Europe, in the form of trade credits and the purchase of American securities. The billions that Europeans plowed into railroad bonds during London's go-go years financed the imports of rails and steam engines from booming British industrial cities like Birmingham. In each of the three decades following the Civil War, net capital flows from Europe, almost all from England, averaged more than $10 billion in today's currency.

The trade balance with Europe began to shift into America's favor in the late 1870s. American exports continued to grow strongly, but imports flattened out; by the end of the 1880s, America no longer had to go to Europe to shop for high-quality steel. And by the 1890s, following the lead of Rockefeller's Standard Oil, American manufacturers were already attacking Europeans in their home markets. Rockefeller, from the earliest days, had recognized that the industrial economies of Europe were the natural market for his refined petroleum products. Even in the 1870s, exports accounted for about 70 percent of his sales, and he grimly fought off challenges through the 1880s from the Royal Dutch Company, which had made big new finds in the Dutch East Indies, and Great Britain's Shell, which had discovered important Russian fields.

The reversal of the trade deficit happened very quickly, much like the reversal in the trade deficit between America and Japan a century later. After the financial crises of the mid-1870s—the same ones that allowed Gould to take control of the Union Pacific—Europeans temporarily withdrew capital from America, forcing a sharp reduction in American imports. From that point, the merchandise trade balance, including agricultural products, was persistently in America's favor. From the late 1870s on, the United States typically ran a 25 to 30 percent merchandise trade surplus with the rest of the world, with much larger surpluses when Europe was at war. The trade balance in manufactured goods took only a bit longer: it was still almost $2\frac{1}{2}$ times in Europe's favor in 1875 ($241 million to $102 million), but had competely reversed by 1890, when American manufactured exports outstripped manufactured imports, $485 million to $337 million.

At first, Europe funded its new trade deficit by repatriating earnings from its American investments, but by about 1895, capital flows shifted dramatically, and Americans suddenly became net investors in Europe—to the tune of about $250 million a year in the second half of the decade. Americans were now supplying the loans, trade credits, and purchases of securities that permitted Europe to keep on buying American goods, rather than the other way around. The shift in capital flows simply reflected economic reality. By the eve of the Great War, the United States economy was the world's biggest—two and half times bigger than England's or Germany's and four times bigger than that of France. On a per capita basis, American citizens were the world's richest by a very large margin.

The shift in capital flows inevitably meant that America, and specifically New York, supplanted London as the world's financial capital, although it took almost a generation for that realization to sink in. Forty years of breakneck American growth had resulted in an enormous accumulation of capital. During its entire period of industrialization, American savings rates were very high, averaging some 25 to 30 percent of total national product—which is fairly typical for developing economies; it takes a while for worker bees to learn how to consume. With the federal government paying off its war debt as rapidly as it could, America no longer needed Europe to finance its relentless industrial expansion, and as the shift in capital flows suggest, it had enough money left over to finance some European, Asian, and Latin American catch-up as well.

The position of the American investment banks was radically altered. When Europe was the primary font of American capital, a bank like Morgan or Kuhn, Loeb could raise funds merely by tapping into the long-established European financial pipeline. But now that domestic savings had become the main source of finance, a new plumbing infrastructure was required to channel the wealth of households and small businesses into the big pools of capital that were the lifeblood of a burgeoning industrial superpower. Some smaller banks attempted direct retail marketing of bonds and stocks in the years before the war, but the amounts of money involved were small, and the promotions were sufficiently outrageous—glossy brochures, absurd claims, misleading financials—as to prompt a wave of "blue sky" state securities regulation.

The primary intermediaries of domestic savings were the commercial banks and the booming life insurance companies. The sudden prominence of life insurance is itself a measure of how fast the economy had monetized. Barely a half century before, when one could still talk of "frontier families," the best way to provide for the future was simply to have more children. But by the turn of the century, even many working-class families were plunking a few cents, or a few dollars, a week into life insurance policies. Commercial banks and insurance companies needed to invest their deposit and policy money in conservative bonds, while the New York investment banks needed a reliable network of buyers for their securities. Within a very few years, the new financial pipeline had organized itself into a relatively stable set of financing syndicates that reformers like Louis Brandeis and Lincoln Steffens immortalized as "the Money Trust."

The image of a Money Trust—a latter-day version of Andrew Jackson's "Monster Bank"—was firmly fixed in the public mind by the 1912–13 Congressional Pujo hearings. The hearings were named after the subcommittee chairman, Arsène P. Pujo, a congressman from Louisiana, but the guiding force was the subcommittee counsel, Samuel Untermyer, a Wall Street lawyer turned reformer, who had made his fortune in mergers and buyouts and knew where all the bodies were buried. As Untermyer stated the case shortly before the commencement of the hearings:

> If it is expected that any Congressional or other investigation will expose the existence of a "money trust" in the sense in which we use the word "trust" as applied to unlawful industrial combinations, that expectation will not be realized. Of course there is no such thing. . . . If, however, we mean by this loose, elastic term "trust" as applied to the concentration of the "Money Power," that there is a close and well-defined "community of interest" and understanding among the men who dominate the financial destinies of our country and who wield fabulous power over the fortunes of others through their control of corporate funds belonging to other people, our investigators will find a situation confronting us more serious than is popularly supposed to exist.

That there was a fabulous concentration of power is not to be doubted, with the prime exhibit being, as always, J. P. Morgan and Company. Morgan's firm, and Morgan's close friend George Baker, were the biggest shareholders in the First National Bank of New York, while Morgan was a major shareholder in the National City Bank and was the majority shareholder in the Equitable Life Assurance Society. Morgan partners also controlled both Bankers Trust and the Guaranty Trust Company of New York. All together, the Morgan firm disposed of well over $1 billion in assets. The investment committees at Equitable, First National, National City, Bankers Trust, and Guaranty Trust were so intertwined with the

Morgan operations that, for all practical purposes, the Morgan partners simply allocated their flotations among those institutions as if they were all part of the same company—as, after a fashion, they were. Cascading down from the center of power were a host of smaller entities, like the regional banks who regularly subscribed to New York issues, and firms like White, Weld and Company, which made its living primarily by participating in Morgan syndicates and reselling their share through retail branches. Kidder, Peabody and Lee, Higginson held a leadership position in Boston similar to Morgan's in New York.

Ironically, Morgan had fueled the legend of his power by returning from Europe and semiretirement to take charge of a near-panic during a sharp stock market break in 1907. By dint of his powerful personality, and at considerable risk to his own firm's capital, he coordinated a rescue of a number of tottering firms and headed off a much more serious crisis. Once the smoke cleared, instead of showering him with thanks, as he thought he deserved, opinion makers expressed horror at such a stunning demonstration of one man's influence over the financial markets. Morgan's intervention, as much as any other factor, made the creation of a the Federal Reserve system a major plank of the Democrats' 1912 election platform. No longer would the United States credit system be so much at the mercy of a single individual.

Although Untermyer succeeded splendidly in dramatizing the concentration of power, there was little legislative followup, in part because he failed to show that Morgan and his coterie had abused their power. The crusty integrity that Morgan and Jacob Schiff, the lead partner at Kuhn, Loeb, had imbibed from the old merchant banker tradition was still the surest protection against scandal. At bottom, Untermyer was claiming that the members of the Money Trust used their power to bilk their corporate customers, but a long parade of the alleged victims respectfully disagreed—they greatly admired Mr. Morgan, were proud to be his customers, and benefited enormously from their association with him.

More important, Untermyer was really documenting a fading

ancien régime: the financial system was broadening and deepening so fast that the old-line firms were inevitably losing their grip on Wall Street anyway. The elite firms like Morgan, Kidder, and Kuhn, Loeb had developed primarily as bankers to the railroads and to American heavy industry. But as middle-class and working-class America joined the monetary economy, a host of new retail and light manufacturing businesses, like Sears, Roebuck and United Cigar Manufacturers, began to build national franchises, and new banking firms like Goldman, Sachs and Lehman Brothers grew up along with them. At the same time, regional firms, like Halsey, Stuart, had their eye on the business of newer commercial centers like Chicago, while the larger insurance companies like Equitable, and the bigger commercial banks, chafing at their role as passive buyers of securities, were beginning to challenge for a share of the lucrative originating business.

The coming of the war vastly increased the demand for capital, at the same time that the economic boom from supplying the European war machine put a great deal more money in the hands of the common man. The entire financial system expanded mightily, and just as happened in Amsterdam in the 1780s and in London in the 1870s, once the capital-gathering machinery was extended beyond the small circle of cognoscenti, even if only to the upper-middle-class segment of the population, risk and instability increased dramatically.

The World's Banker

When war broke out in Europe in 1914, exchanges closed throughout the world, including in America. Initially, the value of the dollar fell sharply: European bankers insisted on payments in gold—mostly, it seems, out of a century-long habit of viewing the dollar as a weak currency. The immediate crisis for American investment banks was figuring out how to ship gold overseas so their wealthy customers who happened to be traveling could pay their hotel bills. In 1914, the United States was still a net debtor country—two decades of trade surpluses had not yet reversed balances built up over many years—and Europeans began dumping American securities for gold. The international jitters ended when the New York financial community, led by the Morgan bank, organized a $100 million gold pool, clearly enough to withstand any foreseeable assaults. The dumping stopped almost immediately, and from that point, the world effectively was on a dollar standard. The value of the dollar rose sharply in terms of other currencies, and by the end of 1915 the United States had accumulated the largest gold reserve of any nation in history.

It took a while for the European powers to realize that they would have to finance their war in America. England executed a backdoor American financing by issuing government bonds to the British public in exchange for American securities, which it then resold in the American market. But by 1915, all the belligerents were lining up for American loans. The Wilson administration, in accord with its neutralist stance, announced that it was not opposed to foreign flotations; Wall Street was not so sure. Influential voices were concerned about a scarcity of credit in the United States and wondered if foreign loans were really safe investments—would any country, including England or France, pay their debt if they lost the war? Repudiations had routinely followed struggles much less devastating than the European war was shaping up to be.

The Morgan bank effectively ended the debate by floating a massive $500 million Anglo-French loan, at that time one of the largest single flotations ever, and certainly the largest foreign flotation ever in the United States. The bank presented the loan as "trade finance," not a "war bond," arguing that it would stimulate the American economy, just as British capital had once fueled a boom in British exports to America. Despite a massive syndication effort that attempted to reach regional and retail markets, the loan was taken up mostly by large corporations and financial houses. The DuPont interests and Bethlehem Steel, both heavily involved in arms manufacturing, together bought more than 10 percent of the offering. For some years, it was the custom of manufacturers of explosives to distribute the loan certificates in lieu of dividends.

The Anglo-French loan also pointed up tricky ethnic contentions. Kuhn, Loeb did not participate in the syndicate because part of the proceeds was earmarked for czarist Russia, where the government had encouraged anti-Jewish pogroms. Germans and pro-German Irish were incensed by the loan, especially in Chicago, where the president of one participating bank received so much threatening mail that he hired armed guards. There was an assassination attempt against Jack Morgan, Pierpont's son and successor at the bank; the assassin, an ethnic German, was probably an isolated lunatic, although Morgan always believed that the assault was an organized terrorist retaliation for the loan. The Morgan firm was unabashedly pro-British: besides their underwritings, they acted as the British government's purchasing agent for war materiel, abetted British intelligence operations, and helped fend off an attempted German buyout of Bethlehem Steel. Kuhn, Loeb handled some financings for the German government, but none after the *Lusitania* incident. Overall, American bankers managed about $3 billion in European wartime financings. Almost half of the proceeds went to Great Britain—a testimony to the long-standing ties between British and American merchant bankers—and just a bit over 10 percent to Germany.

The Birth of Retail Brokerage

By the time the United States entered the war in 1917, there was already fear among the bankers that American capital markets were tapped out. When Congress authorized a $5 billion "Liberty Loan," some bankers advised that they would be lucky to float a fifth, or even a tenth, of that amount. It was the Treasury Secretary, William McAdoo who, in the face of much professional skepticism, devised a strategy of going directly to the retail market—and thereby propelled Wall Street into a whole new era. Instead of the normal practice of having a few large houses buy up the loan and then redistribute it through syndicates, McAdoo insisted the bonds be issued in $100 denominations and sold directly to consumers. The Treasury financed a massive nationwide advertising campaign, stressing the high rate of interest the bonds carried (3½ percent), the probability that they would appreciate, and the patriotism of a purchase. McAdoo even offered installment purchase plans.

It was not the first time that the government had sponsored retail bond sales. When a Civil War bond issue failed in 1862, the government enlisted the services of a prominent Philadelphia banker, Jay Cooke, who had once successfully managed a retail distribution of Pennsylvania bonds. Cooke geared up a nationwide sales operation and publicity campaign—at one point, he had 2,500 salesmen in his employ. He quickly sold out the issue and went on to place a total of $362 million for the Union. (Cooke charged only ¹⁄₁₆ of 1 percent for his services but developed a profitable business dealing in the secondary market for the bonds.) After the war, he attempted to apply the same techniques to railroad bonds and lost his bank as a consequence. (He got caught between slow bond sales and a railroad management, the Northern Pacific's, that insisted on overdrawing its account in anticipation of the bond proceeds.) Cooke's failure helped precipitate the crash of 1873 and squelched any incipient interest in retail brokerage among his competitors, if indeed there had been any.

Once again, in 1917, consumers proved to be enthusiastic buyers of war bonds, and the first issue—for $2 billion—was oversubscribed by half. All together, the Treasury floated the staggering total of $17 billion in Liberty Loans in 1917 and 1918, plus an additional $4.5 billion Victory Loan in 1919. By the time of the 1919 flotation, the process of tapping into the consumer market had been honed almost to a science. The bonds were distributed through Federal Reserve branches to retail commercial and savings banks, insurance companies, and other financial intermediaries in every town of any size throughout the country. Distribution was coordinated with a massive publicity campaign and selling effort that even utilized corps of volunteer sales personnel. The Treasury was only slightly exaggerating when it called the 1919 loan "the greatest financial achievement in all history." Measured by the size of the issue and the breadth of the placement, it was true. Bankers advising McAdoo on the first Liberty Loan had estimated that there were at most 350,000 bond buyers in America. They were off by a factor of about 60. The Liberty and Victory bonds were registered in the names of some 23 million different individuals, or about a fourth of the population.

This time the bankers noticed. The government placements were so huge and the sales effort so widespread that by the time the war ended a highly developed infrastructure for retail security sales was in place. A number of second-tier firms originally got their start as local distributors of Liberty Bonds, and many of them, like the Guaranty Trust Company of New York, became substantial underwriters in their own right after the war. The fact that one start-up firm in Chicago had a "women's division" and a "foreign-language division" gives a sense of the intensely retail flavor of the enterprise. There was also plenty of fraud, especially in the secondary market. Just as happened after the Civil War, sharp operators bilked consumers by taking their bonds in exchange for worthless securities that promised astronomical returns. There were some stirrings of regulatory attention near the war's end, but it did not survive the victory.

The decade of the 1920s opened with an acute awareness that the country had embarked on new financial waters. As Paul M. Warburg of Kuhn, Loeb put it, "Where heretofore investment banking addressed itself primarily to the comparatively few possessed of large incomes . . . successful distribution of large volumes of new securities can only be carried on by following wealth into the millions of small rivulets and channels into which it now flows." Certainly, American industry was capital-starved. The big government flotations had preempted the credit markets, and by the end of the war, any substantial private financing required specific government approval to ensure that it was war-related. At the same time, industry had grown enormously. Bethlehem Steel's order book, for instance, had shot up from less than $50 million in 1914 to $650 million by 1918. Despite the Federal Reserve's best efforts to restrict credit flowing into Wall Street, there was a stock market boom in 1916 and a series of mini-booms thereafter. And as one scholar noted, "The war fervor . . . [had] placed government bonds in the hands of millions of people who had never before possessed such instruments of credit." The country was primed for the Roaring Twenties.

Crash

By 1929, Frederick Lewis Allen writes in *Only Yesterday:*

> The rich man's chauffeur drove with his ears laid back to catch the news of an impending move in Bethlehem Steel; he held fifty shares himself on a twenty-point margin. The window-cleaner at the broker's office paused to watch the ticker, for he was thinking of converting his laboriously accumulated savings into a few shares of Simmons. . . . [Rumors] told of a broker's valet who had made nearly a quarter of a million in the market, of a trained nurse who cleaned up thirty thousand following the tips given her by grateful patients; and of a Wyoming cattleman, thirty miles from the nearest railroad, who bought or sold a thousand shares a day.

Allen exaggerates. At most, only about 1.5 to 3 million Americans held stock in the 1920s, and only about 600,000 people, including a large number of business firms, bought stock on margin (that is, with borrowed money). By traditional measures, those were very large numbers, but not many chauffeurs and window washers were actually playing the market.

The causes of the Depression are still poorly understood. Many different factors interacted to produce a worst-case result, including the fall in world trade following enactment of the punitive 1930 Smoot-Hawley tariffs by the United States; a stubbornly difficult recovery in Europe; an agricultural crisis in Germany; Winston Churchill's 1925 decision to force England back on the gold standard at an unsupportably high prewar exchange rate; foolishly restrictive monetary policies on the part of the world's central banks during the immediate post-crash period; and probably many others. The Great Depression was not caused by the stock market crash of 1929—indeed, the crash was probably an event of relatively minor significance—but it remains a central metaphor for the entire sad period. And the crash and its subsequent investigations shed a pitiless light on the methods and ethics of Wall Street.

The 1920s were good times in America. The economy had recovered from a sharp postwar recession by the end of 1921, and real annual growth averaged in the 4 to 5 percent range for the rest of the decade. The new Federal Reserve system seems to have performed creditably enough, despite later charges that easy credit fueled the stock market boom. The broader monetary aggregates grew about 4.5 percent per year during the decade, which seems just about right, and interest rates were fairly stable after 1922. The period of speculative frenzy was concentrated in just a very few years, and appears completely unconnected with events in the real economy. It took from 1921 to 1927 for the Standard and Poor's index of common stocks to double, but then the index almost doubled again by 1929. The growth of new common stock issuances is even more impressive, rising from $200 million in 1921 to $700 million in 1927, and then leaping ahead to more than $2 billion in 1928 and $5 billion in 1929. A large percentage of the new issues were simply garbage. Just as with Jay Gould in the 1870s, the opportunity to gull the greedy proved irresistible. At the very end of the cycle, even the House of Morgan abandoned its long tradition of crusty integrity for the chance to line its partners' pockets.

The financial markets' magic potion was the "investment trust," what we now call mutual funds, which were common in England at the time but relatively rare in America. By themselves, investment trusts offered a sensible way for the small investor to acquire a diversified portfolio and the benefits of professional management. Wall Street, however, discovered the marvels of the *leveraged* investment trust. That is, if a trust financed part of its stock purchases by borrowing, apparent returns would go up that much faster. Since no one expected the market to fall, few people seem to have noticed that leverage also works the other way. Even better than leveraged trusts were *pyramided* leveraged trusts. If you create a leveraged trust that buys shares of other leveraged trusts, the degree of leverage can be raised *ad infinitum*. (For example, a $100 million trust financed 50 percent by borrowing and 50 percent by equity issuances could buy all the equity of two other similarly leveraged trusts of the same size, and those two trusts could buy all the equity in *four* similar trusts, and so on.)

Wall Street's shadier practices were laid out in excruciating detail by the Pecora investigations—a probe by a bipartisan Senate subcommittee under the staff direction of Ferdinand Pecora, a pugnacious, Progressive, Sicilian-born former New York district attorney. All the financial industry's leading figures were paraded in front of the committee, most to their lasting embarrassment. The hitherto highly reputable Boston firm of Lee, Higginson was found to have sold $250 million in shares of companies owned by Ivar Krueger, the "Swedish Match-king," both directly and through investment trusts. The stock was almost totally worthless, and when Krueger committed suicide in Paris in 1932, it was revealed that Lee, Higginson had never examined Krueger's books or checked to see that the promised collateral was in place. The Goldman, Sachs Trading Corporation was launched in late 1928 with the sale of $100 million in shares at $100 par value. It then merged with another trust, and its stock price more than doubled, to a value more than twice the merged company's actual assets. The price run-up, it subsequently became clear, stemmed from the fact that the trust had bought almost $60 million of its own stock. In mid-1929, Goldman launched two more large leveraged trusts, floating almost $250 million in new paper, with the Trading Corporation buying a substantial portion of both issues. When the smoke cleared from the market crash, the original $100 shares in the Trading Corporation were selling for $1.75.

The firm of Dillon, Read sold an unsuspecting public some $1.5 billion of Central and South American bonds which turned out to be nearly worthless, and were early masters of the investment trust. They launched the United States and Foreign Securities Corporation (US&FS) in 1924, with 250,000 first preferred shares, 50,000 second preferred shares, and 1,000,000 shares of common. Dillon sold the first preferred to the public at $100 a share, raising $25 million, allocating one share of common for each preferred share. The Dillon partners then bought the entire block of second preferreds for $5 million and took the rest of the common, thereby becoming majority owners while putting up only a sixth of the total investment. Dillon followed up by organizing another trust, the United States and International Securities Corporation (US&IS), that was twice as big as US&FS but with the same structure. The first preferred and a quarter of the common were sold to the public for $50 million, while US&FS bought the rest. Dillon had thereby parlayed its initial $5 million investment into majority ownership of trusts disposing of $75 million of the public's money, while earning substantial underwriting fees along the way. When Clarence Dillon, the firm's senior partner, was asked whether the public had been fairly treated, he seemed incredulous: "We could have taken 100 percent," he said. "We could have taken all that profit." A senator wound up the discussion by quoting Clive of India: "When I consider my opportunities, I marvel at my moderation."

The notorious pyramiding of the Insull electric utility holdings throughout the Midwest was accomplished primarily with incestuous investment trusts. Insull actually received much more blame than he deserved, and his utility securities performed better than most during the Depression. His downfall was precipitated by a bear raid led by the Morgan bank as part of a war with the Chicago firm of Halsey, Stuart for control of Midwestern utilities financing. Insull's initial pyramiding of his utility holdings was a device to protect his voting control against New York–financed interlopers; on the evidence, he never expected the wild run-up in stock prices that ensued. He fled to Europe at the height of the crisis but returned to stand trial and was quickly, and it seems fairly, acquitted. He returned to Europe and died penniless in a Paris metro station. The destructiveness of the utilities financing wars suggests near-total irresponsibility on the part of the bankers.

Every day seemed to bring more shocking revelations. The National City Bank's chairman, Charles Mitchell, admitted that they had used their securities affiliate to clear their books of more than $100 million of questionable loans to Brazil, Peru, and Chile by dumping them on the public, and that they had similarly dumped very large holdings of Anaconda Copper when there was a sharp break in the copper market. The securities affiliate traded actively in the parent's stock, and aggressively "bulled" the stock to very high levels in 1928. It also raised $25 million in a public flotation of a "General Sugar Corporation" that was used to purchase a portfolio of defaulted sugar industry loans from the parent that had a book value of $1.

If anything, Albert Wiggin's record at Chase was worse than Mitchell's at City. Wiggin, once dubbed the "most popular banker" in America, shamelessly intermingled his own finances and the bank's, masking his speculations through a series of family-owned corporations. Even as he led a bankers' group trying to stabilize the market in the wake of the crash, Wiggin— shades of Daniel Drew—borrowed $8 million from Chase to finance a bear raid on Chase stock. When the market continued its dive, he made a $4 million profit. The Morgan partners' reputations were tarnished by revelations that they had indulged in transparent tax-evasion schemes, had distributed new issues of stock among influential politicians at highly favorable prices, and despite their long aversion to equity, had finally launched two leveraged investment trusts of their own. Almost all the big firms and their leading corporate clients routinely participated in "pools" to manipulate the price of big-company stocks.

The only leading financial figure actually to be convicted of a crime was Richard Whitney, a vice president of the New York Stock Exchange and the brother of a senior Morgan partner, who had embezzled funds to feed a gambling addiction. His Wall Street friends, however, had made him numerous loans under circumstances that should have raised questions about his behavior and insatiable need for money. Whitney's brother and Thomas Lamont, both senior Morgan partners, knew of his crimes some months before prosecutors did, and could have been prosecuted for misprision of a felony.

The lesson could not have been clearer. "Following wealth into the millions of small rivulets and channels," as Warburg had put it, was unquestionably a good idea—good for the finance industry, its clients, and the country. The vast new demands for industrial capital, the shift in the balance of wealth from Europe to America, and the accumulation of savings by America's emerging new middle class all demanded a radically new approach to finance, and the development of the world's first retail financial industry was a brilliant innovation. But the integrity of the financial system had always depended on bankers' honor, and honor, unfortunately, proved an elastic concept that could be relied upon only within their own small circle. The Mitchells, the Wiggins, and the Dillons of the world, even if they had done nothing actually criminal, had treated their own stockholders and the investing public as so many sheep to be fleeced by whatever means the ingenuity of accountants and lawyers could devise.

Just as in the 1830s and the 1870s, the financial system's spontaneous innovative reflexes had solved the immediate problem—in this case, how to tap a much broader base of American savings for industrial development—but at the expense of greatly increased risk and instability. The rules of ingroup clubman loyalty—what Pierpont Morgan had once called "character"—didn't apply once the capital markets had been opened to middle-class retail customers. Investing would not be safe for the average person until the whole panoply of regulatory mechanisms and information requirements were in place—a Securities and Exchange Commission; registration and disclosure rules; financial accounting standards; minimum standards for brokers and dealers; rules against conflicts of interest, insider trading, and stock manipulation; and in America at least, strict separation between a firm's advisory and trading operations, and between commercial banking and securities underwriting. The securities regulatory system that evolved through the 1930s is a capstone of New Deal accomplishment, and by most lights, has proven itself the most successful in the world.

Interlude

The close of the creative cycle of 1930s financial regulation also signaled the end of a long wave of financial challenge, response, and innovation. The roughly half century from 1870 to the great crash had seen the rise of the private enterprise corporation as the chosen vehicle for large-scale industrial enterprise; the development of a highly effective and reasonably transparent system for channeling capital from wealthy people into private corporations; the establishment of a minimum competitive code for large corporations; the birth of a national banking and credit system; the shift of world financial leadership from Europe to America; and the democratization—or better, the embourgeoisement—of the financial system, with the establishment of regulatory standards and review procedures to make business investing safe for upper-middle-class households. The fact that the great names from this half-century still resonate in our collective consciousness—the Goulds, the Morgans, the Rockefellers, the Carnegies—attests to the dramatic and fundamental nature of the changes that they brought into being.

The next fifty years were as remarkable for the *lack* of development of financial markets. The 1930s, of course, were dominated by the Great Depression, and the 1940s by world war and recovery. But the American business system that had evolved by the 1950s still bore the visible mark of J. P. Morgan's heavy hand. His bondholders would have been delighted at the comfortable oligopolies that dominated the industrial map: General Motors, Ford, and Chrysler in automobiles; U.S. Steel, Bethlehem, Republic, and a handful of others in steel; Alcoa, Reynolds, and Kaiser in aluminum; General Electric, Westinghouse, Sylvania in electrical motors and appliances. The same pattern prevailed in tobacco, radios and televisions, and most other major industries—stable market shares, informal "price leadership," organization men, conventionalized union bargaining. Since war had destroyed the industrial infrastructure of Europe and Asia, the same companies imposed their system on the entire developed world.

With relatively stable inflation and interest rates—inflation of more than 1 percent was considered alarming—corporate finance became a "relationship" business. Competing for clients was mostly a matter of golf and lunch. Banking was the ideal career for the sons of the upper classes—the slow learners could always be placed in the bond department. The stock market was dominated by retail customers, drawn mostly from the upper-income brackets. Big institutional investors, like insurance companies and pension funds, usually did not invest in stocks at all, and were often legally barred from doing so. Brokerage was another relationship business, with only rudimentary notions of portfolio performance standards.

Very fat corporate balance sheets led to a brief spurt of buyout activity in the 1960s. A newly minted crop of postwar business school graduates ran down their surpluses with a half decade's buying and selling of one another. It was a sign of degeneracy rather than creativity—bored executives, out of touch with their shop floors, amusing themselves by shifting the chits on the table. Standard Oil went into the office-machinery business, while Mobil bought a circus and a department store. Andrew Carnegie would have been appalled. The bills fell due when Asian freighters started unloading Toyota cars and Panasonic TVs. It was only after the searing experiences of the 1970s— runaway inflation, the "hollowing out" of the industrial sector— that the financial engine clicked into high gear once again, and it played a critical role in the industrial restructuring of the 1980s and 1990s.

During all this period, one major financial innovation stands out, and it was sponsored by government rather than by the private sector, with its roots in New Deal recovery legislation: An innovative system of housing finance worked almost magically in the decades after World War II to make America the world's first nation of home owners. But after operating splendidly for a full generation or more, its critical assumptions finally broke down and led to one of the greatest financial crises in our history.

Chapter Four

WHITE-COLLAR WILLIE
SUTTONS

In the early 1980s, some imaginative real estate developers discovered a wonderful new magic lantern. First, buy an S&L—you had to put up only about 1 percent of its assets, and you didn't need cash. Make your real estate company a loan, say $1 million, to buy some raw land, and pay yourself a nice development fee, say $100,000. Stick a hefty rate of interest on the loan—say, 20 percent—and *prepay* the interest. You do that by rolling the land loan, the development fee, and, say, the first five years of interest into one big loan totaling $2.1 million ($1 million for the land, 5 years of 20 percent interest, plus the $100,000 fee). When the interest is due, you just draw down more of the loan. Your S&L's books look rosy: interest is being paid, and your loan seems to be earning a healthy profit. Since you own the S&L, you can even declare a dividend. But the weedy little piece of raw land isn't earning any profit at all, and sooner or later, your genie will run out of tricks. By the time all the magic lanterns ran down, the cost to the taxpayer was at least $150 billion.

The American S&L scandal is only one recent example of the damage done when governments try to suspend the laws of economics. The decision by West Germany in the the early 1990s to pretend that East German output and productivity was the same as in the West (which was the implication of accepting 1:1 east- and west-mark convertibility) required a wealth transfer of at least a half trillion dollars, and plunged the rest of Europe into a depression that lasted for years. The long conspiracy between the government of Japan, its major financial institutions, and its large-industrial sector to maintain a high rate of investment in unprofitable business has created an S&L-style financial crisis, with cleanup costs that are likely to be two or three times higher than America's.

There are other lessons. The consequences of separating risk from investment are dire. Capital flows toward opportunities for windfall profit, however unsavory, with astonishing speed. Standards of professional conduct are a fragile bulwark against fraud and abuse; they failed in the 1980s, just as in the 1920s. And finally, there is a corollary to Murphy's Law: When things start to go wrong, they get worse than anyone ever imagined they could.

The Savings-and-Loan Industry

Savings cooperatives to finance housing have been around for a century or more, but the modern American savings and loan, or "thrift," industry dates from the spate of social and financial legislation passed in the first years of Franklin Roosevelt's New Deal. To encourage home ownership, a new class of federally chartered savings-and-loan associations was empowered to take customer deposits and make residential mortgage loans, but within strictly defined limits. They could not offer checking accounts, lending was restricted almost solely to mortgages on homes within a fifty-mile radius of the home office, and they had to abide by strict capital and accounting requirements. The trade-off for all the restrictions was that depositors would be federally insured against losses up to $5000, a critical business advantage in a country still staggering from massive Depression-era bank failures. Regulatory authority was centered in a new agency, the Federal Home Loan Bank Board, and the deposit guarantee was provided by the Federal Savings and Loan Insurance Corporation (FSLIC), an agency of the Bank Board. States also had the power to charter thrifts, but state-chartered thrifts could qualify for federal insurance by complying with Bank

Board and FSLIC regulations. By the 1970s, about 80 percent of all S&Ls and thrifts were federally insured.

The savings-and-loan legislation was the foundation stone of an elaborate, and very successful, national housing strategy. The banking theory of the day held that commercial banks, because of the volatility of their core checking account deposits, should concentrate on making short-term working-capital loans to businesses, while savings and loans, with their "stickier" passbook savings accounts, would concentrate on long-term mortgage lending. The geographic restrictions on S&L lending reflected the view that housing was an inherently local industry, and that only local financial institutions could make adequate judgments of housing values and the ability of a home owner to carry a mortgage. The complete package included special tax breaks for home owners, federally insured mortgages, a variety of interest subsidies, and a federally sponsored mortgage corporation that bought up mortgages from banks and S&Ls to help them stay liquid.

For some thirty years, the S&L industry performed pretty much as its creators had hoped. The geographic lending restrictions ensured that S&Ls were small, local enterprises. Residential mortgages turned out to be excellent credit risks, and as household savings rose strongly both during and after the war, the S&L deposit base rose right along with it, increasing about tenfold from 1940 to 1960. Savings-and-loan executives became pillars of the local community and discovered the pleasures of the "3-6-3" rule—take deposits at 3 percent, lend them at 6 percent, and be on the golf course by 3. It was not an industry for anyone hungering after vast riches, but it offered both its executives and its borrowers a pleasant taste of the American good life. The Jimmie Stewart character in Frank Capra's 1946 feel-good *It's a Wonderful Life* is, significantly enough, a savings-and-loan executive.

Warning Signals

The first signs of unraveling came in the mid-1960s. As inflation clouds began to gather, short-term interest rates rose from about 3.5 percent in late 1964 to 5.4 percent two years later, an increase of more than a third. Thrifts and banks competed for deposits by pushing up the rates they paid on savings accounts and CDs. But that exposed the central flaw in the S&L industry—the assumption that they could, over the long term, safely run a radically "unmatched book."

To an S&L or a bank, deposits are liabilities: they represent money owed to customers. The S&L's main assets are its mortgage loans: they are investments that earn interest for the depositors and profits for the institution. Mortgages are long-term investments—on average, they are paid off in about twelve years—and in the 1960s, all S&L mortgages carried fixed rates of interest. But the savings deposits that funded the mortgages turned over faster than the mortgages did and earned a market rate of interest. The mismatched balance sheet of the thrift industry—long-term fixed-rate assets funded by shorter-term, floating-rate liabilities—was not a problem as long as market rates were steady. But once rates began to move up quickly, as they did in the 1960s, S&Ls were trapped in a profit squeeze. The rates they had to pay for their deposits began to approach, or in some cases exceed, the rates they were receiving for their long-term mortgage loans. Paying 6 percent for deposits and getting 5 percent for loans was clearly a mug's game.

Congress rode to the rescue by passing "Regulation Q," effectively outlawing price competition for consumer deposits. Regulation Q set a ceiling on the interest rates that banks and S&Ls could pay depositors—in 1966, it was set at 4 percent for banks, and 4.75 percent for S&Ls, at a time when the U.S. Treasury's short-term borrowing rate (the rate on three-month T-bills) was a bit over 5.25 percent. The higher rate for S&Ls was designed to preserve the housing finance advantage, and to compensate customers for forgoing the richer mix of services, like checking accounts, offered by full-service banks. The S&L deposit ceiling was lower than the T-bill rate, and often substantially lower, in ten of the thirteen years that elapsed before Regulation Q was repealed.

When it passed Regulation Q, Congress characteristically fluffed the opportunity for a much more fundamental fix—permitting S&Ls to make adjustable-rate mortgages. If the interest rates on both mortgages and deposits adjust roughly in parallel, then the asset-liability matching problem mostly disappears. But adjustable-rate mortgages (ARMs) were still beyond the pale—an utterly predictable, fixed-rate, inflation-insensitive home mortgage, it seems, had become an American birthright. Rather than recognize that long-term fixed-rate lending was no longer feasible during a time of gyrating interest rates, Congress voted to repeal the laws of economics.

The oil-price and inflation crises of the 1970s spelled doom for Regulation Q. Federal Reserve Chairman Paul Volcker declared war on inflation in 1979; he clamped down hard on the supply of money, and the T-bill rate shot up to more than twice the allowable passbook savings rate. In 1982, the T-bill rate briefly exceeded 16 percent, and the housing industry plunged into a deep depression. High interest rates also spurred rapid growth of money market mutual funds that were not governed by Regulation Q, and consumer deposits hemorrhaged out of banks and S&Ls chasing yield. The banks were badly hurt too, although not as badly as the thrifts. Most bank lending business was at floating rates, so their balance sheets were never as mismatched as the thrifts', and in addition, they also attracted substantial deposits for transaction purposes. The thrifts were basically defenseless; instant catastrophe was prevented only because consumers were slow to realize what a much better deal the money market funds offered.

Every financial crisis has its own mechanics. In this case, thrifts were forced to sell off mortgages to produce the cash for fleeing depositors. But buyers of mortgages naturally require investment yields that are consistent with market yields. If market yields are higher than the rate of interest on a mortgage, the mortgage must be sold at a discount that will bring the investor's yield into line with the market. When interest rates rose sharply through the 1970s and early 1980s, therefore, the market value of all the low-yielding mortgages on the S&Ls' books was drastically reduced. For example, if an S&L wanted to sell a typical $100,000 mortgage paying 6 percent to an investor looking for a 9 percent annual return, it would have to knock down the price of the mortgage by more than 25 percent. In a 15 percent rate environment, the price of the 6 percent mortgage would fall by more than half, which was truly stomach-churning.*

Most financial institutions are required to revalue their assets on a continuing basis to track the changes caused by interest rate fluctuations ("marking to market"). But S&L accounting rules did not require marking mortgages to market so long as the S&L intended to hold them to term. Since the S&L would eventually recover the face value of the mortgage, it seemed reasonable to record it at face value on the books. But when an S&L was forced to sell off its mortgages at less than face value, those were realized losses that had to be reflected on the financial statements. By the time Congress got seriously to work legislating yet another fix in 1982, the great majority of S&L mortgages still had not been marked to market, but a true mark-to-market accounting would have shown that the industry was insolvent to the tune of tens of billions of dollars. S&Ls desperate for cash were holding off selling their mortgages to avoid recognizing their true losses, but the lid could not be kept on much longer.

---

*The value of any fixed-rate long-term instrument is very sensitive to changes in interest rates. Assume you paid $100 for a default-proof bond that pays interest of $5 per year and repays your $100 principal investment thirty years from now. Because an assumption of, say, 3 percent average inflation over thirty years makes the principal repayment close to worthless in today's dollars, the value of the bond is determined almost entirely by the stream of interest payments. But if interest rates rise to 10 percent—that is, newly issued bonds just like yours return $10 per year for every $100 invested—the market value of a bond that returns only $5 a year would fall to only about $50. A 1 percent rise in interest rates therefore causes roughly a 10 percent loss in the value of the bond. With a short-term security like a three-month Treasury bill, on the other hand, the cash flow is dominated by the return of principal, so fluctuations in interest rates have minimal impact on capital values.

Garn–St. Germain

The S&L rescue legislation of 1982, embodied in the Garn–St. Germain bill, named after its sponsors, Senator Jake Garn of Texas and Congressman Fernand J. St. Germain of Rhode Island, both Democrats, is usually viewed as a prime example of government idiocy on stilts. But it is worth recalling that almost no one opposed the basic thrust of the rescue effort. The few analysts who did express concerns did so in decidedly low-key voices, and none anticipated the catastrophe that actually ensued. The rescue effort also had broad support across the political spectrum. The basic moves toward deregulating the thrift industry had begun with the Carter administration, and were consistent with its more or less successful program of deregulation in the trucking, air passenger, and railroad industries. The incoming Reagan administration was even more committed to deregulation and supported the Garn–St. Germain legislation as strongly as the Democratic majority in the Congress. Given the depth of ideological disagreement between Reaganauts and Democrats on most other issues, the Garn–St. Germain rescue program became law with remarkably little partisan tussling. The day after the bill passed, St. Germain, in one of the great famous-last-words pronouncements in American financial history, bragged, "This is a no-cost situation. It's not a bailout."

The key elements of the legislation were:

- The Bank Board was given authority to substantially lower S&L capital requirements, to defer the recognition of losses on mortgages sold out of portfolios, and to ease many of the other restrictions that applied to S&L ownership, deposits, and other business practices.
- S&Ls were permitted to enter a broad range of other lending businesses and to offer a range of customer services much like those of commercial banks.
- The ceiling on insured deposits was raised from $40,000 to $100,000. (When it was first enacted, the $40,000 ceiling

was equivalent to about $66,000 in 1982 dollars, while the original $5,000 ceiling was equivalent to about $35,000.)

Damaging as all these changes turned out to be, the rescue legislation was not completely crazy. Congress assumed that once Volcker had wrung inflation out of the economy, rates would drop back to more normal levels, mortgage assets would rise in value, and housing starts would pick up again—all of which actually happened. Temporizing seemed like the better part of wisdom. Shutting down the industry at the lowest point in the economic cycle would require immediate recognition of all the industry's losses and billions in payments to depositors. Waiting a bit made a great deal of sense. In addition, since there was now much more competition in the residential mortgage business, especially from banks, it seemed only fair that S&Ls be allowed to compete for broader lines of financial business too.

In hindsight, the reductions in S&L capital requirements are usually viewed as the most damaging of all the changes ushered in by Garn–St. Germain. Capital represents the owners' investment. In a bank or thrift, it is the firebreak standing between bad loans and depositors' money—if a bank suffers losses, they are charged against owners' capital first. Previously, S&Ls had been required to maintain a capital ratio of 5 percent—against $1000 of mortgages and other assets, an S&L would offset a minimum of $50 in owners' investment and a maximum of $950 in deposits. At least 5 percent of the S&L's loans would have to go bad, that is, before depositors' money, or the deposit insurance funds, would be at risk. The new rules dropped the capital requirement to only 3 percent and allowed a five-year grace period to come up to the 3 percent level. If an S&L was growing rapidly, it could work the grace period rules to get by with an actual capital ratio of only about 1 percent.

Less obviously, nominal industry capital was inflated by much more generous treatment of regulatory "goodwill," an accountant's term for intangibles like the going concern value of a business. In the early 1980s, the Bank Board was trying to force deeply insolvent thrifts to merge with solvent ones but needed to come up with heavy capital infusions to make up for the negative value of the insolvent merger partner. Since even healthy thrifts were very thinly capitalized, and the Bank Board did not have any money, they papered over the problem by approving very large goodwill write-ups for the merged entities. The additional goodwill on the asset side of the balance sheet was automatically balanced by an increase in shareholders' equity—purely an accounting fiction so the balance sheet balanced—making the capital base of a merged entity look much stronger than it actually was.

But even the tinkering with capital rules was not quite as foolish as it looks in cold summary. The losses caused by funding low-yielding mortgages with high-rate deposits had eaten up most of the industry's capital anyway. More important, S&L executives had *never* had much of their own capital at risk. Through the 1970s, almost all thrifts were organized as mutual companies, rather than stock companies. The "capital" on the books belonged to the depositors, not to the managers, and represented accumulated earnings that had not been distributed as interest. (The passbook account holders theoretically stood in the shoes of equity investors, but few of them knew it, so they did not exercise even the minimal supervisory role played by shareholders in stock companies.) The tradition of conservative management behavior didn't spring from a *homo economicus* desire to protect a personal equity stake; it was simply the way S&L managers always behaved.

The really critical changes were quite subtle. The truly crucial but unarticulated assumption of a temporizing strategy was that even with all the rule changes, the people who ran the S&L industry would continue to behave in their old conservative ways. But the constraint-loosening tendencies of Garn–St. Germain were greatly amplified by Richard Pratt, a Wall Street veteran, a deregulatory ideologue, and the Reaganaut S&L regulator. Pratt, with a fervor that seems almost malign, exploited the openings in Garn–St. Germain to push through a series of rule changes virtually designed to draw a whole new breed of high rollers into the industry. To make matters worse, the new rules came into force at a time when heavy staff cuts were being imposed on an already undermanned and poorly paid regulatory apparatus.

To begin with, thrifts were encouraged to convert from mutual to stock company status, but the old rule was dropped that required a thrift to have at least four hundred stockholders, with no individual shareholder controlling more than 25 percent of the stock. This had been a key prophylactic against self-dealing. At the same time, long-standing loan-to-value rules were dropped, and lending authority was broadened to include almost any type of asset, including raw land and development properties. Previously, a thrift could lend no more than 80 percent, in some cases 90 percent, of a house or a developed commercial property's appraised value. Under the new rules, it was possible to lend 100 percent against almost anything, or if one knew a friendly appraiser, even more than 100 percent. And thrifts were allowed to own a variety of subsidiaries—real estate development or hotel companies, for instance—and even worse, lend to their own subsidiaries.

Within the economic equivalent of a nanosecond, sharp operators of every variety perceived that the S&L industry offered some very interesting opportunities. It was now possible for a single individual—a real estate developer or a builder, say—to take ownership control of a thrift, with a capital investment of no more than about 1 percent of the assets, and use the deposits to finance his real estate development business. Even the 1 percent could be raised without putting up any cash. One could contribute, say, the equity in a real estate development subsidiary, or some form of goodwill, or perhaps the appraised value of raw land in excess of the debt that the land carried. And the new loan-to-value rules meant that the developer no longer had to put any of his own money into his real estate business: he could build whatever he wanted, and borrow 100 percent of the capital from his own thrift, or borrow *110 percent* of the capital and pay himself a nice development fee.

If that were not inducement enough, a new owner could grow his thrift as fast as he pleased, without the drudgery of building up a local deposit base. Besides the increase in the deposit insurance ceiling to $100,000, the Bank Board eliminated restrictions on brokered deposits. Financial institutions have always traded deposits. Big-city, "money center" banks, for instance, typically have more lending opportunities than they have savings customers, so they purchase deposits from regional banks, which tend to be deposit-rich. S&Ls had also been allowed to top up their books with purchased deposits to keep up with, say, a sudden increase in local development activity, as long as purchased deposits did not exceed 5 percent of the total. But with the restrictions eliminated, an S&L owner looking for supercharged growth needed only to place a phone call to a proliferating new breed of "deposit brokers" and order up whatever amount he chose. If he was a plunger, he didn't mind paying above-market interest rates for the new deposits. Top-drawer Wall Street firms, like Merrill Lynch, developed a thriving business packaging up customer deposits in brokerage accounts or money market funds into $100,000 chunks and spreading them around the riskiest thrifts. Brokerage commissions were as high as 2 percent. Even if an S&L went under, Garn–St. Germain required the federal government to make good on *both* the lost principal and the lost interest, no matter how outrageous the contracted interest rates. For the Wall Street firms, it was just business. Although "deposit broker" conjures up an image of an oily fast talker in a silk suit, in reality they were the same clean-cut kids who man the phone lines at today's big mutual funds.

Since S&L operators therefore had unlimited access to high-interest deposits, while putting almost none of their own money at risk, it made perfect sense to splurge on high-risk real estate development, or junk bonds, or new varieties of mortgage-backed derivatives. If the high-risk investment paid off, everybody made a lot of money; if it didn't, you just turned over the keys to the government. While Garn–St. Germain sprayed a combustible house with kerosene, in other words, the Pratt-era regulatory changes dropped lit matches in every room. The only extenuating circumstance was that some state regulatory bodies, like California's, had started one-upping the feds in rule loosening, in order to tempt thrifts back into state regulatory orbits. (If there are no state-chartered thrifts, there are no jobs for state regulators.)

But even the radically changed supervisory environment does not fully account for the S&L disaster. While the Congress and the Bank Board were busily creating the preconditions for catastrophe, circumstances in the larger economy were conspiring to ensure that it would be as bad as ever it could possibly be.

A Plungers' Paradise

Amid the bull-market peaks of the 1990s, it is hard to remember how depressed financial markets were two decades ago. The Dow Jones Industrial average broke 1000 for the first time in 1968, quickly dropped back to about 800, and did not break 1000 again until 1982. After inflation, the Dow *lost* more than a third of its value over the period, while the broader market averages did only somewhat better. Successive oil crises fueled runaway inflation, and the bond market collapsed under the pressure of soaring interest rates. Flagship American companies, like General Motors and RCA, watched their markets disappear before the onslaught of an aggressive new breed of Asian competitors, and stock and bond underwritings shrank to a trickle. In the late 1970s, an experienced Wall Street bond trader might get paid $30,000 a year, and was lucky to be working at all. Senior investment banking executives had salaries and bonuses in the low six figures. Turmoil in the markets precipitated a flight from financial assets into inflation hedges, like real estate and art. The price of an ounce of gold jumped from $35 in 1971 to $850 in 1979.

Deep demographic tides recarved the face of the country. The depression in Rust Bowl industries and the soaring price of oil—with a big boost from mass-market air conditioning—prompted a vast population shift from older Northeastern and Midwestern cities to the South and West. Sunbelt cities from Florida through Texas to California grew from sleepy backwaters to booming metropolises. By 1980, Los Angeles was the nation's second city, and Houston was closing in on third. At the same time, the baby boom generation, the massive "pig in a python" birth cohort born in the decade after World War II, entered the labor force, with consequent rising unemployment, lower average worker skills, and downward pressure on real wages.

The economy seemed to go from bad to worse when Paul Volcker's war on inflation plunged the nation into the 1981 recession, one of the steepest on record. In fact, although it was hard to see amid all the gloom, the preconditions for a vast economic and financial expansion were already in place.

- The boomers were moving into their thirties and forties, getting married, and settling down into permanent housing. At the same time, because of very rapid increases in social security payments, older people, for the first time, could keep their homes instead of moving in with their kids. Quite suddenly, there was a serious shortage of housing, which was only exacerbated by mass population relocations. With home prices already bid up by inflation hedgers, the stage was set for a real estate bubble.

- The shortage of commercial real estate was at least as pressing. The first half of the 1980s was the great age of shopping malls—in the Sun Belt especially, they were often enough giant, enclosed, air-conditioned demi-cities. As financial services and high-tech industries rushed to the burgeoning new metropolises, opportunities bloomed for the development of office space, industrial parks, and medical complexes. Tax breaks made the returns from commercial real estate very high.

- It gradually dawned on market professionals that fifteen years in the doldrums had left the stock market seriously undervalued. An industrial restructuring had been quietly gathering steam for some years, and throughout the 1980s

American manufacturing productivity rose very rapidly, making up all or most of the ground lost to the Germans and Japanese. But in 1982, the 500 largest stocks were selling at only a little more than seven times earnings, close to an all-time low.

- The oil price shocks finally fed through into much greater energy efficiency; after about 1982 real oil prices, and then interest rates, fell steadily for a decade.

Just as the national moroseness at the end of the 1970s was overdone, the exuberant bounceback of the 1980s was bound to be a little crazy. Once entrepreneurs like T. Boone Pickens figured out that most oil companies, for example, had a market capitalization (share price times shares outstanding) that was less than the value of their recoverable reserves, it was obvious that one could borrow money to buy a controlling block of stock, sell the oil, pay off the loan, and keep the difference. By 1983, the leveraged-buyout boom was in full swing and stock prices were soaring. Average households had an LBO boom of their own, financing expensive homes with huge mortgages, and totting up big paper equity returns as home prices kept climbing. Developers flocked to the Sunbelt, chasing huge profits in commercial real estate. When the government tried to slow the real estate craze by eliminating most of its special tax breaks in 1986, the boom actually accelerated, as developers rushed to start projects to beat the tax-change deadline. More square feet of office space was built in the 1980s than in the entire previous history of the country.

. . . And the Inevitable Ensues

By the mid-1980s, it was clear that the real estate boom had badly overshot. In Sunbelt cities like Fort Worth and Houston, brand-new office towers stood absolutely empty, and developers were offering preposterous deals to entice tenants into their buildings—five years of free rent on a ten-year lease was fairly common. By the end of the decade, in most major cities, office vacancy rates were in the 15 to 20 percent range, and in some cases much higher.

When the building frenzy ended, virtually all major financial institutions found themselves in serious trouble. More than half of all commercial bank lending in the first half of the 1980s had been in real estate, mostly commercial real estate. Citibank, the nation's largest, admitted to $3 billion in bad real estate loans in 1992, and was forced into a humiliating deal with the regulatory authorities giving the government veto power over future business expansions. Two-thirds of the $2.5 billion in commercial mortgages on the books of the giant Equitable Life Assurance Society were in default in 1991. Its capital had dropped to an S&L-like level of only 1.8 percent of liabilities, and it was forced into the arms of the Axa Groupe, a French financial conglomerate. The giant Canadian developer, Olympia and York, with flagship properties in lower Manhattan, declared bankruptcy the same year. When some analysts began to talk up a real estate recovery in 1992, *Barron's* commented, "Why real estate? you may ask. Why not toxic waste or resort hotels in Yugoslavia?"

As the weakest of all financial services players, the S&L industry was therefore bound to be in fundamental crisis. By authorizing entry into the commercial real estate market just at the frothiest stage of the upswing, however, Garn–St. Germain had made the inevitable crisis much worse. And then the villains whom the Bank Board's perverse regulatory incentives enticed into the industry turned a hopeless financial mess into a near-total catastrophe. A reasonable guess might be that of the final $150 billion cleanup cost, a third was the locked-in cost of the 1982 decision not to fold up the weaker thrifts. Another third resulted from the thrifts' plunge into unfamiliar lending territory. And the rest came from sharp practices, political chicanery, and cowardly or misconceived regulation. The villains helped a lot, that is, but the popular perception that the industry was brought down by a small band of criminals is a gross oversimplification. In the daily press, for instance, the S&L disaster was most frequently linked to the contemporaneous "junk bond" scandals, but only about 9 percent of all thrift assets were in high-yield bonds, with 90 percent of them held by just a half dozen institutions. For most thrifts, the problem, first and last, was real estate.

It is worth reiterating that if the thrift industry and the Bank Board had maintained the old tradition of stodgy management, the industry might have survived Garn–St. Germain. Asset values improved sharply once interest rates began to fall after 1982, and prudent managers could have found plenty of profitable lending opportunities, while they used the accounting grace period to shed old low-yielding assets. With cautious diversification of lending and forced mergers of the weakest thrifts, the whole industry could have limped along for a decade or so, until it was finally absorbed by the commercial banks. The odds of such a rosy scenario coming to pass may have been low, but they were not completely outside the realm of plausibility.

When abusive practices cropped up almost immediately upon the passage of Garn–St. Germain and the new Pratt-era rules, the Bank Board found itself eyeball-to-eyeball with reckless operators. It blinked, and from that point, the sluice gates were open. The Empire Savings Bank of Texas zoomed from $17 million in deposits in 1982 to $300 million in 1984, and the Beverly Hills Savings and Loan shot up from $600 million in assets at the end of 1981 to $2.8 billion in 1984. In both cases, they funded their rapid growth by heavy reliance on high-cost brokered deposits, which they invested in high-yield but very high-risk development loans, loans for raw land, and in the case of Beverly Hills, junk bonds. The Bank Board could have cracked down; even with the new watered-down regulations, you still needed permission to grow faster than 25 percent a year. But the Board looked the other way when the operators thumbed their noses at the growth rules. From that point on, unscrupulous operators had a near–carte blanche to plunder the industry.

Prefunding interest on shaky loans was a standard ploy. You borrowed the future interest payments on a loan as well as the principal value. The interest portion stayed in the bank, but was drawn down each year to make it look as if the loan was current.

All of the money, of course, came from deposits being shifted from one column to another to look like profits. The transaction worked even better if the S&L owners also acted as the developers, because then they could disburse the loan to themselves, frequently on land they had acquired for much less. Mortgage sales staff and their developer-clients had good laughs about their "trash-for-cash" deals. The hall-of-fame scamshop, perhaps, was the Vernon Savings Bank of Texas, which was taken over by a Dallas developer who revved up its assets from $82 million to $1.8 billion in a bit more than a year, buying himself a half dozen Lear jets in the process. When the regulators finally looked under the lid, they found that 96 percent of the loans on Vernon's books were delinquent.

The problem with scams like these is that they had a limited life. In the example above, when the prefunded interest ran out, the worthlessness of the asset would be exposed for all to see, which could be a serious embarrassment, unless the S&L operators had planned to decamp for Brazil. The alternative was to pyramid again—bury the worthless assets in a cloud of new, equally worthless assets, also carrying prefunded interest, so total income would look like it was still rising strongly. And here's where the true evil of brokered deposits made itself felt: The requirement to match each dollar of loan expansion with a dollar in deposits had always been a brake on reckless growth, but when operators could order up whatever amount of deposits they needed just by calling a broker, the brakes were gone. Brokers naturally insisted on the highest rates from the most reckless S&Ls, which naturally pushed them toward ever more reckless lending to book the highest possible yields. Even white-shoe Wall Street firms couldn't resist the high returns. Merrill Lynch, which stuffily insisted that it sold deposits only to "investment-grade" institutions, shoveled more than a quarter *billion* in deposits into just two S&Ls in the six months before the Bank Board shut them down.

Rapid growth was therefore a sure sign of S&Ls on the road to hell. The twenty fastest-growing S&Ls during 1985 (averaging a 73 percent growth rate in the first six months of the year alone) had a tangible capital deficit (i.e., not counting goodwill) of almost $6 billion by 1988. (Contemporaneous estimates of capital deficits, like this one, are probably much too low. Actual cleanup costs were 7 to 8 times higher than even pessimistic 1988 estimates.) More amazingly, 132 *insolvent* Texas thrifts were *still* growing in 1988, 16 of them at rates in excess of 25 percent annually, and 47 at rates in the 10 to 25 percent range.

Charles Knapp's Financial Corporation of America (FCA), with operations in California and Arizona, and credited with coining the "trash for cash" sales pitch, may have been the paradigm case. The Stockton, California, operation pyramided $1.7 billion in assets in 1980 to $5.8 billion in 1982, and to $10.2 billion by mid-1983. It then acquired a healthy Arizona S&L and took off on a growth path of $10 billion every six months, making a mockery of the 25 percent per year rule. William Popejoy, an experienced banker, was brought in by the Bank Board after they finally forced out Knapp in 1984. Popejoy tried to work his way out of FCA's mess by investing in derivative securities that amounted to big, unhedged bets on the direction of interest rates that mostly turned out badly. By 1988, FCA's stated negative net worth was $1.2 billion and falling rapidly. When the government finally sold the California operations to Bass Brothers, a Texas investment vehicle, later in the year, it was estimated that loan values were overstated by $3 billion. (The government kept the bad loans, and it paid $1.7 billion to depositors. Bass Brothers, which had bought a 70 percent stake for $350 million, brought in an experienced executive who quickly put the bank on the lending and operational straight-and-narrow. The following year the bank actually made a $215 million profit, 30 percent of which went to the government.)

Most disheartening, perhaps, was the evidence of a systemic lack of ethics within the legal and accounting professions. Most of the investor safeguards in the nation's securities laws are built around the requirement for outside legal and accounting reviews by independent auditors and lawyers, whose work is governed by detailed canons of professional practice. But the most prestigious accounting firms and law firms repeatedly misrepresented conditions to regulators, or certified the books of the most flagrantly abusive S&Ls, or assisted in stonewalling investigations, and in some cases actually invented misleading documentation. Aggressive prosecution of claims by the government later led to enormous settlements. Among the accounting firms, Ernst and Young paid $400 million and Arthur Andersen, $79 million; and among the law firms, Jones, Day, Reavis, and Pogue paid $51 million; Kaye, Scholer, $41 million; and the venerable Paul, Weiss, Rifkind, a reported $40 to 45 million. The accounting profession spent almost $800 million in 1992 alone, or about 14 percent of revenues, on S&L litigation and settlement costs, and at one point faced some $31 billion in claims. (To some degree the settlements merely represented asset shifting among law firms. Cravath, Swain was only the best known of the law firms that made tens of millions pursuing other professionals on behalf of the government.)

Wall Street firms, which perhaps did not have reputations to lose, also took full advantage of their opportunities. "They were much more sophisticated than the S&Ls," said one investment banker who had acquired an S&L. "And they could sell them anything they didn't want to hold themselves—the tail ends of mortgage-backeds, pieces of LBO loan syndications. The S&L would look at the names on the paper and think they were playing in the big leagues, but often didn't understand the risks involved." Martin Mayer wrote that when the traditional operators met Wall Street, "It was like the Indian tribes when the white settlers brought them measles."

Charles Keating's Lincoln Savings of California was a kind of Typhoid Mary for political and professional reputations. Keating and his partners bought Lincoln in early 1984, when it had about $1.1 billion in deposits, none of them brokered, with about half of its lending in home mortgages. As part of the purchase application, Keating committed to retain present management, to maintain a cautious rate of growth, and to emphasize home mortgage lending. But upon taking control, he immediately fired the old managers and began an all-out growth drive. Within two years, assets had almost tripled, to $2.8 billion, more than a third of deposits were brokered, and home mortgage lending had dropped to 15 percent of total assets. When regulators attempted to crack down, they were met by an all-out legal and political onslaught. At one point, Keating was reported to have eighty law firms working for Lincoln—"They knock you flat, they overwhelm you," said a frustrated regulator. Even Alan Greenspan, soon-to-be Federal Reserve Chairman, was on the Keating payroll, duly attesting to regulators that Lincoln had "transformed itself into a financially strong institution that presents no foreseeable risk to the [government]."

The famed "Keating Five"—Senators Alan Cranston, Donald Riegle, Dennis deConcini, John Glenn, and John McCain—collectively accepted some $1.3 million in campaign contributions from Keating, and numerous other perks, like vacation trips. They intervened repeatedly and heavy-handedly to block regulatory actions against Keating, and when local regulators revealed that they planned to file criminal charges, succeeded in transferring regulatory oversight back to D.C. Bank Board, allowing Keating to wreak havoc with taxpayers' money for more than another year. Decisive action came only in the summer of 1989. But by then, the political atmosphere had turned decidedly antithrift, Lincoln had been linked with Ivan Boesky's insider-trading scandals, and the "Keating Five" were desperately scrambling to return Keating's money. (Politically, only Glenn and McCain survived the scandal.) By that time, Lincoln's assets had jumped to $5.8 billion, some $2.6 billion of which was invested in Keating-controlled subsidiaries. Home mortgages were now only 2 percent of total assets. The eventual cost of closing down Lincoln was well in excess of $1 billion.

Scorched Earth

By 1989, the S&L debacle was much too big to hide, and estimates of the cost of cleanup rose almost daily. As the headlines trumpeted the doings of the likes of Keating, the S&L scandals became linked in the public mind with the Wall Street junk-bond and insider-trading scandals emblematic of the by-now-notorious "eighties." To the Bush administration's surprise, when it proposed remedial legislation early in the year, an anti-S&L mood seized the Congress, and the legislation, the Financial Institutions Reform, Recovery, and Enforcement Act of 1989, or "FIRREA," was much tougher than anyone had thought possible. The old separate regulatory apparatus was blown away, and thrifts were brought under the control of the banking authorities and the FDIC (Federal Deposit Insurance Corporation), which had performed much more creditably during the parallel crisis in commercial and mutual savings banks (the latter are thriftlike institutions which, for historical reasons, were regulated separately from S&Ls). Minimum capital-to-asset ratios were raised in rapid steps from 3 percent to 8 percent, "grace-period" gaming was ended, and most intangibles, like goodwill, were disallowed as regulatory capital. The Resolution Trust Corp. (RTC) was authorized to issue long-term bonds to take over insolvent institutions, pay off the depositors, and sell off the assets. Within two years, the original $50 billion cleanup-cost estimate escalated to $150 billion.

The same Wall Street firms that had made a bundle on the way into the crisis made a bundle on the way out. The RTC, under the the control of Albert V. Casey, a hard-driving former airline executive, has been much criticized for the speed with which it acted to acquire and sell off troubled properties. Properties of all kinds—apartment buildings, office developments, shopping malls—were assembled in huge pools and sold off at rock-bottom prices in speculators' auctions. The big investment banks eagerly bid for the commissions from chopping up pools of S&L mortgages into exotic new bonds to sell into the capital markets, again at highly favorable prices. Big investors, fresh from the LBO game, like Bass Brothers, and Kohlberg, Kravis, and Roberts, picnicked on the healthy remnants of failed S&Ls. The New York investor Ronald O. Perelman bought a string of failed Texas S&Ls for $160 million, and reportedly made 170 percent profit the first year.

In theory, if the RTC had not acted so precipitately, it could have realized much better returns. A number of analysts correctly anticipated that with the collapse of the commercial construction market, all those new empty office buildings would sooner or later fill up, as indeed they did. Cities like Houston, which had been badly battered by the 1980s oil-patch recession, made a strong comeback, with much more diversified and office-based economies. But the notion of an RTC sitting tight to await a market recovery seems utterly unrealistic. Keeping such an enormous portfolio of properties under government control would have created the potential for almost unimaginable corruption and scandals. Admitting all cases where speculators made outrageous profits, Casey's broad policy of getting the whole mess off the government's plate as fast as possible surely made sense.

Lessons

The most striking aspect of the S&L experience, perhaps, is that massive as it was, by the mid-1990s it was hard to detect any lingering economic effects. In a $7 trillion economy, it seems, $150 billion just isn't such a big deal. The RTC bond sales undoubtedly roiled world capital markets, but their effects are impossible to untangle from, say, the 1991 Gulf War or post–Cold War developments in Europe. There was a price rollback in both residential and commercial real estate markets to absorb the overbuilding, and the construction industry had several tough years, but real estate and construction both recovered strongly, as did the big real estate lenders, like Citibank and the Equitable. The most lasting effects, fittingly enough, may have been political, for it was problems with a failed S&L that first triggered the Whitewater scandals, which bedeviled the Clinton administration from its very earliest days.

The lessons may be twofold. The first is that a huge and deeply liquid economy like that of the United States has impressive healing power. But the second is that financial viruses now propagate with explosive speed. Governments once could jiggle the laws of economics a bit, as with Regulation Q in the 1960s, and temporizing policies still looked quasi-plausible in 1982. But contramarket interventions are probably always doomed in today's high-octane financial system, and they risk making crises worse than anyone imagined they could be.

Chapter Five

MEPHISTOPHELES

Michael Milken was sentenced to ten years in prison on November 21, 1990. "When a man of your power," sentencing judge Kimba Wood told him, ". . . repeatedly conspires to violate, and violates, securities and tax laws in order to achieve more power and wealth for himself and his wealthy clients, and commits financial crimes that are particularly hard to detect, a significant prison term is required to deter others." The sentence, of which Milken was to serve more than half, was by far the most severe handed out to any of the defendants in the 1980s insider-trading and junk-bond scandals, and was on top of roughly $1.2 billion in fines and civil settlements. For James Stewart, the *Wall Street Journal* reporter who covered the scandals almost from the day they first came to light in 1986, and wrote the best-selling book *Den of Thieves,* it was the denouement of a criminal conspiracy that "dwarfs any comparable financial crime." "During this crime wave," Stewart continues, "the ownership of entire corporations changed hands. . . . Household names . . . vanished in takeovers. . . . Thousands of workers lost their jobs, companies loaded up with debt. . . . Profits were sacrificed. . . . Bondholders and shareholders lost many millions more."

The junk-bond market that Milken had created was staggered by the revelations. RJR Nabisco bonds, for example, lost almost 30 percent of their value from November 1989 to November 1990, and the same year saw a long list of junk-bond-funded companies fail completely—Integrated Resources, Federated Department Stores, Continental Airlines, Pan American, Revco, Allied Stores.

Junk-bond indices were down by more than 11 percent for the year, while Tom Wolfe's *Bonfire of the Vanities,* the story of the fall of an erstwhile Milken-like "Master of the Universe," was on the best-seller list for many weeks. The "Decade of Greed," it seemed, had come to its inglorious end.

Well, not exactly. Barely a half dozen years after Milken's sentencing, junk bonds—or "high-yield bonds," as they are now normally called—are an established part of almost any reasonably diversified investment portfolio, with an excellent long-term performance record. The RJR paper that looked so shaky in 1990 was selling at a premium a year later, and has long since been paid off. Many of the noisiest failures, like Federated and Continental, have emerged from bankruptcy and are doing fine. The gloom that suffused the American economy during the 1992 election campaign had dissipated within the year. The often violent restructuring of American industry during the 1980s, it became clear, had led to very large increases in efficiency and productivity—manufacturing productivity grew especially rapidly during the 1980s—and America has now recaptured leadership from the Europeans and Japanese in most key industries. Instead of shareholders losing "many millions," stock market valuations increased by more than a trillion dollars between 1982 and 1989. Michael Milken is out of jail, probably still a billionaire when the assets of his family and foundations are taken into account, and is working mostly on philanthropy. While he is hardly the reincarnation of Mother Teresa that his public relations flacks claim, his crimes actually appear fairly paltry in light of the severity of his sentence.

The growth of the junk-bond market and the leveraged buyout, or "LBO," industry in the 1980s would have happened with or without Michael Milken, for it was a response to forces that far transcended the ups and downs of any individual's career. Contrary to legend, neither the junk bond nor the leveraged buyout was a Milken invention. Jay Gould was a master of the LBO, and built his railroad empire on a wobbly superstructure of bonds, the like of which has hardly been seen since. Morgan created U.S. Steel with a billion dollars of borrowed money and layers of exotic bonds and mortgages. When railroads got into financial difficulty in the 1950s and 1960s, mostly because of increased competition from over-the-road trucking, their bailouts often involved "income bonds," or instruments expressly tied to the company's performance, with a high rate of interest and a high risk of default. Junk bonds were just one convenient way to finance leveraged buyouts, and Jerome Kohlberg, a founder of the very successful buyout firm of Kohlberg, Kravis, Roberts, Inc. (KKR), was doing LBOs at Bear, Stearns in the 1960s when Milken was still in college. Back then they were called bootstraps.

Junk Bonds

The American bond market that developed after the war reflected the comfortably oligopolistic structure of American big business. Only the hundred or so companies that dominated the country's business profile—the U.S. Steels, the General Motors and Fords, the Chase Manhattans, the AT&Ts—routinely issued bonds, and only their bonds, along with the bonds issued by the federal government or high-rated state and local governments, were considered "investment-grade." The primary buyers of bonds were life insurance companies and pension funds, who needed to invest a relatively constant revenue stream to fund distant liabilities. By law, regulation, or simply long-established practice, pension and insurance investing was limited almost solely to high-grade bonds. Much like their colleagues in the savings-and-loan industry, insurance executives had their own version of the "3–6–3" rule. Sell life insurance policies that paid a return of 3 percent, or even less; invest in high-grade bonds that paid 5 to 6 percent; and race their S&L colleagues to be first off the tees in the afternoon.*

---

*Insurance company financial crises tended to hit rather late in the 1980s, well after the S&Ls and the commercial banks had gone through their versions of financial hell. Life insurance liabilities have a very long tail—a half century may elapse between an initial payment and a claim—so balance sheet mismatches can take a long time to show up. Insurance policies moreover, are so complicated that policyholders rarely understand their conversion options, so they sat on low-return policies long after S&L and bank depositors had shifted their savings into mutual funds.

The 1973 threefold price increase for Arab oil was like a clap of doom for the post–World War II American industrial and financial dispensation. All the cracks crisscrossing the smooth face of American capitalism were suddenly blown wide open. For the bond market it was a double whammy. The annual increase in the Consumer Price Index exceeded 10 percent in four of the eight years from 1974 through 1981, while the 1980 CPI rate of 13.5 percent was the highest in history. (Average CPI change from 1960 through 1965, by contrast, was about 1.3 percent. An inflation rate of 1.7 percent was a major issue during the 1960 presidential campaign.) Besides compensating a buyer for the use of his money and for the issuer's credit risk, a bond's interest rate has to fully compensate for future inflation—otherwise the bond buyer's investment will shrink by the year. But in the 1970s, new issues of long-term bonds, like newly issued mortgages, were often priced at *less* than the current rate of inflation, and long-term financings, understandably enough, became almost impossible.

The impact on existing bond portfolios was devastating. A long-term bond loses roughly half its value when interest rates double, and as interest rates trailed inflation rates skyward, the value of portfolio holdings dropped like a stone. By the mid-1970s, bank and insurance regulators, the SEC, and accounting-standards bodies began to require financial institutions to start marking their portfolios to market. Since writedowns in financial asset values are directly reflected in income statements, profits were battered at any firm that carried substantial bond inventories. On top of that, in the real economy, any company caught on the wrong side of the inflation surge, like suppliers of goods under long-term contracts, found themselves in serious trouble. Bankruptcies and business failures increased sharply, disrupting the credit markets even more.

Financial markets typically overreact to new information. Dreadful as conditions in 1970s credit markets actually were, the drop in bond values was overdone. Often enough, traders could find no buyers for even decent-quality bonds at almost any price. Inevitably, canny investors realized that there were opportunities in underpriced bonds, and the junk-bond market was born. The first junk-bond portfolios were typically assembled from so-called fallen angels, bonds from companies or governments that were struggling financially. Railroad bonds, and for a while New York City bonds, were particular favorites of the bottom feeders. (The city defaulted on interest payments in 1975, and its bonds fell to 50 to 60 cents on the dollar. The state stepped in within a year, city bonds very quickly moved back near par, and speculators reaped huge profits.)

The success of the junk-bond traders suggested that the bond rating system and the rigid division of bonds into the categories of investment-grade and all others* were excessively conservative. A famous 1943 paper by the economist W. Braddock Hickman bore out the optimists. Hickman had tracked the performance of a large sample of bonds and found that differences in the default rates of high-rated and low-rated bonds were much smaller than the ratings suggested. Investors, that is, were being overcompensated for the risk in low-rated bonds, to such an extent that low-rated bonds actually were better values than highly rated bonds. Hickman's conclusions may have been exaggerated, for his results were skewed by the experience during the Depression, when a wave of failures among highly rated companies blurred the relation between ratings and returns. But his paper lent an air of academic respectability to the advocates for junk.

At the same time, new technologies and major demographic changes gave rise to a host of new businesses that needed financing. Banks did not make long-term loans, and low valuations made stock market financing very expensive from a business's perspective. Rapidly spreading cable television networks, with their promise of steady revenues and low operating costs, proved ideal candidates for high-yield bond financing, paving the way

---

*Third-party rating agencies—primarily Moody's, Standard and Poor's, and Fitch—use similar letter-grade rating systems to rate the credit risk of a bond. Standard and Poor's, for instance, denotes a gold-plated credit with an AAA designation. Investment-grade bonds run the gamut down to BBB, while lower-rated bonds, from BB down, are considered speculative, or "junk." A C usually identifies a bond on which no interest is paid, while a D company is currently in default. There can be a relatively wide pricing spread between the best and the worst junk.

for more adventurous financings like MCI and Turner Broadcasting. The good performance of the high-yield bonds issued in connection with the Chrysler bailout also helped to make junk respectable.

Milken joined Drexel in 1969, while still in business school. He focused on the opportunity in high-yields from the very start, and by the late 1970s ran the largest high-yield trading operation on Wall Street. In 1977, he underwrote the first original issue of high-yield debt—as opposed to just buying and selling fallen angels. By the end of the 1970s, several Wall Street firms, including Merrill Lynch, were doing an active high-yield financing business. By that time, Milken had moved his Drexel operation to the West Coast, where he worked with almost total independence, under the later-notorious arrangement that allocated half the profits from his high-yield business to him and his department. None of his early deals had anything to do with buyouts.

LBOs

Leveraged financings have been part of the financial landscape for a very long time, just as junk bonds have. The average American household has much of its wealth tied up in leveraged home financing, and homeowners learned the delights of mortgage roulette during the 1970s/early-1980s boom in real estate prices. Buy a $150,000 house; put down $30,000 and borrow the rest. A few years later, sell the house for $300,000, pay off the $120,000 mortgage, and bank a nice fivefold return on the initial investment. Or better yet, roll the profit over into a much bigger house, with a much bigger mortgage, and start the process all over again. Buying and selling a business works much the same way. If investors expect the value of the business to rise, they can maximize their gains by investing as little of their own money as possible and borrowing the rest of the purchase price. The catch in both cases is that a low initial investment implies a high level of debt service, so leveraged buyers must be sure they have the cash flow to manage the debt service during hard times. A default on business debt or a home mortgage puts the asset in the hands of the banks or the bond-holders, and the owners lose everything.

The primary criterion for a classic leveraged buyout, therefore, is predictable unencumbered cash flow. That is why LBOs are so rare in fast-moving industries like software and semiconductors that require a very high rate of reinvestment just to keep pace. (Even as they fell on very difficult times, companies like Apple and DEC still kept their balance sheets virtually free of debt.) Andrew Carnegie ran his steel company much like a modern semiconductor company, relentlessly plowing back operating profits to push technology faster and faster. But once Morgan completed his leveraged capitalization of U.S. Steel, cash flows were diverted to debt service, and the entire industry settled into the prolonged technological stagnation that Gary and Morgan called "stability." They got away with it until the 1970s, when old-line American companies were battered by invaders from Japan and Korea, and by American upstarts like Nucor, who think about steel much the same way Carnegie did.

When stocks are substantially undervalued, however, almost any moderately successful company is a plausible LBO candidate, because the debt required to buy up the stock doesn't make much of a dent in cash flows. The very low stock prices of the early 1980s therefore created a unique opportunity for LBOs. In 1982, Standard and Poor's composite index of the stock prices of the 500 largest companies, the S&P 500, was priced at less than 7.5 times their previous year's net earnings, or only about half the normal price/earnings ratio. (By 1987, the price/earnings ratio had shot up to about 22.) Leveraged investors could therefore expect that the typical company could easily service buyout debt, and that they would make astonishing profits if market valuations merely returned to normal levels.

A few early deals focused Wall Street's attention. Wesray, a partnership comanaged by William E. Simon, Treasury secretary in the Nixon administration, bought Gibson Greeting Cards in 1982 for $80 million, putting up only $1 million of its own money and borrowing the rest. Less than a year and a half later, with stock prices rising strongly, it put the company back on the stock market at a valuation of $290 million. The Wesray partners used the public offering proceeds to pay off the debt, pocketed $48 million from selling some of their own stock in the offering, and were left owning stock worth about $190 million and rising, for an eye-popping annual return on their cash investment of a bit over 2,000 percent. Forstmann, Little, one of the most successful, and most conservative, of the 1980s buyout firms, bought the soft drink company Dr Pepper in 1983 for $623 million, or 24 times the previous year's earnings, a price analysts thought was shockingly high. The deal was heavily leveraged, with only $30 million in equity underpinning almost $600 million in debt. But Forstmann immediately reduced the debt to about $170 million, by selling off real estate, bottling plants, and a Canadian business line. Leaned-down overhead brought operating profits (before debt service) to $60 million, up from about $40 million. The next year, Coca-Cola, looking to round out its soft drink lines, bought the entire company for $470 million, including the remaining debt, leaving $300 million proceeds for Forstmann—not a bad return for a couple of years' work. Less spectacular deals, like the LBO of the dressmaker Leslie Fay in 1982, routinely racked up annual gains of 100 percent or even more.

The Gibson deal suggests how much the early LBO movement was simply an arbitrage on an underpriced market. Gibson had a small niche in a business dominated by big players like Hallmark. Over a five-year period it had doubled its market share, with an innovative strategy involving easy-to-use store racks, computerized inventory systems, and the use of popular cartoon characters like Garfield, a strategy that was paying off well before the LBO. Wesray's contribution was mostly to focus the market's attention. The partners' high profile on Wall Street ensured a glittering public offering (at quite a reasonable multiple of earnings) of a previously obscure little firm that they had snapped up for only a fraction of its true worth.

Sober observers were scandalized by the huge profits from the 1984 Metromedia LBO, but it was another case where the Street just got the numbers wrong. Metromedia was a grab bag of TV and radio stations and random entertainment properties like the

Harlem Globetrotters, and had been controlled for twenty-five years by Jack Kluge, who was sixty-eight in 1984. The subtext of a series of analyst reports and articles in the financial press throughout 1983 was that Kluge had lost it—the company's assets made no strategic sense, accounting was seriously deficient, and Kluge was plunging, at very high prices, into a string of unprofitable cellular and paging properties. When the stock dropped from about 120 to below 20, Kluge felt vulnerable to a hostile purchaser. Neither Bear, Stearns nor Lehman Brothers could find a friendly buyer, so he organized a buyout himself. Shareholders got $30 in cash, plus paper with a market value of about $10, for stock that was trading at $24.50 just before the announcement. There were no competing bidders. Moody's downgraded the buyout debt shortly after it was issued, and the deal almost came unstuck when Kluge missed one of the first interest payments. Within a year, TV stations and cellular were white-hot, and by 1987, Kluge had sold off the company's assets for five times the buyout price, pocketing a cool $3 billion himself. It's not clear whether Kluge was smart or just dumb-lucky, but it's hard to make a case that he cheated anybody.

Oil industry stocks were especially ripe for repricing. A set of rather obvious calculations showed, for example, that Gulf Oil's recoverable oil reserves were worth more than $100 a share in 1983 (i.e., the total value of Gulf's reserves divided by the total number of Gulf shares outstanding), when the market price of Gulf shares was hovering at only about $47. So Mesa Petroleum, run by the Texas oilman T. Boone Pickens, started buying up Gulf shares and announced that it was lining up financing to buy the whole company. Once Mesa won control, Pickens said, it would dismantle the company, sell off the oil, pay down the debt, and pocket the difference. The management of Gulf, who considered themselves one of James Stewart's "household names," huffed and puffed about Pickens's effrontery, generating a clamor in Congress. But to no avail, for Pickens had focused a spotlight on just how sloppily Gulf was run. He exaggerated when he argued that the difference between the stock price and the value of Gulf's assets measured the negative contribution of its managers, but he clearly had a point. Standard Oil of California finally came to the rescue and bought out the company for $80 a share. Gulf shareholders almost doubled their money and shed few tears for departed management. Pickens made about $400 million. One footnote for buffs: While he was looking for bank financing, Pickens paid a visit to Drexel and asked James Blagan, one of Drexel's senior executives, whether junk bonds couldn't also be used for LBOs. Blagan thought that was quite a good idea, and as he later recalled, "the rest is history."

Academics love talking about efficient markets. The experience of the early 1980s, however, suggests that markets more often react like mules—they eventually get where they're supposed to be, but at their own pace, and they sometimes have to be hit with an ax handle to get started. The mispricing of American stocks persisted through most of the first half of the 1980s, to the point where it was hard for an LBO to go wrong. Theodore Forstmann, the senior partner in Forstmann, Little, bragged in 1985 that his firm was racking up annual gains in the 80 percent range. But merely buying the S&P 500 index in 1982 with 90 percent leverage would have produced a 70 percent annual return by 1986, without any of the high drama or heavy expenses of deal making. (Federal Reserve margin requirements prohibit stock purchasers from borrowing more than 50 percent of the purchase price of a stock. In a real sense, then, LBOs were simply a way that big players could leverage up beyond the margin rules. Bank regulations regarding LBO lending were changed in 1989 to bring them into closer conformity with stock purchase rules.) The great success of the early LBO deals, in short, is less striking than the fact that it took literally hundreds of successful deals before stock prices recovered to levels that more accurately reflected company values.

Excess

Slow-footed or not, markets inevitably *do* correct for mispricing. By about 1986, stocks were arguably fully valued—indeed, as the sharp 1987 market break suggested, they may have been overvalued by a substantial amount. But the spectacular returns from the early deals had spawned legions of imitators, and any investment bank or entrepreneur worthy of the name had put together a buy-out fund.

From a fund organizer's point of view, the numbers were irresistible. Consider a fairly typical $100 million buyout fund arrangement. The organizers would put up $1 million of their own money and raise the rest by subscription from pension funds and insurance companies. At an average 90 percent leverage ratio, which is conservative, $100 million would generate $1 billion in deals. Assume, again very conservatively, that the deals are sold out of portfolio at an average 25 percent increase over the purchase price four years later. What do the fund managers get? They get a 1 to 2 percent annual management fee on the equity fund, or $1 to 2 million a year. They get perhaps 0.5 to 1 percent deal fees on the gross value of the completed deals, for a total of $5 to 10 million. They get a consulting contract to oversee the purchased firms—$1 million a year would be modest. The gross proceeds from the deals are $350 million ($1.25 billion minus $900 million in debt). The managers get their 1 percent share of that—$3.5 million—plus 20 percent of the limited partners' net profits, or $36 million. Total revenues over the five-year period are therefore about $50 million, against an initial investment of $1 million and annual expenses, before bonuses, of perhaps $2 to 3 million. Not bad. Fee income covers expenses, and the deal profits are spectacular, even assuming a very modest 25 percent pickup on the deals. And if only a few of the deals are sold out of portfolio at Dr Pepper–type gains, the partners can retire and become philanthropists.

But the limited partners have no complaint. With just the 25 percent selloff profit, their $99 million investment would have turned into $311 million in five years (the $350 million less the fund managers' share), for an annual gain of about 26 percent, much better than is usually available from public market securities. And since the early-1980s buyout deals had such spectacular returns, any minimally experienced fund manager could trot out a track record promising annual gains of 40 to 50 percent or more. Even very conservative pension fund and insurance asset managers who could fully appreciate the risks inherent in buyout funds took it for granted that some small portion of their assets should be al-located to buyout funds—the potential profits were just too big to ignore.

The commercial banks and investment banks came salivating into the fray, their appetites whetted after the penitential hell of the 1970s. About half the capitalization of a typical leveraged deal would be conventional bank debt, and big banks, like Chase and Citi, earned very large fees organizing loan syndicates, sometimes comprising 100 or more banks from throughout the world. The investment banks got even higher fees for underwriting the high-yield layers—and as long as the bonds sold out quickly, very little of their own capital was at risk. Lights burned late at Wall Street law firms, accountancies, and financial printers, keeping the money wheel spinning. Times were flush for restaurants, bars, limo services, and makers of silk ties and custom shirts.

The "Decade of Greed" probably lasted four years, from about 1985 to about 1989. By 1985, buyout funds had accumulated billions in subscriptions, so fund managers had to generate a massive deal flow to deliver the hoped-for fees and subscriber returns. (KKR alone had an uncommitted war chest of $5.6 billion in 1987.) Informed estimates calculated that commercial and investment banks could come up with $250 billion in deal financing. For a brief period almost any company was in play—it was common to see buyout books circulating on Wall Street for major public companies that had no idea that someone was trying to gin up a transaction.

It was a time of real opportunity for sharks and sharpsters. "Greenmailers" were frequent raiders, like Pickens, or the Dart Group, run by Herbert and Robert Haft, a father-and-son team from Baltimore, who probably had little interest in completing deals. In 1986, for example, Dart mounted a hostile raid on Safeway Stores, a big Western supermarket chain. A bidding war ensued, and management finally allied with KKR, who completed a $4.9 billion transaction. The Hafts made $100 million on their stock accumulation and were paid an additional $59 million to release an option to purchase some Safeway stores. For the winning side, KKR collected a $60 million deal fee, Drexel made $15 million for underwriting the junk bonds, and a long lineup of invest-ment and commercial banks, lawyers, accountants, printers, and consultants divided $110 million more. When the deal closed there was insufficient cash to service the bank debt, and the new company's solvency depended on selling off real estate and stores, and laying off about 25,000 employees. Within the same few months as it closed the Safeway deal, KKR, which comprised just a handful of executives, also bought the Owens-Illinois Glass Company for $3.3 billion and Beatrice Foods for $6.2 billion.

Long after rising stock prices had eliminated slam-dunk mis-pricing plays of the Gibson and Gulf variety, the huge overhang of unspent money in the buyout funds pushed fund managers into riskier and riskier ventures. As soon as a deal was mooted, bidders appeared from every side, while Wall Street "arbs," who made a living guessing on takeover stocks, added to the price momentum. Youthful analysts with Lotus models spun out ever more inge-nious, and ever more precarious, financial structures. In 1970s-vintage leveraged deals, borrowings were usually secured by hard assets, like land or salable commodities. The early 1980s shifted the emphasis to cash flows—balance-sheet assets didn't matter so much if future cash flows could comfortably support debt service. As deal prices kept rising, promoters began projecting *increasing* cash flows from operational improvements and layoffs, as in the Safeway deal. Finally, when cash-flow projections had been stretched beyond the point of fantasy, the emphasis shifted to breakup value—what the pieces of the company might be worth if they were carved out and sold separately.

The more implausible the company's business projections, the more exotic the outlying layers of junk bonds became. Junior se-curity holders took for granted, of course, that they would have to wait to get their principal back, but it soon became customary to defer interest as well ("zero-coupon bonds"). When even deferred interest payments looked implausible, the investment bankers cre-ated "PIKs" or payment-in-kind securities—the company had the choice of paying interest either in cash or by issuing new stock. Or instead of PIKs, investors might take an IRN, an "increasing-rate note"—the longer interest payments were deferred, the higher the interest rate. The RJR Nabisco deal included "reset PIKs"—the interest rate would keep rising to keep the price always at par. Wall street called it the "death spiral"; if the company faltered, the PIKs would eat it alive. There was a radical downshift in the quality of new issues: in the period of 1977 through 1984, only about 60 percent of junk-bond offerings were in the lowest rating grades; by 1988, fully 86 percent were. As new-issue quality deteriorated, investment banks competing for lucrative fee business were forced to buy the riskiest debt layers themselves. A heavy inventory of junk bonds brought First Boston to the brink of insolvency, and eventually forced it into the arms of Crédit Suisse.*

Selling the junk was obviously the key to a successful deal, and that was the source of Michael Milken's power. Working sixteen-hour days at the legendary black X-shaped desk at his Beverly Hills office, Milken, by dint of almost maniacal hard work, superb research, and brutally tough trading tactics, had acquired a near-stranglehold on the junk-bond business. At the peak of the takeover boom, Milken had personally managed half or more of all junk-bond financings since the inception of the market, and had about three times the market position of the number-two player, Merrill, Lynch. Drexel routinely carried junk-bond inventories of $3 billion or more; in a market where there were relatively few buyers and sellers, Milken's trades could push prices in almost any direction he pleased. No other investment bank could match the "Milken network"—a close set of working relationship with a number of pension funds, insurance companies, and S&Ls that had earned very high returns from his paper, trusted him absolutely, and would buy whatever he was selling. (Milken reportedly managed some of his network members' portfolios as if they were his own, more or less commingling the Drexel and network portfolios, much as Morgan did in the days of the "Money Trust.")

---

*The RJR Nabisco deal included five layers of bank debt, six layers of "permanent debt"—so-called partnership debt securities, subordinated floating rate notes, subordinated discount debentures, PIK subordinated debentures, subordinated extendible reset debentures, and subordinated debentures—and two layers of "reset PIKs," all of which were on top of the company's already very complicated pre-buyout debt structure. The deal pushed the outer limits of the plausible, but all of the debt was paid on schedule.

A "highly confident" financing letter from Milken, therefore, was as good as money in the bank. Buyout specialists beat a path to his door because he offered the best and cheapest financing in town. However arrogantly he wielded it, Milken had earned his power.

The enormous sums of money washing around the deals business were an intolerable strain on the always-fragile ethics of Wall Street. The Dennis Levine–Ivan Boesky insider-trading scandals surfaced in 1986, and the stain spread for the rest of the decade. More prevalent, because not illegal, were conflicts of interest between management, shareholders, and obligations to employees. It was routine for managements to recommend "going-private" LBO transactions, supported by projections showing sharp improvements in operations. The obvious question was, Why hadn't they delivered similar performance when the company was owned by shareholders? And management enrichment, as often as not, came out of the hides of employees, as in the Safeway deal. During the 1989 RJR Nabisco LBO, the biggest ever at $23 billion, the company CEO, Ross Johnson, pursued his self-interest to a degree that even Wall Street found unseemly. (Johnson's side lost, to much quiet cheering.) A favorite ploy was to finance a deal by raiding employee retirement funds, or ESOPs, under the guise of "employee ownership." Polaroid's and Macmillan's management both used ESOPs to fend off raiders, while the $1.75 billion ESOP-funded buyout of Avis Corporation in 1987—the fifth buyout of the company in eight years—was an all-time ESOP record. Wesray had bought Avis from KKR for $265 million plus debt in 1986, unloaded $400 million worth of assets, and sold the remainder to the employees only a year later for $750 million plus assumption of the debt. Avis's management supervised the deal as "fiduciaries" for the employees, kept their jobs, and pocketed $157 million for themselves when Avis was sold again almost ten years later. The employees did much less well.

Bruce Wasserstein ("Bid-'Em-Up Bruce"), chairman of the buyout firm Wasserstein, Parella, raised the practice of Wall Street ethics to the level of comic art form. Investment bankers are theoretically governed by a canon of ethics, just as (tongue-in-cheek) lawyers and accountants are. Part of an investment banker's practice consists in rendering "fairness opinions": as an independent professional advising a company's directors in the discharge of their fiduciary duties, the banker opines whether a transaction is reasonably valued and in the best interest of shareholders. During three successive deals—Macmillan, Interco, and Time-Warner—Wasserstein repeatedly changed valuation estimates in a way that reinforced management's position. In the Macmillan deal, for example, he advised management that their stock was worth in the $63 to $68 range, and then opined that successive unwanted offers of $64, $75, and $80/share were inadequate. He also apparently tipped KKR on a competing bid, which the Delaware court said "violated every principle of fair dealing." When Time-Warner and Paramount found themselves in a bidding contest with offers and counteroffers flying in every direction, Wasserstein declared a $200/share cash offer from Paramount to be clearly inadequate, although he had earlier valued Time stock at a much lower level when a lower valuation was in management's interest. He projected that the final deal, which was the one management preferred, would produce a stock price of up to $400 in four years. He was off by a factor of about four, despite a generally strong stock market.

The failure of the United Airlines transaction in the summer of 1989, as much as any other event, marked the end of the deals craze. The CEO, Stephen Wolfe, who held stock options that could have been worth $100 million after an LBO, had engineered a sharp improvement in the company's performance just as airlines were becoming hot LBO targets. (Most airlines owned their planes. Selling the planes and leasing them back could generate a big one-time cash bonanza, producing a new source of LBO financing at a time when the deals market was flagging.) The stock was languishing at about $90 a share in early 1989, although analysts estimated that intrinsic values might justify as much as $150. When the buyout artist Martin Davis began acquiring UAL stock in the spring, bidding started in earnest. The stock jumped $80 in one week and roared past $200 in midsummer, and a deal was concluded at $300 in August. But a few weeks later, the bank syndicate managers, Chase and Citi, admitted that they could not sell the transaction to the global banking community. Wolfe later tried to put together a deal at less than two-thirds the August price, but could find no takers. At about the same time, First Boston was forced to withdraw a $475 million junk-bond offering for a mattress company for lack of buyers. A whole series of deals, involving Lear Siegler, Gillette, and Goodyear were quietly shelved, and the entire high-yield market went into a severe tailspin.

In January 1990, Federated Department Stores, the owner of Bloomingdale's, defaulted on $800 million in junk bonds, only thirteen months after their issuance. (Bondholders eventually recovered only about a third of their capital—and these were "sophisticated" investors!) Integrated Resources, a $2 billion insurance and S&L conglomerate, and a key member of the Milken network, defaulted almost simultaneously. Then followed in rapid succession Allied Department stores (Brooks Brothers, Zales' etc.), Southland (7–11 stores), Revco (drugstores), Baldwin-United (financial services), and a whole string of others. Subsequent analysis showed that Revco had been insolvent on the day it completed its deal, although $80 million was extracted in deal fees. To make matters much worse, Drexel, the primary trading support of the entire high-yield market, filed for bankruptcy protection in February.* Piling on, the new FIRREA S&L regulations forced thrifts to sell off all their junk-bond holdings, driving prices down further. More than $40 billion worth of junk bonds, or about 20 percent of the outstandings, defaulted through 1990 and 1991. There was not a single junk-bond-financed LBO deal in 1990, and the world screamed for Milken's scalp.

---

*Prosecutors pursuing the insider-trading cases used RICO pressure to force Milken out of Drexel in December 1988, and later to extract heavy settlements from Drexel itself, which was a major factor in the firm's demise. RICO was an antimob law that empowered prosecutors to seize a target's assets during an investigation. In effect, if Drexel had not cooperated against Milken, prosecutors could have shut the firm down, as they had earlier shut down another firm, Princeton-Newport. Its use in the Wall Street cases, effectively imposing a penalty without a trial, or even an indictment, was abusive. The use of RICO was later sharply restricted by Congress.

The Rest of the Story: Leverage, Junk, and American Restructuring

The 1980s was about more than takeover battles, greenmailers and white knights, trading scandals, and ripoff fees. The spumy froth of Wall Street's "Decade of Greed" obscured a fundamental restructuring of American industry and finance. The old industrial dispensation that had carried the country from World War I through the 1960s was taken apart and put back together. American cars, for example, still carried Big Three nameplates, but the individual components—doors, brake systems, engine blocks, fuel-injection systems, axles and wheels, individual castings—were as often as not made by specialist manufacturers selling to all the major companies. Internet Foundries, the biggest supplier of engine blocks and other castings for automobiles, built itself out of a ragtag collection of small foundries snapped up at bargain prices, often with debt financing, from floundering manufacturing conglomerates like Mead. By the mid-1980s, it was the biggest independent foundry in the world, able to meet and beat Asian competitors on price and quality, featuring highly automated production lines, one-day delivery schedules, and triple the productivity of the old in-house automobile company foundries. The dis-integration of the old monoliths meant greatly improved car quality, longer warranty periods, and longer average car lives, and substantially closed the once-yawning productivity gap between American and Japanese carmakers.

Numbers are elusive, but the vast majority of LBO transactions were "friendly"—that is, usually involving management, and almost always helping to de-conglomerate an old-line company.* Unwieldy 1960s- and 1970s-style business empires had become

---

*Officially, only a tiny fraction of 1980s acquisitions were "hostile"—that is, against the wishes of current management. But the number of transactions that were *initiated* by a hostile move was much higher. Both the Gulf and Safeway transactions mentioned earlier, for example, would have been classified as "friendly," although both were driven into friendly deals by hostile raids. The great majority of junk-bond financings, however, had nothing to do with buyouts.

slothful bureaucracies that were getting thoroughly whipped by foreign competitors. Despite all the wasted energy and money, and the hypercharged *Sturm und Drang* of the deals frenzy, the gross direction of the restructuring movement was to increase specialization and focus and to move top management closer to the shop floor. USX (the old U.S. Steel) sold off its railroad business in a junk-bond-financed transaction organized by the railroad's management. Revlon financed its LBO by getting out of health care products and focusing on cosmetics. Beatrice paid off its first round of junk bonds by selling its Playtex division to management, and gradually trimmed down to a small group of related food companies. Gordon Cain used junk-bond financing to assemble one of the most productive specialty chemical businesses in the world. He eventually sold out at $100 million personal profit, and distributed $537 million among his 1,350 employees. All the American textile companies, almost all of which were involved one way or the other in LBOs, radically reconfigured their operations, becoming high-technology, high-productivity specialists—West Point Pepperell and Fieldcrest Cannon in towels and sheets, J. P. Stevens and Collins and Aikman in auto body cloth, and so on. Sometimes it took the threat of an LBO to generate action. Union Carbide sold off a grab bag of consumer product and other businesses to return to its roots in ethylene-based chemicals, while the possibility of a hostile raid forced Goodyear to divest its hotel and aerospace business.

Lexmark, one of America's major computer printer manufacturers, is a nice example of an overstretched management deciding on a leveraged spinoff on its own. Through the 1980s, IBM, Lexmark's parent, became notorious for its layers of overhead process management, and as its business fragmented, it found itself competing in a host of different industries—mainframes, minicomputers, PCs, software, networks, semiconductors, office equipment. Lexmark was created in 1990 when IBM spun off its typewriter and low-end printer businesses in a $1.6 billion leveraged transaction developed with the buyout firm Clayton, Dubillier. Freed from bureaucracy, the unit's managers quickly reduced overhead, radically reorganized production lines, and reduced parts counts for individual products by as much as a factor of five—thereby improving ease of manufacture, quality control, and operating reliability. In a brutally competitive business, Lexmark is a technology leader, and as of 1997 held a solid second place behind Hewlett-Packard, the global market leader. Sales had more than doubled since the buyout, to more than $2.6 billion, and the company was virtually debt-free.

It is easy to forget how gloomy the consensus outlook for American business was in the late 1980s and early 1990s. Even business leaders as astute as Intel's Andrew Grove were predicting that America was about to become a "techno-colony" of Japan, and a host of pundits, prominently including academics like MIT's Lester Thurow, were pleading for government subsidies in a host of industries from televisions to computer chips. The low point may have been George Bush's 1992 trip to Japan with American automobile executives, effectively begging for respite from competition. (That was the trip that ended, ignominiously enough, with the President vomiting into the Japanese Prime Minister's lap.) The view from 1998 could not be more different—robust economic growth, low inflation, good productivity, the lowest unemployment rate in decades. American companies are the clear market leaders in a host of industries from microprocessors and financial services to passenger airplanes. They have turned back Asian challenges in diesel engines and construction equipment and are recapturing lost ground in automobiles. Countries around the world, especially in Europe, are fiercely debating whether they must adopt the "American model" to succeed, and foreign investment managers moving their money into American stocks routinely speak of the "American economic miracle."

The human cost of the transition was very high. It would hardly have consoled the 25,000 Safeway employees who lost their jobs in 1986 if they had been told they were contributing to a fundamental change of economic direction. And the couple hundred million in fees extracted from the deal would have paid for a lot of grocery clerks. But fees or no fees, all the old-line supermarkets had to rethink their staffing. A virtual revolution in the supermarket business was under way during the mid-1980s, and the competitive battles are still savage, with a high degree of automation (ordering and inventory control), paper-thin profit margins, operating costs pared to the bone, and many new services—delis, bakeries, fresh fish counters, pharmacies—all to enhance a local edge. The older chains, like Safeway and A&P, either had to restructure or die, and the Safeway transaction ultimately turned out to be quite successful.

Rational discussion of the 1980s is almost foreclosed by the refusal of economic conservatives to recognize the real costs of the national restructuring, and the refusal of economic liberals to recognize the real gains. A major restructuring was clearly long overdue by the 1980s, and no one would want to relive the economic malaise of the 1970s. That said, the huge profits racked up by the buyout firms and the junk-bond salesmen, the crudeness of the conspicuous consumption on Wall Street, and the arrogance of the young spreadsheet jockeys pushing the "delete" button on hundreds of thousands of workers are all offensive. One of the lasting taints of the buyout era has been the obscene ballooning of senior executive incomes, even while average worker incomes have barely kept up with inflation. Investment bankers typically get paid a small percentage of a deal's value, and made huge sums as company values skyrocketed. Once executives realized what their advisers were making, they insisted on a share of the pie. Big-company executive salaries have jumped by a factor of ten or more over the past dozen years or so. The necessity for restructuring didn't make the process any less wasteful or ugly.

Junk bonds played a critical role in the national realignment. In *Den of Thieves,* James Stewart trumpets the 11.2 percent negative annual return of junk bonds in 1990, and derisively quotes a former Milken loyalist: "Some people believed whatever Mike Milken said [but] bondholders got all the risk and very little of the upside." But most of what Milken said turned out to be true. In the decade 1986–96, which includes all the very worst years for junk, high-yield bonds experienced an 11.5 percent annual average *positive* return, with less than half the return volatility of stocks, after taking into account all the much-publicized defaults. The return from stocks was higher, but the Sharpe ratio, a widely used measure that adjusts absolute return for volatility, shows that high-yields actually outperformed stocks and, of course, all other classes of bonds.

High-yields routinely outperformed most other classes of instruments right through the first half of 1998. The yield spread of high-yields over treasuries—the best measure of perceived risk—narrowed to just a couple of hundred basis points on the better grade of "junk" and the yield spread between the better- and worse-rated issues was probably much thinner than it should have been. All bonds, however, except for the most highly rated instruments like U.S. treasuries, were hit very hard by the liquidity squeeze that followed in the wake of the Russian default and the collapse of Long Term Capital Management in the late summer and fall of 1998. (See Chapters Seven and Nine.) For a few months, the losses on high-yields were as bad as at any time since 1989, far more than was justified by the inherent value of the instruments. The high-yield market had begun a substantial recovery by the end of the year, although liquidity was still comparatively tight. Even amid the rough sailing of late 1998, however, there was no longer any question that high-yields had come to own a permanent place in the spectrum of standard financial instruments.

Junk bonds were never the "democratic revolution" that market promoters sometimes claimed. But they *were* something of a bourgeois uprising. High-yield financing, pioneered by Michael Milken, helped fuel high-growth companies like Hospital Corporation of America, especially in nontraditional industries. They helped break the aristocratic stranglehold on the American financial markets and were a critical element in a vast, and largely successful, restructuring and modernizing of American industry, which will pay dividends, financial and otherwise, for years to come.

Just as in the 1870s and 1880s, when Jay Gould turned the financial markets upside down, a period of high innovation came at the price of greatly increased risk and anxiety, alarums on Wall Street, the misdirection of huge sums of money, temporary chaos in important companies, and the vast, and unjust, enrichment of a lucky, or clever, few. Hardly anyone begrudges Bill Gates his billions, absurd though his wealth has become. After all, he has built a huge business over twenty-plus years. But the hundreds of millions changing hands on Wall Street almost in the flick of an eye tended to stick in the craw, especially since the restructuring movement often caused so much short-term pain.

In contrast to the 1870s and 1880s, however, the period of high risk and financial turmoil was blessedly brief. The same pattern we have seen in earlier financial episodes seems to have prevailed. Fundamental factors in the larger economy call forth financial innovation; the innovation is initially successful but generates turmoil and increased risk; until finally, after a period of instability, the innovation is absorbed and the markets settle into a new state of normalcy. And with the much smoother economic sailing of the 1990s, the benefits of the 1980s restructurings are finally being realized, despite the visible scars that still persist, like the skewing of executive and worker incomes.

Postscript: What Was Milken Guilty Of?

Highly successful entrepreneurs are frequently not very nice people, and Milken, all the slick public relations to the contrary, seems to have been a particularly unattractive personality—fanatically driven, greedy, arrogant, obsessive, unfeeling to his subordinates, brutal in negotiations. He is also a criminal, because he pleaded guilty to specific felonies. But are claims by authors like Stewart that he was kingpin of "the greatest criminal conspiracy the financial world has ever known" really justified?

Milken actually pleaded guilty to six offenses. One was assisting in tax evasion by an investment partnership run by a longtime correspondent, David Solomon. Solomon wanted to take a tax loss on two illiquid investments, so he sold them to Milken and bought them back at a lower price, with the assurance that Milken would make up the difference later. The transaction looks sleazy, but when Solomon defended his case, as Milken did not, the court ruled that there had been no tax evasion, for Solomon had taken a real loss, and Milken had paid taxes on his profit. Solomon would have evaded taxes only if Milken's bare promise could be treated as taxable income, which it clearly was not.

A second charge is almost absurdly technical, and also involves Solomon. Solomon did part of his trading through Milken, and at one point Milken insisted on increasing his trading fee, although within the bid-ask spread for the securities being traded. (Traders conventionally have considerable latitude in settling an actual price within the bid-ask spread.) Solomon agreed, but did not update his prospectus to inform his investors of the change, as he should have done, although it is highly unlikely that they would have cared. Milken pleaded guilty to unlawful failure to disclose the change in the trading arrangement—not to Solomon's investors, for that wasn't his obligation, but to *Solomon,* in the written trade confirmations that followed each transaction.

The final four charges all involved alleged "stock parking" with Ivan Boesky, a Wall Street arbitrageur who had admitted to numerous insider-trading offenses, involving one famous incident of buying inside information with a suitcase full of cash delivered in a hotel lobby. Boesky pleaded guilty to a series of lesser charges in return for turning state's evidence, primarily against Milken, and the stock-parking charges depended heavily on his testimony. The offense of stock parking dates only from 1968, when Congress responded to a flurry of takeover activity by amending the securities laws to require, among other things, that investors make declarations of intent when they exceed certain accumulation thresholds. (If the investors declare that the accumulation is in preparation for a takeover, detailed rules of procedure come into play.) Stock parking might take place, for instance, if a raider asks a confederate to accumulate stock without declaring that they are acting as a "group" to avoid crossing one of the triggering thresholds. No stock-parking violation had ever been prosecuted as a criminal matter. One firm had been ordered by the SEC to disgorge its profits from a transaction, while all other cases had been dealt with by various forms of administrative wrist slapping.

The most notorious of the Boesky allegations involved an engineering company, Fischbach, that had been subject to a hostile raid by a Drexel client. The company bought back the raider's stock, and negotiated a standstill agreement, barring another takeover attempt unless some new raider acquired a 10 percent stock position in the company. Boesky later acquired a 10 percent position in Fischbach, allegedly at Milken's behest, and made a takeover declaration, opening the door to an eventual takeover by yet another Milken client. The "parking" violation consisted in whether, as Stewart puts it in his book, "Milken assured Boesky that . . . he would guarantee Boesky against any losses," which would have been illegal parking. Milken said that he had merely advised Boesky that Fischbach was a great opportunity, but that he had never made guarantees.* Boesky's testimony to the prosecutors actually tends to support Milken's version:

> Q. O.K. And did Milken say to you in that conversation that he would guarantee you against loss?
> A. Those were not the words, never were the words.
> Q. It's the code you were talking about, the Wall Street code?
> A. I never used that word either. It was an understanding.
> Q. O.K. What were the words you remember Milken using?
> A. "Just buy it, don't worry about it," something to that effect. . . . I've forgotten the exact language of the specific conversation.

This seems thin gruel, to say the least, which is all the more remarkable since Boesky clearly was doing his best to incriminate Milken. Milken's version of events is equally plausible, for he had a long track record of putting loyal correspondents into profitable investments, and he was so much in the center of the nation's deal

---

*Boesky's investment actually turned out badly, for just as a takeover was heating up, Fischbach was indicted for bid rigging. A deal eventually went through anyway, and the stock recovered, but not to the level Boesky had paid. Stewart alleges that Boesky sold out his position to the winning bidder at a loss but at an above-market price. Boesky bought the stock at $50; the sale was allegedly at $45 compared with a current market of $40, which Stewart takes as evidence of the Milken guarantee (although obviously not one "against any losses"). The sale probably happened as Stewart says, although it was executed offshore and there is no clear trail, and the sale by itself hardly incriminates Milken. The company may have had good reason to pay a modest premium to get rid of a very large and potentially troublesome shareholder like Boesky. In short, while it's possible that an arrangement existed as Boesky said, the evidence for it is very weak.

flow that if a favored correspondent took a loss on a recommended investment, he could easily give him first crack at others to make up for it.

There were two other allegations, one of a Drexel stock purchase from Boesky and another by Boesky from a third party on Milken's recommendation. In both cases, the transactions arguably served a larger Drexel purpose, and Boesky alleged that there had been mutual guarantees that would qualify the transactions as stock parking. Once again, there was little conflict between Milken's and Boesky's versions of events. Some kind of vague "assurances" were certainly made. The question was whether there were ever specific "guarantees," which is probably impossible to prove one way or the other.

The final charge was of a generalized conspiracy between Boesky, Solomon, and Milken to enter into illegal stock-parking arrangements. The primary evidence for the conspiracy was a $5.3 million "consulting fee" payment that Milken extracted from Boesky, which the prosecutors, and Stewart, allege was a payment for the net amount owed by Boesky for all the illegal stock-parking schemes agreed by him and Milken. The backup for the payment was a series of ledgers that included many other transactions that no one claimed were illegal. Moreover, Drexel's and Boesky's ledgers were conflicting, despite repeated attempts to reach a reconciliation. Milken finally strong-armed Boesky by threatening, at virtually the last minute, to torpedo a major financing for Boesky unless he was paid the $5.3 million. The Milken version is that the payment was tagged a "consulting fee" because the state of the ledgers didn't permit tying it to individual trades; Boesky says that the "consulting" rubric was used to conceal that the payment was for illegal transactions. Either version would have been very hard to prove in court, but the burden of proof, of course, lay with Boesky and the prosecution.

After Milken had pleaded, the prosecutors, worried that the offenses pleaded to would not carry a sufficiently harsh penalty, prepared a pre-sentence report that included seventy pages of alleged "other crimes" that Milken had committed. The judge in the case, Kimba Wood, thereupon invoked an unusual procedure called a "Fatico" hearing, in which prosecutors were permitted twenty hours to present evidence of other crimes in order to impeach Milken's character. Milken could mount a normal defense, but the prosecution did not have to meet a "reasonable doubt" criminal evidentiary standard. The prosecutors concentrated on four allegations. The first was that Milken had obstructed justice by instructing, or hinting to, employees that they should destroy files. (He probably did, and Judge Wood concluded as much, but the evidence was sketchy—mostly oblique insinuations and vague suggestions, much as in the Boesky allegations.) The rest involved detailed charges of illegal actions with respect to three specific transactions that one must assume represented the most damning cases that the government had. Remarkably, even under the relaxed standards of a Fatico hearing, the government failed to carry its case. One charge was that Milken had directed a course of manipulation to push the stock of Wickes to $6^{1}/_{8}$, which would have triggered a transaction in Drexel's interest. The prosecution's primary evidence was a trader's testimony—a trader who had admitted lying in a number of other instances—that Milken had walked by his desk and said, "Peter. Wickes. $6^{1}/_{8}$," which was at best, "fairly ambiguous," as Wood commented. The other two cases were even weaker, for the government's own witnesses contradicted the charges. Wood ruled that the evidence did not clearly support either the government's or Milken's version of events, which suggests how very flimsy the government case against Milken may have been. (Stewart's book *Den of Thieves* conveniently leaves out the Fatico hearing, except for a brief mention in an endnote in the back of the book.)

Given the fast-and-loose way Milken ran his operation, it is almost inconceivable that he didn't often run afoul of security regulations. (Moving bonds in and out of his customers' portfolios could easily amount to stock parking.) But people rarely, if ever, went to jail for those kinds of technical violations. And Milken has never admitted, and the government never succeeded in showing, that he engaged in the kind of insider-trading abuses that were Boesky's specialty, or again unlike Boesky, that very much, if any, of his great wealth was due to illegal activities. The prosecution's weak showing at the Fatico hearing suggests that Milken might well have gotten off had he chosen not to plead. Quite possibly he concluded that a plea and a short jail term were preferable to the possibility of years in court. Similarly, paying a billion in settlements may have seemed a small price for peace. (A billion isn't so much if you have a billion left over.) In any case, the ten-year sentence handed down by Wood was shockingly severe—a case of an inexperienced judge playing to the headline writers calling for blood. Perhaps twelve to eighteen months of the sentence could be attributed to the crimes Milken had pleaded to; the remainder was the price exacted for being a "symbol of greed."

Chapter Six

A QUESTION OF SCALE

The early 1980s were a time of turmoil in government bond markets. Federal deficits from the Reagan-era tax cuts and two straight smash-mouth recessions required trillions in new government issues. At the same time, the Federal Reserve's war on inflation ratcheted interest rates up to the highest levels in modern history, causing wild gyrations in bond prices. Wall Street bond departments, longtime sinecures for the dimmer sons of the upper classes, suddenly became scary, exciting places where hundreds of millions could disappear in the turn of an eyelash.

In the spring of 1982, Peter Demmer was a thirty-eight-year-old Chase Manhattan vice president. He had started at the bank while still working his way through college and had risen through various back-office jobs to a comfortable position in Chase's "custody" operations. Bank custody departments service big investors like trusts and pension funds, carrying out the mundane tasks of receiving and delivering securities, maintaining position records, collecting interest and dividends, and storing paper certificates.

Demmer had built up a profitable side business by standing in the middle of a short-term financing method called "repurchase agreements," or "repos." Instead of borrowing money at a stated rate of interest, a firm that needed cash would ostensibly sell securities and contract to buy them back later at a higher price. The agreed price premium was equivalent to interest, so the transaction worked just like a short-term loan. But since repos were fully collateralized—the party providing the cash held the securities—they could be done very quickly with minimum documentation. "Reverse repos"—put up the cash and borrow the securities—were also a perfect solution for high-volume traders scratching for inventory. Demmer was paid for setting up accounts for the repo counterparties, receiving securities from one and cash from the other, collecting the interest due when the repo expired, and settling the transaction. There didn't seem to be any risk involved for Chase, since it was only acting as agent, or so Demmer and his superiors believed.

One of the reasons Wall Street used middlemen like Demmer on repos was so traders could keep their positions secret. If it was known that a trader needed securities to close out a position, his buddies at other desks could squeeze him on price. So when Demmer stood in the middle of a repo, the tickets he sent to the two counterparties usually did not disclose the other side's name. Chase's Wall Street division, however, assured him that that was normal "Street practice."

Demmer's most rapidly growing "no-name" repo customer was a small brokerage named Drysdale Securities. Although the firm had been in business for almost a century, it was new to trading governments, and its chief trader, David Heuwetter, had a reputation as a flashy loudmouth. To the chagrin of the old-line government dealers, Heuwetter quickly became one of the biggest players on Wall Street and a special force in the repo market. In early 1982, Drysdale announced that it would apply to become a primary dealer, one of the handful of elite firms that could buy directly for its customers at government auctions. Heuwetter was telling his drinking companions that he was making tens of millions of dollars and soon hoped to be able to corner an entire government issue.

It didn't take long for other traders to figure out what Heuwetter was doing. Treasury notes and bonds pay interest semiannually. In between coupon dates, their market price includes the interest that has been accrued, so an otherwise identical bond that is a month away from an interest payment is worth more than one that is five months away. But because the repo market got started when rates were comparatively low, the calculation of repo cash collateral didn't include accrued interest. Heuwetter was doing reverses, borrowing securities and supplying cash. But he always picked securities that were near their coupon date, so they were worth more than his cash collateral. He would then sell the securities and have free use of the extra cash during the repo period. Since Heuwetter was a plunger, he naturally used the free cash to borrow more securities and ratchet up his positions.

By the time traders were on to his game, Heuwetter's positions had gotten so large that he was an easy mark—he was constantly in the market for near-coupon treasuries either to work his cash gimmick or to return securities from repos that were closing out. Although his positions were supposed to be secret, the treasuries Heuwetter liked best became known as "Drysdales," and traders gleefully marked up their prices whenever he was in the market. Heuwetter was actually losing money on most of his transactions, because trading costs ate up his free cash, but his losses were obscured as long as his positions kept getting bigger.

Heuwetter's doom was sealed by the arithmetic of his trading, but the tightly knit government dealing community detested his flashiness and upstart bragging, and ganged up in late April and early May of 1982 to bring him down with a crash. There is no evidence of an explicit conspiracy, but there didn't need to be one—it was almost too easy. The bulk of Heuwetter's repos had no fixed term, meaning that his counterparties could ask for their securities whenever they pleased. All at once, a number of counterparties demanded their securities back. Then the Street watched and steadily raised their prices as Heuwetter scrambled like a bug in a bottle trying to cover his positions.

Demmer had not a clue as to what was going on. His information system was designed to track transaction execution, so he didn't even know how big Heuwetter's position was. He got worried when he received a series of calls from traders in late April asking him if Chase was agent or principal on its no-name repos, but Chase's law department apparently assured him that he was okay. Then in the first week of May, Heuwetter bounced a check for $10 million. It was quickly covered, but for the first time, Demmer began looking at Heuwetter's total positions and was shocked to discover that they exceeded $4 billion. A few days later,

Heuwetter visited Demmer to say that the Street was squeezing him, and he might be up to $40 million short of a $160 million interest payment that was due on the seventeenth, the next Monday. Demmer alerted top officials of the bank—most of whom hadn't known his operation existed—but the primary worry was that Chase faced a public relations embarrassment, not that it had any financial liability.

By late Saturday, it was clear that Heuwetter could not meet *any* of the interest payments due on Monday. His books were in wild disarray, and in a hallucinatory meeting on Sunday at which he and the Chase staff tried to reconstruct his positions, he estimated that his "eventual loss could be between 50 million and a billion dollars." Unaware of what a sitting duck it was, Chase determined to act the good citizen, and organized a meeting of Heuwetter's counterparties, which included virtually all the top government trading desks, at the New York Federal Reserve on Tuesday. The bank explained what had happened, and offered to contribute working capital to a trading pool to work out Heuwetter's positions. The Wall Street firms listened politely, but the next day when the meeting reconvened, they said they had no idea what Chase was talking about. They had never done business with Drysdale or Heuwetter—the only name on their repo tickets was Chase's, and they expected Chase to pay up. Rubbing it in, Morgan Stanley, for one, had been offsetting its positions with Drysdale by borrowing short-term from Chase. When Chase failed to deliver Morgan's repo interest, Morgan just stopped paying Chase on its loans.

For at least two scary days, until Chase caved, the repo market came to a grinding halt. Positions were so intertwined that they could have taken weeks to unwind. Starved of cash, Street firms could have fallen like tenpins. Ironically, the traders who pulled the plug on Heuwetter thought he was *lying* about how big his positions were, so their little frolic almost turned into a Jonestown. Chase's CEO, Willard Butcher, denied that the Federal Reserve put any pressure on him to pay up, which is risible. But even without that pressure, there was panic at Chase over the possible damage suits if one of Heuwetter's counterparties failed—numbers like

$20 billion were bouncing around the boardroom meetings. Chase's ultimate losses were estimated at $250 million; Manufacturers Hanover, which was in a similar but smaller position, took a hit about a fifth as large. Chase got its revenge by firing Demmer.

Once blood pressures recovered, the Drysdale episode quickly washed out of Wall Street's collective memory. Repo collateral requirements were adjusted to include accrued interest; Chase lost about a quarter's earnings; few people noticed when Drysdale closed its doors. The real significance of Drysdale, however, is that it was one of the first demonstrations of the consequences of the shift in scale that was taking place on Wall Street. Mere grit in the ball bearings, once shrugged off as beneath traders' notice, was suddenly revealed to hold the potential for enormous profits or cataclysmic losses.

Wall Street's Scale Shift

The New York Stock Exchange had its first million-share trading day in 1886, and it took until 1961 for turnover to reach 4 million shares. Turnover growth accelerated rapidly in the 1970s. The first 100 million–share day came in 1982, the first 200 million–share day in 1992, and the first billion-share day in 1997. Average annual turnover growth had dawdled along in the low single digits through most of the exchange's history, but jumped to almost 40 percent in the 1990s. Change on this scale reflects, as always, deeper tidal forces in the economy.

For the entire period after World War II, the number of America's over-sixty-fives has grown more than twice as fast as the rest of the population. The trend has been quite stable—about 2.4 percent per year for the over-sixty-fives compared with 1.1 percent for everybody else—and long predates the recent spate of worries about the aging of the baby boomers. Two of the landmark legislative actions of the 1970s can be traced directly to growing greybeard political power. The social security reforms of 1973 engineered major increases in benefits and indexed future payments to the rate of inflation. And after several well-publicized failures of private-sector pension plans, the Employee Retirement Income Security Act (ERISA) of 1974 created government insurance for private-sector pensions and set rules for maintaining plan solvency and protecting the rights of employees and retirees.

The economic effects of oldsters' new spending power are well known. But ERISA's long-run effects have been almost as profound, for the pressure to achieve adequately funded retirement plans generated very rapid growth of institutionally managed financial assets. The trend was reinforced when New York City's 1975 fiscal crisis spotlighted the funding problem in public pensions; within the next few years ERISA-like laws on state and local government pensions were passed throughout the country. Pressures for adequate funding naturally focused attention on plan earnings, and by the end of the decade pension plan investments were moving decisively away from ultraconservative bonds into stocks and even more exotic instruments. The state employees pension fund for Oregon, for example, was one of the earliest members of Michael Milken's junk-bond network (and did extremely well). At least since the mid-1980s, pension portfolios have been a major source of capital for LBOs, mortgage-backeds, and venture capital funds, and have been among the most important customers for Wall Street's new generation of rocket scientists. At the same time, pension funds trained the talent and provided the role models for the retail mutual fund industry. The numbers in the table speak for themselves.

To put the table into perspective, the total value of mutual funds and pension funds was only 29 percent of GDP in 1973, but had grown to 113 percent of GDP by 1995. The value of stocks

Dollars in billions	1973	1980	1985	1990	1995	CAGR
Money market mutual funds	1.0	62.2	193.3	364.9	451.6	32.0%
Other mutual funds	38.7	45.6	197.9	467.8	1582.9	18.4%
Pension reserves	358.5	1056.2	2047.0	3388.2	6257.7	13.9%
Totals	398.2	1164.0	2438.2	4220.9	8292.2	14.8%

and bonds held directly by households also grew strongly during the same period, but not nearly as fast. In 1973, individual stock and bond holdings were almost twice as big as mutual funds and pension funds; by 1981, funds' assets had drawn even with individual holdings, and were more than 40 percent larger in 1995. In 1992, for the first time, pension fund reserves exceeded the value of the equity that Americans held in their homes; by 1997, so did mutual fund holdings. The shift of power to institutional portfolio managers was signaled as early as 1975, when the SEC's "Big Bang" reforms prohibited fixed commissions for stock brokerage; within a few years negotiated fees had made institutional trading nearly costless. Individuals accounted for the bulk of trading on Wall Street in the 1970s; by the 1990s, more than 80 percent of all trading was by institutions.

Professional poker players say that in a typical five-handed pickup game, there is usually one other competent player at the table. The pros spot each other within a hand or two, systematically bet against the duffers, and walk off with all the winnings. Traditional investment theory, enshrined in the famous 1934 Benjamin Graham–David Dodd textbook *Security Analysis,* and most prominently espoused today by Warren Buffett, works the same way. Investment, according to the fundamentalists, is a process of company-by-company analysis—of balance sheets, income statements, competitive technologies, and the like—to find the opportunities the dumbos have missed.

The average investor probably is a fool. One recent study of 100,000 trades shows that individuals consistently make the worst of all possible choices, typically buying stocks that are about to fall—probably because they've been hot—and selling stocks that are about to rise, which should create plenty of opportunities for the pros. But that logic breaks down when professionals account for almost all trading—the idea that *you* can find stocks everyone else has missed gets implausible. The growing dominance of institutional portfolios, that is, calls into question the basic premises of fundamental investing. A growing body of data since the 1960s suggests that professionals make a lot of dumb decisions too, which makes the fundamentalist case even weaker. Intuitively, when professionals do all the trading, some professional is buying whatever another professional is selling, and they can't both be right. In any event, sheer practicalities argue for other approaches. Generalized advice about sniffing out bargains simply isn't much help when you've got $6 trillion to place.

The rise of institutional investing coincided with the rapid development of the academic theory of finance—Eugene Fama, William Sharpe, and Jack Treynor are a few of the prominent names. Academics like to think about *portfolios* rather than individual securities. From the perspective of a pension fund manager, it is the riskiness of his portfolio that matters, not the riskiness of each security. (Buying a risky stock can reduce overall portfolio risk if it is likely to move in the opposite direction of some other risky stock.) Riskiness can be quantified as volatility, or "beta," and analyzing portfolio beta forces one to think about *classes* of instruments rather than individual stocks or bonds.

The very nature of pension fund investing required an entirely new perspective on risk. The job of a pension fund manager is not to "beat the market" as traditionalists would have it, but to fund a stream of well-defined future liabilities at the lowest cost. In principle, one could completely "immunize" pension liabilities by constructing a portfolio of treasuries with cash flows that precisely matched the expected pension outflows. Since treasury returns are low, however, that would be a very expensive approach to funding. By the mid-1980s, it had become standard practice for pension advisers to construct hypothetical fully immunized portfolios, then apply optimization mathematics to substitute riskier but higher-return assets to reach a mix of risk and cost that the client could live with. While it would be foolish to fund a short-term liability with high-volatility stocks, for instance, history suggests that such stocks will have higher-than-average long-term returns, so it is perfectly sensible to use them to fund obligations in the distant future. There is still room for stock picking in portfolio construction, but it is subordinate to a more generalized discipline of analyzing how well classes of securities match up against the liabilities that are being provided for. A manager at Merrill Lynch said, "CALPERS [the California pension system, one of the biggest of all investors] just can't decide to dump $10 billion in equities. It can't be done. So you have to discuss what kind of asset profile they're trying to achieve, what kind of volatility, what kind of floors and caps, and then use all the technology at your disposal to achieve that position."

Arbitrage, Indexing, and Triple Witching

The combination of mammoth institutional portfolios, academic theory, huge leaps in accessible computer power, and burgeoning options and futures markets in financial instruments utterly changed the nature of professional trading.

A trading technique known as "yield-curve arbitrage" is a good example. Treasury notes or bonds can be deconstructed into a series of zero-coupon bonds, each representing the separate interest and principal payments. (For example, a $1000 ten-year note, with a 6 percent coupon paid semiannually, can be broken up into twenty separate contracts paying $30, one in six months, one in a year, one in eighteen months, and so on, plus a contract to pay $1000 at the end of ten years. The separate contracts are called "zero-coupons" because each one pays out only at the end of its term.) Since the treasury market is so deep and liquid, one can create a "synthetic" treasury of almost any maturity by cutting and pasting together a string of interest and principal payments culled from the whole universe of eligible notes and bonds.

In principle, if the market is priced right, the outlay for creating a synthetic treasury should be exactly the same as the price of an ordinary one, taking into account transaction costs. In fact, in the 1980s, especially when interest rates were bouncing up and down, that tended not to be so—pricing simply wasn't yet that precise. Traders at Greenwich Capital Management in Connecticut may have been the first to systematically exploit the opportunity, and they made very large trading profits before the rest of the market caught up. Although there were many wrinkles on the strategy, the basic trading technique was simplicity itself. Whenever your computers spotted an opportunity to create a synthetic instrument with a significantly different price from a real one, you simultaneously bought the side that was cheap and sold the side that was expensive. Bingo. Markets abhor riskless profits, so it didn't last. Within a relatively short time, there were a lot of trading computers searching out arbitrages in treasury synthetics, so prices tightened and squeezed out the easy profits. Bond market arbitrages are much harder to find today and usually involve complex multicurrency, multicountry deals.

Stock index arbitrage is much better known, and has exceeded any other derivatives products in its capacity to outrage traditional Graham-Dodd-style investors. Two separate developments made it possible. The first was the rapid-spread of "index" investing during the 1980s, and the second was the development of futures and options markets in indexes.

STOCK INDEXES Index investing was invented at Wells Fargo Bank in the early 1970s; it expressly repudiated the principle of assembling portfolios by fundamental securities analysis. Academic theory suggested that as markets professionalized and information flow became more efficient, stock pickers could not consistently beat market averages. Instead of trading actively in and out of the market, therefore, it is logical, and cheaper, simply to instruct your computer to create a portfolio that precisely replicates some broad cross section of the market and sit still. The Standard & Poor's 500 Stocks and 100 Stocks, and the Major Market Index, based on the biggest Dow Jones stocks, are among the more popular indexes.

To the chagrin of traditional analysts, by the late 1970s a growing body of data suggested that such "passive" portfolios usually outperformed ones that were actively managed. The savings on transaction costs and management fees accounted for much of the difference, but not all—just like individuals, professional managers may have a built-in tendency to persist in bad strategies. By about 1990, possibly a third of all pension assets were passively invested in index funds replicating a great variety of equity, bond, and foreign security positions; at the same time, stock index funds, like those popularized by the Vanguard Group, were becoming increasingly popular for individuals as well.

The principled complaint against indexing is that if everyone indexed, the market would cease performing its role as a price discriminator—a company's stock price would be determined merely by its position in an index rather than by its economic performance. Reaching an all-indexed position, however, is hardly plausible, for as the proportion of indexers increases beyond some point, the advantage will shift back to stock pickers. As of 1997, only about 15 percent of market assets were indexed, and the record of the past ten years suggests that on the whole, indexers have had much better results than active managers. Indexing, however, works well only in deep, efficient markets. In more opaque markets, like those in Southeast Asia, where information is more likely to confer an advantage, active managers generally outperform indexers.

INDEX FUTURES Futures are firm contracts to buy or sell some commodity at some future date. (See the next chapter for a broader picture of the use of futures and options in modern financial markets.) Traditional futures markets grew up around agricultural products, like corn and wheat, spread to foreign currency trading in the 1960s and 1970s, and have recently expanded to a wide range of financial instruments.

The main advantage of futures is that they offer an extremely efficient and inexpensive way to enter and exit the market, because traders need to put up only a small portion of the actual cash value of the contract, usually in the 5 to 10 percent range. But low initial margin requirements are counterbalanced, in financial futures markets, by the obligation to *cash-settle* daily. Suppose I buy a 90-day T-bond futures contract that's worth $100,000 and make an initial margin deposit of $10,000. If the value of the contract falls $1000 on the next day, I will have to make an additional $1000 deposit; conversely, if the value rises, I can take back an equivalent value of margin. So my daily profits and losses will follow precisely those of the bonds. On the last day of the contract, the price of the future has to converge precisely to that of the underlying bonds. (It has become, in effect, a contract to take delivery of the bonds on that day.) So the net cash outcome should be exactly the same as if I bought the $100,000 worth of T-bonds in the first place.

Note how simple cash settlement makes the process. With a small outlay of cash, I've taken a position in $100,000 worth of bonds for 90 days. If the bonds rise in value, I'll get cash in exactly the amount of that rise; and if they fall, I will shell out cash to that amount. There's no necessity actually to take possession of the bonds, and the vast majority of financial futures contracts are settled up in cash, without the actual instruments ever changing hands.

With the increased popularity of indexing, it was only a small step to futures and options on indexes. The Kansas City Board of Trade was first off the mark in 1982, with a futures contract on a group of stocks selected by the Value Line investment service, but that was quickly eclipsed by the Chicago Mercantile Exchange's futures contract on the Standard & Poor's 500 stocks, and within a few years contracts were available on a wide variety of index futures, index options, and options on futures, allowing big traders to move quickly in and out of large positions and hedge against falling markets. A 1992 Goldman, Sachs study documented the efficiency savings on the futures markets. It cost seven times as much (0.77 percent) to buy the S&P 500 stocks in the stock market as it did to replicate the position in the futures market (0.11 percent). Futures markets' relative lack of friction pushed them into the stock price leadership role by the mid-1980s. Significant moves in stock prices now show up in futures markets first, and only some minutes or hours later in stock markets.

INDEX ARBITRAGE   Stock index arbitrage, like yield-curve arbitrage, is a way for large traders to take advantage of small price misalignments in theoretically equivalent instruments. Buying a futures contract on, say, the S&P 500 index that expires in 90 days, in principle, is the same as buying the underlying stocks and holding them for 90 days, except that you don't get any dividends and you can earn interest on your free cash. So the price of an index futures contract should precisely reflect the current price of the underlying stocks adjusted for interest and dividends. Like all financial futures, stock index futures are settled in cash daily, and as time goes on, the owner of the futures will make or lose money as the value of the futures contract fluctuates along with the underlying stocks.* If the position is maintained until the end of the contract, the profits and loss on the stock and futures positions should be exactly the same.

The key word in that last sentence is *should* be exactly the same. Since trading is an inexact art, there are almost always tiny misalignments between actual futures prices and the theoretically correct ones. When the misalignments are greater than the cost of trading, it pays to engage in arbitrage. If futures are more expensive than they should be, for instance, the trader will sell the future and buy the stock. At expiration, the contract will be closed out based on the value of the stock, and the trader will pocket the excess profit from the sale of the future. Conversely, if the future is too cheap, the trader will short the stock and buy the future, and then use the future to fulfill his short contract. Academics praise such trading as an essential market corrective. If futures prices drift too far down, the possibility of arbitrage sparks a wave of buying, which by itself drives prices back up again, keeping stock and futures prices locked tightly together.

A detailed analysis of 2,600 index arbitrage trades in 1990 found that arbitrage opportunities lasted, on average, only about three minutes. About 70 percent of all positions were unwound as soon as they were profitable, and earned about 5 percent more than the treasury bill rate. More than a third of the positions were

---

*The stocks in the S&P 500 are chosen by a Standard & Poor's committee, and the index is computed from the average of the prices of the stocks weighted by issuer market capitalization. The futures contract price is the index multiplied by $250. (A mini-contract—index times $50—was recently added to make the contract accessible to smaller investors.) On December 16, 1997, e.g., the S&P 500 index closed at 964.25, and the March '98 index futures closed at 975.40, with the difference reflecting interest and dividend adjustments. One March contract therefore had the value of 975.40 × $250 = $243,850. For a qualified nonmember trader, the minimum initial margin requirement was $12,563 per contract, or about 5.2 percent of the contract value (as compared with 50 percent in the stock market). Margin is thereafter adjusted based on fluctuations in the total contract value. So if the index falls by five points, the trader would have to increase her margin reserve by that amount (5 × $250 = $1250), or the same as the mark-to-market loss she would have incurred if she had actually owned the underlying stock portfolio. If the index rises, so does the equity in her margin account, and she can withdraw the excess over the minimum required, in effect realizing her mark-to-market gain immediately.

not actually risk-free, since the two legs were not closed out at the same time. The period of "legging"—when the trader was exposed on one side or the other—extended from a few minutes to as long as a day or two. Risk was also increased slightly by traders' preference for buying and selling only a subset of stocks in an index to save transaction costs, so there was almost always some degree of mismatch between the indexes and actual stock portfolios.

What churns the stomachs of Graham-Dodd traditionalists is that strategies like index arbitrage imply huge volumes of trading, since the margins available are so razor-thin. One well-known fundamentalist adviser grumped in the mid-1980s that "in the last three months, the market has made ten distinct, important moves without any rational explanation other than [arbitrage] trading." As a practical matter, computers take over the trading desk—constantly monitoring the markets for pricing misalignments, and immediately entering large pre-programmed trades with little or no human intervention, and occasionally unpredictable consequences. The "triple witching hour" was for several years the prime exhibit of the anti-arbitrage forces. Four times each year, in January, March, June, and September, index futures contracts, index options, and options on index futures all expire on the same Friday, frequently triggering a rush of trading just before the markets closed. Holders of in-the-money options had to exercise them before they expired, at the same time as index arbitrageurs were rushing to close out their positions. Often enough, there were big trading clots in the last hour or so of those Fridays, and wild moves in stock prices.

As far as the anti-arbitrageurs are concerned, all these phenomena came home to roost during the "Black Monday" market crash of 1987, when the Dow Jones Industrial Average fell by 23 percent in a single day, exceeding in percentage terms—and massively in dollar terms—even the Great Crash of 1929.

Black Monday, Portfolio Insurance, and Computerized Trading

The Dow Jones Industrial Average hit a new record of 2700 in August 1987, marking more than a threefold increase in just five years, then began a slow, nervous slide through the early fall to stand just above 2500 on Wednesday, October 13. The jitters seemed well founded. Traditional indicators, like the ratio of dividend yields to bond yields, all signaled an overpriced market, and economic portents, like the soaring American budget and trade deficits, were ominous. The breaking news on Wednesday morning was all bad. Trade deficit numbers were much worse than anyone expected; long-bond yields jumped past 10 percent for the first time in two years; and a key House committee proposed tax penalties on corporate takeovers. Professional traders started dumping takeover stocks, and there was heavy institutional selling throughout the day. The Dow ended Wednesday down 95 points, or almost 4 percent.

Overnight market breaks in both Tokyo and London were even worse than in New York, and the Thursday morning futures markets opened with heavy selling by "portfolio insurers." Portfolio insurance was a set of strategies developed by two California academics, Hayne Leland and Mark Rubinstein, to protect large institutional portfolios against market drops. In principle, one can protect a portfolio against price drops by buying put options, which give the right, but not the obligation, to sell at a specific price. If the right combinations of options are available, one can achieve a mix of stock and options that will never fall more than, say, 5 percent; or that will even behave just like cash (see next chapter). The difficulty was that in 1987 the options markets weren't deep enough to make such a strategy practical. But Leland and Rubinstein showed how traders could create "synthetic puts" by a disciplined strategy of selling a precise number of index futures whenever the market drops—the faster the drop, the more futures sales. In the months leading up to the crash, big institutions became avid buyers of portfolio insurance, and by October, "insured" assets totaled about $100 billion, about half of it supervised by a firm owned by Leland and Rubinstein. There had been some insurance-based selling on Wednesday, but the strategy was often implemented with a one-day lag to minimize trading costs, so the main impact was delayed until Thursday.

When futures markets opened on Thursday, the initial insurance-impelled plunge was so sharp that stocks had trouble catching up. Futures were therefore at a discount to stocks for much of the day, although they conventionally trade at a premium. By late afternoon, index arbitrage—buying futures and selling stocks—had brought the two markets back into line, and a brief rally allowed the Dow to recover most of the morning's losses. But a burst of trading in the last half hour, much of it from portfolio insurers and index arbitrageurs, brought the market down 57 points for the day. Friday saw the same pattern of heavy model-driven selling. To make matters worse, an Iranian gunboat attacked an oil tanker, so traders got *really* jumpy. The Dow lost another 108 points, its biggest point drop ever. Over the three days, the Dow had fallen more than 250 points, or about 10 percent. Friday also saw the first substantial sales by non-trading-oriented institutions, who normally stuck with their portfolios in heavy weather.

The weekend news was all bad. America bombed an Iranian oil platform. There was a public spat between the American treasury secretary and European finance ministers. The dollar fell against almost all major currencies. Long-bond yields rose a full half percent. American mutual fund managers dumped stocks in London. All major stock markets were down sharply. Professional traders knew that portfolio insurance models called for even heavier selling on Monday, and were poised to sell into the hurricane at the opening bell.

On Monday, the markets staggered from breakdown to breakdown. Many of the largest New York Stock Exchange stocks did not open until about 10:30 because specialists* could not handle the volume of sell orders, and the NYSE "DOT" computerized trading system, which is available to big block

---

*On the major stock exchanges, floor orders are routed to a specialist assigned to each stock, who is responsible for maintaining "orderly" prices, committing his own capital as necessary to adjust order imbalances. Futures markets use an "open outcry" system, which operates pretty much as the phrase implies. The difference between the systems is narrowing, as more and more institutional trading is executed without the assistance of the specialists. Block trades on the NYSE (more than 10,000 shares) are routed through the "upstairs" market, the block-trading desks of the big brokerages, who match up buyers and sellers directly, while computerized "program" trades are input directly to the DOT, now "SuperDOT," automated trading system. In the aftermath of the crash, a number of specialists were disciplined for trading defensively instead of risking their capital to stem the downward price pressure. Minimum capital requirements for specialist firms on the NYSE were subsequently raised from $100,000 to $1 million.

traders, was badly backed up from the opening bell. In Chicago, stock futures were in free fall, and the futures discount was historically wide. The discount was an illusion, because a number of stocks that had not opened on time were still being listed at Friday's closing prices, but the mispricing burned a number of pros whose arbitrages blew up when stocks opened much lower than they had expected.

Once all stocks were open, arbitrage pulled the futures market back up, but a brief stock rally in the eleven o'clock hour was snuffed out by more selling pressures from portfolio insurers. By early afternoon rumors were circulating that the market might close. One portfolio insurer alone pumped out thirteen consecutive $100 million sell orders. The DOT system effectively ceased functioning by late afternoon, eliminating the possibility of index arbitrage and breaking the link between the stock and futures market. The futures contract plummeted to a level that implied a 29 percent drop in the Dow. In New York, the fall was slowed only by the backup of orders, and the market stumbled to a close of 1738, down 23 percent, the worst one-day performance in its history. Total volume exceeded 600 million shares, twice the previous record, and triple the rate for a typical heavy trading day. Portfolio insurers accounted for about 10 percent of NYSE sales and about 20 percent of the futures sales in Chicago, or twice that amount if market-maker trades are excluded.

Bottom fishing and warm words from the Federal Reserve sparked an early-morning rally on Tuesday, but by about 10:30, another wave of portfolio insurance selling drove futures prices down. The NYSE temporarily barred the use of the DOT system to index arbitrageurs, once again breaking the futures-stock pricing link. With no check from arbitrageurs, the futures market plunged to a level that implied a Dow of only 1400, and rumors swirled of an exchange failure. Growing panic was finally arrested when a blue-ribbon list of American companies announced stock buybacks worth more than $6 billion. The Dow rallied 170 points in late afternoon, but last-minute profit taking shaved the full-day gain to 100 points, still almost a 6 percent pickup and a new record for a one-day point gain. Even with the improvement on Tuesday, the one-week loss in stock market capitalization was in excess of a half trillion dollars.

As soon as the smoke cleared, a plethora of high-level study groups and commissions were convened to clarify what went wrong and to recommend policy responses. The most prominent was the "Brady Commission," a presidential task force chaired by Dillon Read Chairman Nicholas Brady, soon to be treasury secretary. It produced an almost minute-by-minute account of the week's events that pointed a finger squarely at the apparently mindless computer-driven trading of the portfolio insurers and index arbitrageurs:

> The Task Force concludes that the precipitous decline in the market was characterized by large sales by a limited number of institutional investors throughout the interrelated system of markets—stocks, futures, and stock options. The massive volume, violent price volatility, and staggering demands on clearing and credit raised the possibility of a full-scale financial system breakdown.

The task force recommended a unified regulatory system under the Federal Reserve, and some system tinkering—including "circuit breakers," or mandatory trading halts during sharp upturns or downturns, and increased margin requirements in the futures markets.

The academics were briefly cowed by the obvious failure of their much-touted portfolio insurance. (They had made a fundamental and very simple error. Their strategy assumed that there would always be *buyers* in the futures market at the trigger prices. When buyers hung back, prices went into free fall, triggering yet more futures sales, which frightened off the buyers even more.) But the academics soon struck back with a series of analyses and reports of their own.

The core of the academic argument was simply that government had no obligation to protect investors against bear markets, and that anyway the scale of the downturn may have been about right. The NYSE Composite Index, comprising all NYSE-traded stocks, for example, fell 55 points, or 29 percent, from October 13 through October 20, but it had recovered only 20 points by the following summer, and it took almost two years to get back to its early-October level—suggesting that it was pre-crash exuberance that had been excessive, not the October correction. The crash, moreover, was a worldwide phenomenon: it actually started in most countries earlier than in the United States, and American markets did not have the steepest drop. Since only the United States had adopted highly computerized trading technologies, they could hardly have been a primary cause. Finally, academics did not see why the *speed* of the fall should be such an issue. Technology and derivatives had sharply lowered the cost of trading, so markets could be expected to react much faster than previously. The real problem, in the academic view, was that the exchanges' computer systems couldn't keep up with the order flow. Markets had been most disorderly when computer problems prevented index arbitrage from maintaining price parity between the futures and stock markets.

At the end of the day, while academics may have lost on the public relations front, none of the more radical post-crash recommendations—consolidating regulatory jurisdictions, eliminating index arbitrage or computerized trading, substantially raising margin requirements on the futures exchanges—was put into effect, or even received serious support from regulators. The major exchanges did adopt coordinated circuit breaker rules, some of them fairly subtle. For example, once the Dow moves 50 points from its previous close, index arbitrage must be "stabilizing"—aimed at narrowing stock-futures pricing gaps—and once the S&P 500 futures falls 12 index points, the NYSE slows its computerized trades by five minutes. (Academic warnings of potential dire effects from interrupting pricing information have not, so far at least, been borne out.)

The most important post-crash adjustment, however, may be simply that the exchanges have gotten their computer systems up to snuff. Black Monday's 600-million-share volume no longer even counts among the top ten trading days. During a sharp market break in October 1997, NYSE share volumes exceeded 600 million every day for more than a week, and hit 1.2 billion on Tuesday, October 28, when the market made a substantial recovery. NYSE staff later bragged that they could have easily handled twice the volume. Coordinated circuit breakers kicked in three times during the Dow's 554-point drop—only about a third as great in percentage terms as on Black Monday—but there was little sign of system strain either in the stock market or the futures market. October volume on the Chicago Merc was up 55 percent on the year, with minimal, if any, bottlenecks. Significantly, too, much of Tuesday's buying volume came from small investors, in striking contrast to 1987, when they typically could not even get through to their brokers.

The consensus following the 1997 mini-crash was that the circuit breakers worked reasonably well but growth in market values had made the bands too narrow. An early-1998 agreement provides for a system of moving bands, based on a percentage of the Dow, which makes much more sense. The 50-point index-arbitrage "collar" has also become much too constraining and is triggered much too frequently, but as of early 1998 it had not yet been loosened. Professional traders also seemed uniformly unhappy with the early trading halt on October 27—as opposed to the temporary trading pauses during the day—since it allowed that much more time for Fear and Doubt to build before the next day's market opening, but the 1998 agreements still specifically provide for early closings.

There is other evidence that the markets have successfully adjusted to the shift in scale. A few simple "sunshine" rules have largely tamed the once-feared triple-witching trading. Orders for the fifty biggest stocks now must be placed before the opening of a triple-witching Friday, and again thirty minutes before the close, so there is time for specialists to work off order imbalances. Index arbitrage is now well understood, and seems to have settled into a kind of steady background buzz. Computerized "program" trades routinely constitute some 15 to 20 percent of all NYSE transactions. The use of futures and options to hone institutional portfolios is simply taken for granted, and there is a much more refined understanding of the interactions between cash and derivatives markets. One study after another shows that while *intra*day price volatility may have increased slightly, day-to-day volatility, measured in percentage terms, has been quite stable for a long time. Intraday fluctuations, in any case, should be of little interest to anyone except professional traders. (Interday market volatility may have increased slightly in 1997, but that is fairly typical in the late stages of a bull market.) Fifteen years of probing every market crevice for arbitrage opportunities—in interest rates, treasury coupons, derivative and cash markets, mortgages and bonds—has generated a state of remarkably consistent, almost seamless, pricing, at least across most American financial markets.

If the financial media were any indicator, Wall Street's scale shift has made little impression on the public consciousness. Popular television financial programs, like Louis Rukeyser's *Wall Street Week,* and CNN's *Money Line,* typically feature parades of market gurus—who always disagree with one another—variously suggesting that investors should be "selling cyclicals" or "increasing their weighting of technologies" and recommending some obscure undervalued stocks. The implication is that the average investor is an active trader, calling market turns, making bets on interest rates, buying and selling shares according to some obscure "strategy"—which is not a very sensible way to behave even for professional investors and would be the height of folly for the rest of us.

Gurus notwithstanding, households seem to be accepting the academic argument that stock picking is a foolish way to manage a nest egg, as evidenced by the increased market shares of no-load funds, index funds, and similar products. Stockbrokers have long since restyled themselves as "financial consultants" and are now as likely to push mutual funds as individual stocks. The discount stock brokerage, Charles Schwab, offers its customers 1100 mutual funds, most on a no-load basis, and derived more than a fifth of its 1996 revenues from mutual fund fees and commissions. At the outset of the 1980s–1990s bull market, household mutual fund holdings were only about 5 percent of individual share holdings; now they are a third as much. The sheer fun of playing the market may justify paying high fees and enduring poor performance, but in an investment field covered with the footprints of very large animals, it's no longer a sensible way to look after one's life savings.

If there were any remaining doubts on that score in the early 1990s, a long string of fiascos in derivatives markets showed that even many of the gurus hadn't a clue to what was going on in their own businesses.

Chapter Seven

BLACK MAGIC

GNMAs, or "Ginnie Maes," are bondlike instruments that pay investors the interest and principal payments from underlying pools of mortgages. In the spring of 1987, Howard Rubin, a star trader at Merrill Lynch, was racking up profits by selling the interest coupons (Interest Onlys, or IOs) and the principal obligations (POs) from GNMAs as separate securities, a practice called "stripping." His profits came from the fact that he could buy the whole GNMAs for slightly less than customers were willing to pay for the strips. Merrill Lynch understood that Rubin's activities entailed some capital risk, since he obviously had to hold GNMAs in his trading portfolio during the short time it took to buy them, reconstitute them as strips, and sell them off to customers.

GNMA strips are much more volatile than whole GNMAs. Like any bond, GNMAs fall in value when rates rise, but because of special features of GNMAs, the drop in value is the net effect of a sharp *rise* in the value of the IOs, and an even sharper fall in the POs. Merrill Lynch's implicit assumption in allocating capital to Rubin was that both sets of strips would be sold off at the same time. In early April, Rubin filled a very large IO order from a big customer and was left with a commensurately large position in POs. To make matters worse, the PO position was in excess of his daily trading limit, so he did not enter it into the Merrill accounting system. Inevitably, interest rates spiked sharply over the next several weeks, POs went through the floor, and Merrill discovered it had incurred a $377 million loss.

In December 1994, the Board of Supervisors of Orange County, California, announced that a $7.6 billion investment pool that it managed on behalf of the county and a number of other local jurisdictions, had incurred a $1.5 billion loss. The county official who managed the pool, Robert Citron, had compiled an enviable investment track record, and the local governments had assumed that investment windfalls would continue forever—investment income accounted for fully a third of Orange County's budgeted revenue in the 1994–95 fiscal year.

Citron had compiled his track record by leveraging his $7.6 billion of investable funds into a $20.6 billion portfolio and making a big one-way bet that interest rates would fall continuously. He borrowed short-term funds at low interest rates to buy higher-yield securities with a duration* of about five years. He was therefore terribly exposed when rates rose throughout most of 1994. He either had to sell his long-duration securities at a big loss to pay back his borrowings, or keep rolling over his borrowings at rates higher than he was earning on his portfolio. To make matters worse, he had dramatically increased the risk of his portfolio throughout 1993 and 1994 by investing heavily in "inverse floaters," instruments that fall especially sharply when rates rise; at one point in 1994 they accounted for more than half of his portfolio. At bottom, there was nothing mysterious about what Citron was doing. It was like your Uncle Eddie borrowing money to bet at the racetrack, and always rebetting his winnings so he can't pay you back when he finally loses.

---

*Duration is the average length of time it takes to receive the present-valued cash flows of a bond and is the standard way of expressing an investor's exposure to interest rate changes. A bond with a high-interest coupon will have a shorter duration than a bond with a low-interest coupon, because the high-coupon bond owner gets more cash flow up front. The longer duration of the low-coupon bond means it will be more volatile when interest rates fluctuate. Low-coupon, long-maturity bonds, like municipals, have the highest durations. Consider a five-year treasury with a 6 percent coupon and a 30-year municipal with a 4.5 percent coupon, both priced to yield 8 percent. The treasury has a duration of about 4.4, while the municipal has a duration of about 13. A 1 percent rise in interest rates will therefore cause about a 4.4 percent drop in the value of the treasury and about a 13 percent (!) drop in the value of the municipal. High-grade municipals are "safe" only in the sense that there's little risk of missing interest payments, but their capital values can drop sharply when rates rise. For the mathematically minded, duration is the first derivative of the price curve with respect to yield.

Besides sending shock waves through the municipal bond market—Orange County had a top credit rating—the episode pointed the finger at Merrill Lynch and other investment banks who had been advising Citron and at the same time flogging Orange County bond issues, with full knowledge of how Citron was investing the proceeds. Merrill eventually settled with the county for $420 million, and by the end of 1998, the county had recovered about $800 million from its advisers.

In February 1995, Barings, the venerable banking house that underwrote Thomas Jefferson's Louisiana Purchase, announced that Nicholas Leeson, a twenty-eight-year-old trader in its Singapore branch, had generated more than $2 billion in losses primarily through unauthorized trading in Nikkei futures, a way of making bets on the overall direction of the Japanese stock market. Leeson's bet that the market would trade within a narrow range came undone in January when a massive earthquake destroyed the city of Kobe; then for another month, he made huge bets that the market would recover in the hope of making up his losses. Subsequent investigation showed that Leeson had begun unauthorized trading almost from the day he had been transferred to Singapore in 1992, and that he had repeatedly incurred big losses that he had concealed in secret trading accounts or covered up with phony documentation. He was able to continue his deceptions for so long because he was also in charge of the bookkeeping for his trades, so there were no built-in checks and balances to trip him up. Amazingly, his masters in London had repeatedly met his requests for huge sums to support his trading, including wiring more than a $1 billion in January and February, with hardly a question about what he was up to. Leeson's losses forced Barings to shut down later in the year, selling off its healthy businesses under bankruptcy supervision.

The scandal that helped bring down Kidder, Peabody in the spring of 1994 rivals Leeson's, not in the scale of the loss but in the comic incompetence of his bosses. A young Kidder trader, Joseph Jett, was reconstituting treasury bond interest and principal strips and reselling them as whole bonds, essentially the opposite transaction to Rubin's at Merrill Lynch. Reconstitutions are not a trade, and a reconstitution would not earn a profit unless Jett sold the reconstituted securities to an outside customer for more than he paid for the strips. But Kidder's ancient back-office system had no accounting buckets for reconstitutions, so they were recorded as if they were trades—a notional purchase of the strips and a notional sale of a whole bond.

Treasury strips are sold as zero-coupons. (Assume a five-year treasury with a $5000 coupon paid semiannually; the interest strips will take the form of ten $2500 zero-coupons maturing at six-month intervals.) The problem arose because Jett's department allowed up to five days to settle a reconstitution, which brought into play a special attribute of zeros. Zeros accrue interest instead of paying it currently, so they rise in value with each day closer to the maturity date. Since Kidder's trading system recorded the "purchase" of the strips at the current day's price, and the "sale" of the whole bond at the settlement date five days later, the sale value was always slightly higher than the purchase value, reflecting the additional days of accrued interest. It would therefore briefly appear as if Jett had made a profit. But only briefly, because each day after the trade date, the cost of the "purchase" was restated to reflect the increasing value of the strip, so by the settlement date the illusory profit was extinguished.

Jett, however, discovered that if he always *increased the volume* of his reconstitutions, the illusory profit would not only not disappear, it would keep growing, because the profits that were being eliminated from previous transactions would be more than replaced by those from new ones. Later, the firm's trading rules were changed so that settlement dates could be extended for months, which made the paper profits recorded on the first day of a trade really large. Once Jett climbed on his merry-go-round, he rode it very hard. Starting almost from scratch in late 1991 or early 1992, he built his bond portfolio to $42 billion by the end of 1993, racking up nominal profits of $10 million a month. He was promoted several times and was voted Kidder's "man of the year" in 1993 and awarded a $9 million bonus. The irony was that his appetite for strips, which are thinly traded, was so voracious that his traders had to buy them at a premium, so he was actually losing money on each reconstitution.

The scheme unraveled when General Electric, Kidder's owner, became alarmed at the size of the bond portfolio and ordered that part of it be sold off, which inevitably exposed the true extent of Jett's losses. According to the subsequent SEC investigation, from 1992 through the first quarter of 1994, Jett generated $348 million in fictitious profits while actually causing $83 million in losses. The most remarkable feature of the episode—and the heart of Jett's defense in subsequent litigation—is that Jett had an exceptionally high profile in the company, made little effort to conceal what he was doing, and was subject to frequent reviews by his superiors and internal auditors. It is simply astonishing that accountants could manage to overlook $431 million (348 + 83) in missing cash flow. Jett was ultimately acquitted of fraud, but was forced to repay his bonuses.

The financial news of the late 1980s and early 1990s was peppered with headlines like these—the collapse of Askin Capital, an important mortgage-backed trader, the Daiwa trader who lost $1.1 billion in treasury trading, the $2 billion copper-trading fiasco at Sumitomo Bank. The common threads were that each episode involved a mysterious class of financial instruments called "derivatives" and that the top managements of some of the world's most important financial enterprises did not have a clue about what their subordinates were up to. The sheer volume of derivative contracts outstanding—some $60 trillion worth by mid-1997, or about eight times higher than America's annual GDP—seems sufficient cause for alarm. There have even been moves in Congress to ban the creatures completely.

The Universal Financial Solvent

The term "derivative" refers to any financial instrument whose value depends on some other financial instrument. The value of an option to buy a share of stock, for instance, depends on the price of the stock, and the value of a mortgage-backed depends on the behavior of an underlying mortgage pool. The most fundamental financial derivatives, perhaps, are futures and options, and they illustrate as well as any the powers and the pitfalls of the instruments. Both have long histories, especially in trading agricultural or other commodities.

Options give the right, but not the obligation, to buy or sell something at a specified price within a specified time frame. An option to buy is a "call," and an option to sell is a "put." Take the example of options on IBM shares in late 1997. On December 16, IBM shares closed at 102. On that same day "January calls" on IBM (options that had to be exercised on or before the third Friday of January) at 110 cost $1.75, while January puts at 110 cost $7.63.

If I buy the call I'm betting that the stock will rise sufficiently above 110, the "strike price," so I can cover the cost of the option and still make a profit. So if the stock rises to 115, I'll exercise my option at 110 and make $5 per share less the $1.75 option price, or $3.25, which almost doubles my investment. If the stock doesn't reach 110, however, the option expires worthless, and I've lost my $1.75.

If I buy the put, I'm betting that the stock price will fall. If the price falls to 95, I will sell at 110, for a profit of $7.37 after recovering the $7.63 I paid for the option, ignoring trading costs. On the other hand, at any price above 102⅜ I'll lose money. If it rises to, say, 105, I'll make $5 when I exercise the put, but will still be out $2.63 when I subtract the cost of the option. If it rises above 110, I lose the entire $7.63. Options are obviously much more volatile than stocks, creating the opportunity to make very large profits, doubling or tripling your money, or losing your entire stake, in a matter of days or weeks.

If I *sold* you an option to buy IBM at 110, on the other hand, and it rises to 120, I will lose $8.25 (the $10 I'm losing by selling the stock at less than its market value, offset by the $1.75 you paid me for the call). In the same way, the seller, or "writer," of a put option could suffer heavy losses if a stock falls sharply. In the first week of October 1992, for example, when IBM shares were hovering around 85, January IBM puts at 80 traded at an average price of $4.29 per share. IBM stock fell sharply the rest of the year, and averaged $49.75 in the first week of January, so the puts had risen in value to $30.50 (or approximately the difference between the strike price and the stock price), so the option buyer had made seven times her money in just three months. If the put was exer-

cised that week, the seller would have lost an average of $25.96 a
share, because he was obligated to pay $80 a share for stock worth
only $49.75, offset by the $4.29 he had received for the put, ignoring interest and costs. The buyer of a put or call option, therefore,
is at risk only for the price of the option, while the seller's risk is
much less predictable. The risk of selling calls is theoretically unlimited (in principle, stock prices have no top), and on puts, risk is
limited only by the fact that stock prices can never fall below zero.

Futures, in contrast to options, are firm contracts to buy or
sell—one party to the contract has obligated herself to deliver
goods at a specific price on a specific date, and the other party has
contracted to take them. Unlike options, futures are cash-settled on
a daily basis. So if I have contracted to deliver treasury bonds at 99
sixty days from now, and the price of the bond rises to 101, I will
have to increase my margin deposit by the amount of the difference,
and will have to keep on meeting margin calls as long as the bond
keeps rising. When the sixty days are up, we'll settle in cash; if the
price is 103 on the settlement date, my counterparty gets $4; and if
the price has dropped to 97, the counterparty pays me $2. Finally,
in addition to futures and options, there is also active trading in options on futures, which are simply options whose value depends on
the price movements in futures.

There are more than a dozen futures and options exchanges
throughout the country, most of them in Chicago and New York,
each of them specializing in specific types of contracts. The
Chicago Board of Trade, for example, trades a wide range of treasury bond and other financial futures; the New York Mercantile
Exchange is a leader in a variety of oil future contracts; the
Chicago Board Options Exchange and the New York Stock Exchange both trade stock options and stock index options; and the
Chicago Mercantile Exchange is the leader in the most popular
stock index futures. Exchanges formalize and standardize the
trading process by specifying allowable contracts, delivery dates,
quality standards (e.g., for oil contracts), pricing increments, settlement arrangements, and qualifications for traders and brokers.
Exchanges create a common language for investors ("December
corn is at $3.10"), broadcast prices, and assure deep and liquid

markets. In exchange-traded contracts, the exchange acts as the counterparty on each transaction, matching up buyers and sellers within its own systems, so the individual trader doesn't have to worry about counterparty default.

Exchange trading in financial futures dates only from the 1970s, but "forward" trading, especially in foreign currencies, has a long history. Consider the position of an American importer who has ordered goods from Japan, payment due in yen upon delivery three months from now. From the importer's perspective, a rise in the yen against the dollar is the same as a price increase, because he will have to spend more dollars to buy the requisite yen. By asking his bank to buy yen forward, however, the importer can lock in his exchange rate at the cost of a small premium—in effect, purchasing cheap insurance against currency losses. International companies, like a Ford or a General Motors, that buy supplies from all over the world and frequently move unfinished goods back and forth across borders, track their net foreign-exchange exposure daily and usually stay nearly fully hedged. The vast majority of derivative transactions, like forward foreign-exchange contracts, are conducted off-exchange as "over-the-counter" (OTC) transactions.

The advent of computers and the blossoming of securities mathematics over the past twenty-five years have made quite complicated hedging transactions routine business for portfolio managers. For example, suppose a manager who holds stock would rather hold cash, but for tax reasons wants to avoid selling the stock. One alternative would be to sell call options on his stock portfolio. Assume that the stock in question has a current price of 100, that the exercise price of the option is 102, that the risk-free interest rate is 6 percent, that the stock's volatility is 10 percent, and that the options are good for a year. Options mathematics says that the option is worth $6.19 per share—that is, another trader should be willing to pay $6.19 for the right to buy the stock at 102 at any time in the next year. The same mathematics says that if the portfolio manager sells 10,000 call options for every 6,700 shares of stock, he will be almost perfectly hedged.

The table below shows how the hedge works. If the stock rises by 1 percent, the value of the call options, which are a liability of the manager, will also increase by about 69 cents each, offsetting his stock gain within a few hundred dollars. Conversely, if the stock falls by 1 percent, his profit on the option sale will almost precisely offset the loss on the stock. In effect, although he still owns the stock, within a small margin of error the portfolio now behaves very much like cash.

Stock Portfolio = 6,700 shares @ 100
Sell 10,000 Calls @ 6.19

	Start	*Stock = 101*	*Stock = 99*
Cash (from call sale)	61,900	61,900	61,900
Stock	670,000	676,700	663,300
Liability on calls	-61,900	-68,826	-55,345
Total portfolio	670,000	669,774	669,855

The math used in the example is known as the Black-Scholes Model, developed by the late Fischer Black and Myron Scholes, with the active assistance of Robert Merton. It is one of the most famous of all financial formulas, and is one of the high points of intensive mathematical development in financial theory over the past thirty years. (It earned Scholes and Merton the 1997 Nobel Memorial Prize in Economics. For the model itself, see the Notes on page 268.) After the paper describing the model was turned down by several publications, it was finally published in *The Journal of Political Economy,* in 1973, coinciding with the opening of the Chicago Board Options Exchange. It was almost immediately adopted by exchange traders, and within six months, the model had been incorporated into Texas Instruments' handheld financial calculators. If a trader entered the current stock price, the exercise price, the risk-free interest rate, and a factor for volatility, the calculator would spit out the Black-Scholes option price. In addition, the "hedge ratio"—the ratio of 10,000 options for every 6,700 shares—could be easily derived from the model's treatment of volatility. Options trading exploded, and all major options exchanges now routinely include instantaneous Black-Scholes prices on their trading screens.

The model is not perfect, and it has been refined many times over the past twenty-five years. Its authors themselves have frequently pointed out its many unrealistic assumptions—volatility is never precisely known, for instance, and interest rates will rarely be constant over the life of the option, as the model assumes. Further, the hedged portfolio in the example is hedged only so long as the initial assumptions hold. As time remaining on the options dwindles, or market prices change, the manager must constantly adjust his hedge—another example of routine trading practices that would have been impractical, if not actually impossible, before the spread of desktop computers. Overall, however, the model captures the key elements in option trading, and the empirical evidence is that, on average, its results stand up very well.

One criticism sometimes leveled against option pricing models is that they assume that the past is a reliable guide to the future. But they actually make a much weaker claim—that based on what is *currently known,* the model result is a fair price for the option. There is no assumption about the future, and new information could change the value of the option sharply.

The rich developments in securities mathematics now make it possible for traders to transform assets from one kind to another with an ease that is almost magical. As the example of the hedged stock portfolio showed, risky assets plus options can be made to behave like cash. On the same logic, a cash portfolio plus options can be made to behave just like stock. Combinations of options will be equivalent to futures, and options plus futures can mimic stock, or cash, or any asset at all. Using futures, one can change fixed-rate debt into floating-rate debt or vice versa; or if the futures aren't available—futures with settlement dates much more than a year away are usually hard to find—one can use the same logic, and the same math, to swap one kind of portfolio for another. You can make a dollar portfolio act like a mark portfolio, short-term debt act like long-term debt, a low-volatility stock position act like a high-volatility position. (If you think a bull market is coming, a high-volatility portfolio will react more sharply to an upward move.) For some purposes, it is even useful to analyze a corporate bond as an option on a company's assets, for if the company defaults, the bondholders have, in effect, bought the assets.

Although derivatives can be used to increase leverage, and thereby increase risk, they are probably far more frequently used to *reduce* risk. Interest rate swaps are a good example. In a "plain-vanilla" swap, one party who is earning fixed-rate interest and another earning floating rates agree to swap their income streams. Why would they want to do that? Someone earning floating rates on short-term paper may really want fixed-rate returns but be afraid of tying up her cash in longer-term instruments. By entering into the swap, she can keep her liquid portfolio and still receive a fixed-rate return. The other party could be an S&L who holds fixed-rate mortgages but is paying floating rates to depositors. The swap allows it to receive rates that will move in tandem with the rates it must pay. The same is true for borrowers. A small company may want to borrow at a fixed rate of interest, but banks don't like to make fixed-rate loans, and it is expensive for small companies to tap the bond market. But another company may feel overburdened with fixed-rate debt. If the first company takes out a floating-rate loan, and the two then swap their interest-payment obligations, they will both be better off.

Managing Risk with Derivatives: BancOne

BancOne of Columbus, Ohio, as of 1997, was one of the nation's largest regional banks, with more than 1500 offices through the Midwest and South and some $90 billion in assets. It had grown rapidly by acquisition, increasing its assets by more than tenfold in just fifteen years. The kind of smaller local banks that BancOne liked to acquire almost never made fixed-rate loans, and they raised most of their deposits from savings accounts and CDs that had relatively sticky interest rates. In the jargon, their balance sheets were "asset-sensitive." Over the short term, a rise in interest rates would not affect what they pay their depositors but would greatly affect the income from their loans—if interest rates increase, income will rise sharply, and if rates fall, income will fall.

(This is the opposite of the situation with S&Ls, which were "liability-sensitive." Their loans were of such long maturity that even with relatively sticky deposit rates, their deposits still repriced much faster than their loans. So they *lost* money when rates rose and made money when rates fell.)

BancOne was a pioneer in the use of computers to model its sensitivity to interest rate fluctuations, and through the late 1980s and early 1990s, it engaged in an aggressive program to reduce its overall asset sensitivity, and even to become slightly liability-sensitive. (BancOne's CFO argues that banks "are paid to be liability-sensitive"—converting short-term deposits into longer-term assets, in other words, is what banks are for.) The most straight-forward way to reduce asset sensitivity is simply to make long-term fixed-rate loans, and to a some extent, that's what BancOne did, by buying longer-term treasuries and mortgage pass-throughs. But it found it could accomplish the same objectives much more efficiently through swaps. By entering into "pay-floating/receive-fixed" swaps, it got the best of all worlds: it could maintain a highly liquid portfolio in case it had sudden cash needs, and it avoided weighing down its balance sheet with long-term fixed-rate assets, which lose market value when rates rise, but its asset sensitivity had been reduced just as if it had made a large number of fixed-rate loans.

Looking at the mechanics of BancOne's swaps shows how little actual risk is involved. In the first place, the counterparties don't actually trade assets. When BancOne swaps, say, a floating return from Eurodollar deposits (called LIBOR, or the London Interbank Offering Rate) for fixed-rate interest from mortgage pools, it doesn't assume the risks of the mortgage pools. It keeps its Eurodollar deposits, and the counterparty keeps its mortgage pools; the two simply trade their interest receipts, adjusted so the present values of the two streams are equal. A swap might be negotiated, for example, as LIBOR in exchange for 7 percent fixed, each calculated on a hypothetical, or a "notional," portfolio of $100 million. (The swap rate of, say, LIBOR for 7 percent is set by the current market; if the pay-fixed counterparty has fixed-rate assets that pay more than 7 percent, he keeps the difference, and vice versa.) The two parties settle up each interest period by a payment of the net difference between the two rates. So if the received-fixed rate is 7 percent, and the pay-floating averaged 6 percent, over the course of a year BancOne would collect $1 million (1 percent of $100 million); and if LIBOR rose to 7.5 percent, BancOne would pay $500,000 to its counterparty. The main risk, then, is that the counterparty will default on its obligation; but in that case, BancOne doesn't have to make any payment either. In practice, BancOne protected against counterparty default by swapping only with highly rated counterparties, and usually insisting on collateral—the counterparty had to fund a margin account that provides a cushion against its failing to make a swap payment. While the actual risk, therefore, was not zero, because the failure of a counterparty will disrupt BancOne's asset planning, it was pretty close to negligible.

About 1993, however, BancOne's aggressive use of swaps created considerable consternation in the analyst community. One problem was that the transactions were complicated. In its basic swaps, BancOne was almost always the party that paid floating and received fixed. The pay-floating contracts, however, were usually linked to LIBOR, which is the deepest market. But BancOne's own floating-rate assets were tied to the prime rate, which is much stickier than LIBOR—the prime rate floats in jumps, not smoothly the way LIBOR does. So BancOne covered its pay-floating contracts by entering into "basis" swaps—pay-prime/receive-LIBOR—to minimize the risk of a mismatch between its prime-based income and its LIBOR-based swap obligations. And finally, to avoid getting hurt by a sharp spike in floating rates, it also bought interest caps—options and futures contracts that paid off if rates rose above some threshold level, so BancOne wouldn't be stuck paying very high floating rates. Understandably, some bank analysts were confused.

The huge "notional" value building up on BancOne's financials seemed even more alarming. The swap contract in the example above had a notional value of $100 million. Although the contract would not appear on the bank's balance sheet, the notional value would be entered into a table in the company's financial footnotes. If the company also covered its LIBOR obligation with a "basis" swap (pay-prime/receive-LIBOR) on the same notional value, *another* $100 million in notional value went into the table. And then if the company bought interest rate caps to cover, say, half of its pay-floating obligations, yet another $50 million went into the table. Through the mid-1990s, the notional value of BancOne's swaps fluctuated between $35 and 45 billion, or roughly half its total assets. (Accounting for swaps was substantially revised in 1998; see Chapter 10.)

At one point, at roughly the height of the wave of bad publicity about derivatives, the intricacies of the swaps and the huge notional values involved seemed to panic the analyst community, and the company's stock dropped sharply despite excellent earnings. A frustrated management tried to explain in vain that the bank was actually *safer* with its natural asset sensitivity reduced by swaps, and that using swaps to simulate fixed-rate lending was cheaper, and less risky, than making fixed-rate loans. Notional values, they argued, were irrelevant; what mattered was *value at risk,* and the way the swaps were structured, that was very small.

At the end of the day, the bank seems to have won the argument. Bank officials embarked on an intensive series of analyst presentations, including two all-day sessions in Boston and New York, in which they used academic and other experts to walk analysts through their methodologies. A bank official said, "Several of the bigger banks called us and thanked us for clearing the air. I wouldn't say comprehension of these issues is at 100 percent now, but it's gone from, say, 20 percent to about 90 percent." By 1997, BancOne stock was trading fairly comfortably within the range of its peers, with no evidence of a market penalty due to its derivative activities.

The flurry of derivatives disasters, in a perverse way, may actually have helped BancOne's case, for they sparked dozens of official and semi-official inquiries—by the Federal Reserve Board, the SEC, the General Accounting Office, the Washington-based financial study group, "the Group of Thirty," and many others. Virtually every study concluded that modern derivative technology had become indispensable to a well-functioning financial system, and properly used, served to lower risk and reduce transaction cost. Virtually every study group, as well, noted that derivatives pose tricky accounting and disclosure issues and place a burden on senior managers to know what's going on, but as the Federal Reserve study suggested, management and oversight systems seemed to be catching up rapidly. Within the banking industry, certainly, BancOne-style swaps have become standard procedure.

The analysts' instinct to worry about complicated derivatives structures, however, was a good one. While BancOne's strategies do appear sound, a closer look at a couple of recent fiascos suggests the trouble that they can cause.

Bankers Trust

Gibson Greetings, one of the most famously successful of the early-1980s LBOs, raised $50 million in new capital in the spring of 1991 through a bond issue that carried a fixed interest rate of 9.33 percent. As rates fell sharply over the next year, the debt began to look very expensive, but it was call-protected—meaning the company did not have the right to pay it off. So Gibson's senior financial officers, Ward Cavanaugh and James Johnson, decided they would improve their position with swaps, and turned to Bankers Trust for help. Bankers Trust called in the specialists from their trading subsidiary, BT Securities, and in late 1991, Gibson did a conventional swap covering $30 million of its debt, in which it agreed to pay Bankers a floating interest rate in return for Bankers assuming its fixed-rate payments. (When banks arrange swaps, they usually act as the counterparty. By having a stable of clients whose positions roughly net out overall, the bank avoids the complication of pairing off individual swap clients. It's better for the bank if the counterparties don't know each other, anyway, so they are not tempted to cut the bank out of its fee.)

The swap was a success, but was terminated in mid-1992, because the BT Securities traders had come back with some better ideas. The first was a "Ratio Swap"—Bankers agreed to pay Gibson a fixed rate of 5.5 percent for five years on a notional $30 million, and Gibson agreed to pay Bankers a floating rate equal to LIBOR squared divided by 6 percent. (If LIBOR was at 5 percent, the formula produced (.05 × .05)/.06 = .0417.) But this was no longer a plain-vanilla swap, for the formula introduced a rate gamble. If rates fell, Gibson would be much better off, but if they rose, Bankers would make big profits—if LIBOR went to 9 percent, for instance, Gibson's obligation to Bankers would shoot up to 13.5 percent. In fact, rates fell—which favored Gibson—so Bankers recommended restructuring the swap to change the payoffs. In the new swap, called a Basis Swap, Bankers would pay Gibson up to $42,000 (i.e., 0.14 percent of $30 million) as long as LIBOR did not fall more than 0.29 percent. But if LIBOR fell more than 0.29 percent, Gibson owed Bankers $1500 for each basis point (0.01 percent) fall. If LIBOR fell from 6 percent to 5 percent, for instance, Gibson owed Bankers $106,500. (1 percent − 0.29 percent = 0.71 percent, or 71 basis points × 1500.)

This is confusing enough, but Bankers was just getting warmed up. It then proposed that Gibson enter into a one-year option contract to lock in a spread over seven-year treasuries, called a Spread Lock, but after Gibson entered into the contract, Bankers repeatedly changed the terms. Bankers then proposed that Gibson enter into a second Spread Lock at more or less the original terms, which it also then proceeded to change. Gibson lost money on both Spread Locks, so Bankers designed a "Wedding Band" option contract linking the two Spread Locks, which nominally protected Gibson if interest rates moved outside of a narrow range. It then arranged a complicated series of "Time Trades" in which Bankers paid Gibson $150,000 every six months, but Gibson owed Bankers $7500 for each day that LIBOR varied beyond a specified schedule, although a rapid-fire series of amendments steadily increased Gibson's liability to $13,800 a day.

None of these positions makes any sense in terms of Gibson's relatively simple objectives, but Cavanaugh and Johnson obviously hadn't a clue about what was going on and approved every contract Bankers gave them. In all, from November 1991 through March 1994, Gibson entered into 29 different derivative transactions with Bankers, including amendments to existing contracts. The notional amount of the swaps and option contracts grew from $30 million to $167 million, and Gibson's eventual losses on the positions were estimated at $23 million—all for trying to improve their interest exposure on $30 million in debt.

Gibson sued, and over the next year, seven more Bankers Trust clients came out of the woodwork with similar accusations. Procter & Gamble claimed losses of $195 million; Air Products and Chemicals, $106 million; Sandoz Pharmaceuticals, $50 million. Bankers' defense, of course, was that it was dealing with the most sophisticated clients in the world, the CFOs and treasurers of major corporations—how could they possibly claim that they had been misled? It is standard practice at securities firms, however, to tape traders' conversations, in case there are paperwork disputes. To Bankers' chagrin, all their tapes became evidence in the lawsuits, and of course, traders love to talk tough and dirty. "Funny business, you know?" one trader on the tapes says about a client. "Lure people into that calm and then just totally fuck 'em."

Making all allowances for trading-desk swagger, however, there is no doubt that Bankers was consciously ripping off its clients. Since complex derivatives contracts are one-off transactions, there are no market prices, so they have to be valued by computer simulations. Bankers used proprietary models, which it did not share with its customers, and had considerable latitude to make values come out any way they wanted. In the Gibson case, the SEC found, Bankers "knowingly provided Gibson with values that significantly understated the magnitude of Gibson's losses. As a result . . . Gibson continued to purchase derivatives from BT Securities." The valuations provided to Gibson sometimes "differed by more than 50 percent from the value generated by Bankers Trust's computer model and recorded on Bankers Trust's books." The tapes also suggest that misrepresenting the results of the model was often a device for overcharging customers for their losses, or underpaying them when they won. All in all, the episode represents an extraordinary breakdown in a bank's fiduciary obligation to its clients. As a BT Securities managing director put it to another trader, "From the very beginning, [Gibson] just, you know, really put themselves in our hands, like 96 percent. . . . And we have known that from day one . . . these guys have done some pretty wild stuff. And you know, they probably did not understand it quite as well as they should. I think that they have a pretty good understanding of it, but not perfect. And that's like perfect for us."

The episode was eventually closed when Bankers entered into a consent agreement with the SEC, and individual traders were fined and suspended or barred. Bankers also paid $100 million in fines to the Commodities Futures Trading Commission—the SEC counterpart in most derivatives markets—and entered into substantial out-of-court settlements with a number of its clients, including $14 million for Gibson, $35 million for Procter & Gamble, and $67 million for Air Products and Chemicals.

Alan Abelson, the longtime, and usually jaundiced, market watcher at *Barron's,* summed up the episode: "In derivatives transactions, investors often get killed, which is what is meant when derivatives traders refer to good execution." Abelson goes too far. Derivatives technology introduces wonderful opportunities for managing risk, but exotic instruments, especially in the hands of the unwary or the ignorant, are dangerous things. A financial manager who doesn't understand his positions, or can't explain them to the dumbest member of his board, shouldn't be in them. A second incident illustrates the risks of management's not understanding a complex position, even when it may have been *good* for them.

Metallgesellschaft

In late 1993, Metallgesellschaft AG, a German multinational company that operates in a wide variety of industrial and energy businesses, announced that an American subsidiary, MG Refining and Marketing (MGRM) had lost up to $1.3 billion speculating in oil futures. Loss estimates mounted as the parent tried to unwind the position, and may have been as high as $2 billion.

Although some details of the offending transactions are murky, two professors at the University of Chicago, Christopher Culp and Merton Miller, have reconstructed the underlying trading strategies. Miller is no ordinary professor. He was one of the pioneers of modern financial theory, was a major influence on younger colleagues like Black, Scholes, and Merton, and won the economics

Nobel in 1990. Culp and Miller argue that, in all likelihood, there was *nothing wrong* with MGRM's futures positions, and that the losses stemmed entirely from top management's insistence that the positions be unwound. The reconstruction offers a fascinating insight into the potential and pitfalls of modern derivatives technology.

MGRM had hired W. Arthur Benson, a well-known oil trader, in late 1991 in order to improve its competitive position in the oil and gasoline business. At the time, the wholesale oil market was moving toward fixed-price long-term contracts, which favored major refiners who could store large quantities of oil at very low cost. Benson's objective was to compete with the oil majors by offering long-term fixed-rate supply contracts but assuring his own supply by buying oil in the futures market —in effect, giving MGRM a "synthetic storage" capability. He proceeded to enter into a large number of very long-term fixed-price supply contracts, covering more than 150 million barrels of oil, and extending in some cases for as long as ten years. He then covered his short position (you create a short position when you sell something you do not own) by going long in the futures market—that is, buying oil for future delivery.

The problem was that the oil futures market is deepest in the shortest contracts, and gets very thin as contract dates lengthen, so there was no possible way Benson could match his long-dated delivery obligations with equally long-dated futures contracts. On the surface, he had the same problem as 1980s S&Ls—a long-term fixed income stream that was matched up against expenses that would vary unpredictably. And in fact, not long after Benson got his operation up to speed, he required large cash infusions from the parent. Alarmed, the parent's central board closed down Benson's operation, and using various escape clauses, terminated the delivery contracts, sustaining very large losses in the process.

Based on the information available, Culp and Miller argue both that it *is* possible to hedge long-term contracts with short-dated futures, and that Benson appears to have been doing precisely that. Such a strategy may well entail substantial short-term cash outlays, but the cash flows will balance out over time. Since customers were anxious for the security of fixed-price contracts, they were presumably willing to pay enough to offset the carrying costs of temporary negative cash flows.

If Culp and Miller are correct, Benson's strategy was one of "stacked short-dated hedging." A simplified example shows how it works: Assume that you enter into a one-year contract to supply 1000 barrels of oil a month at $20 a barrel, starting in one month. Assume further that the spot price of oil on the contract date is $17 a barrel, that the best available futures contracts are all one-month contracts, and that the futures price at the start of any month always equals the spot price.* The stacked hedging strategy says that you will immediately purchase futures contracts covering your entire 12,000-barrel delivery obligation. At the end of the first month, after you have delivered the first 1000 barrels, you will purchase futures covering your remaining obligation of 11,000 barrels; and at the end of the second month, you will deliver another 1000 barrels and purchase futures covering 10,000 barrels, and so on.

The two examples in the table on the next page show what happens. Both examples assume that on your first delivery date the spot price is unchanged from $17, the price at which you bought your first futures contract. From that point, the spot price falls at the rate of $1 a month in the first example and rises by $1 a month in the second example.

As each delivery date falls due, you purchase the oil you need in the spot market and settle your futures contract in cash. So at the end of the first month, you buy 1000 barrels of oil at $17 and deliver it to your customer at $20, for a $3000 profit. At the same time, since you bought your futures contracts at $17 and the spot price is still $17, there is no gain or loss on your futures position, so the combined futures and delivery contracts produce a net positive cash flow of $3000. To hedge the second month's obligation, you then buy 11,000 one-month futures at $17.

*This is imprecise but not unrealistic. In general, futures prices equal spot prices plus a factor for cost of carry. In the oil markets, cost of carry includes interest, the physical cost of storage, less a "convenience factor" representing the value of an assured supply. The one-month interest and storage costs are tiny and are often fully offset by the convenience premium. Futures prices are therefore as likely to be slightly lower than the spot prices as they are to be higher. For simplicity, the discussion here also ignores transactions costs, which have only a minor effect on outcomes.

Guaranteed Delivery Contract:
1000 bbl per month @ $20/bl.

Example One: Falling Spot Prices

Mo	Sale Price	Spot Price	Gain on Futures	Gain on Spot	Net CF
1	20	17	0	3,000	3,000
2	20	16	−11,000	4,000	−7,000
3	20	15	−10,000	5,000	−5,000
4	20	14	−9,000	6,000	−3,000
5	20	13	−8,000	7,000	−1,000
6	20	12	−7,000	8,000	1,000
7	20	11	−6,000	9,000	3,000
8	20	10	−5,000	10,000	5,000
9	20	9	−4,000	11,000	7,000
10	20	8	−3,000	12,000	9,000
11	20	7	−2,000	13,000	11,000
12	20	6	−1,000	14,000	13,000
TOTAL			−66,000	102,000	**36,000**

Example Two: Rising Spot Prices

Mo	Sale Price	Spot Price	Gain on Futures	Gain on Spot	Net CF
1	20	17	0	3,000	3,000
2	20	18	11,000	2,000	13,000
3	20	19	10,000	1,000	11,000
4	20	20	9,000	0	9,000
5	20	21	8,000	−1,000	7,000
6	20	22	7,000	−2,000	5,000
7	20	23	6,000	−3,000	3,000
8	20	24	5,000	−4,000	1,000
9	20	25	4,000	−5,000	−1,000
10	20	26	3,000	−6,000	−3,000
11	20	27	2,000	−7,000	−5,000
12	20	28	1,000	−8,000	−7,000
TOTAL			66,000	−30,000	**36,000**

From that point, the two positions diverge sharply. In the case where prices are falling, you make your second-month delivery as before by buying 1000 barrels in the spot market, but for $16, or a $4000 profit. But you take a big loss on your futures position. The 11,000 futures contracts you bought for $17 dollars end up worth only $16, so you have to pony up $11,000 in cash, and you have a combined negative net cash flow of $7000. In the case where prices are rising, on the other hand, you make only $2000 on your delivery contract, since the spot price is at $18, but you make a thumping $11,000 on the futures position for a positive net cash flow of $13,000.

At the end of the twelve months, however, the net cash flows from the two positions are *exactly the same,* at $36,000. In the case where prices fall, the early cash flow hits on the futures are later made up by big gains on the deliveries. When prices are rising, hefty early-stage profits on the futures are offset by the later losses on the deliveries. More strikingly, the $36,000 exactly equals the profit on the initial hedge ($20–$17) times the total number of barrels contracted for delivery. So, yes, it is possible to hedge long-term obligations with short-dated futures, at least if you know what you're about. (Skeptical readers can make the monthly prices in the tables bounce up and down any way they want. The net cash flow always comes out to $36,000.)

And that, of course, is what Culp and Miller believe that Benson was doing. After the Gulf War ended, oil prices fell sharply, and a stacked futures position would have entailed big negative cash flows, just as in the first example above. The bathetic aspect of the parent's reaction, of course, was that by getting *out of* the long-term contracts as soon as the cash flows turned negative, they gave up all the later profits and turned temporary cash outflows into permanent losses. (The delivery customers, of course, must have been delighted, since the price for long-term delivery contracts had been reset to a much lower level.)

A later inquiry by the Commodities Futures Trading Commission faulted MGRM's operations on several counts. Certain provisions of Benson's contracts, the commission determined, such as provisions for cash settlement rather than by actual delivery under certain circumstances, converted them from delivery contracts into futures contracts of a kind that could be traded only on the official exchanges. In addition, during the period of heavy margin calls, the Metallgesellschaft futures trading affiliate that handled MGRM's trading had exhausted its credit lines with the parent without notifying the commission. The violations cited by the commission, however serious, do not go to the basic economics of MGRM's positions.

Metallgesellschaft's fundamental mistake, of course, was getting into a business they didn't understand in the first place, so they couldn't tell whether things were going well or badly or whether Benson's trading was in compliance with commission rules. And for a reputed world-class hedger, Benson clearly hadn't prepared his parent for the possible cash implications of his strategy, and failed to anticipate how exposed he was to topside panic at the first big negative cash flows.

Understanding Risk

Ravi Dattatreya is a senior vice president of the capital-markets subsidiary of Sumitomo Bank and the author of several textbooks on derivatives. His job is structuring transactions for Sumitomo customers, often by distributing pieces of a deal throughout the world to take advantage of tax and accounting regimes. For example, American tax authorities treat a long-term lease of a plane as a conditional sale, while Japanese authorities treat it as a lease. So if a Japanese leasing company borrows money, buys a plane, and leases it to an airline, the Japanese authorities treat the leasing company as the owner and allows it to deduct the interest on the loan and the depreciation on the plane. But if the plane is leased to an American airline, the IRS's "sale" treatment will allow the airline to make those same deductions as well. "Double-dip" tax treatment is enticing, but it opens the parties to a range of currency and interest rate risks. The Japanese investors want a fixed rate of return in yen; the airline's revenues will be in dollars; the financing for the plane may be in yen or dollars and is probably fixed. Complicating matters, the Japanese equity investors will expect to cash out by the airline's exercising a yen purchase option ten or more years down the road.

Structuring the entire transaction may require four or more swaps, including a long-term zero-coupon yen-dollar swap to hedge the purchase option. Not many years ago, such a transaction would have seemed breathtakingly complicated, but it is now almost routine. The market in interest rate, currency, and credit derivatives now dwarfs global stock and bond markets. Big banks and investment banks like Sumitomo, Citibank, and Merrill Lynch are constantly trading positions, balancing their own and their customers' exposures at razor-thin spreads. Under normal market conditions, Sumitomo will be able to execute most of the transactions required for the leveraged airline lease with a few pops on a computer keyboard. The "designer" pieces of the deal, like the zero-coupon yen-dollar swap where the term is too long for the forward markets, will be taken onto its own books and managed as part of Sumitomo's overall exposure. The net effect is that the airline gets a lower cost lease and Japanese investors earn a better return on their equity. Arbitraging away the differences between interest-rate and currency regimes deepens the pool of capital, lowers the costs of financings, and improves market efficiency.

The routinization of transactions like the one described by Dattatreya suggests that financial markets have learned to understand and manage the risks of complex derivative structures. Would that it were so. At the end of 1997, the Union Bank of Switzerland disclosed that it may have lost as much as $700 million by taking a complex position in Japanese equity derivatives. UBS's problem was actually a common one in valuing options—how to value a "deep out-of-the-money" option? Essentially, UBS had sold Japanese bank securities to investors along with a put option: investors could sell them back if bank share prices fell. The strike price of the put option adjusted down if there was a market downturn, but not to the point where UBS would be covered if Japanese bank securities became almost worthless. No one, of course, expected Japanese bank shares to become worthless, so that possibility wasn't factored into the valuation models. But, of course, when Yamaichi Securities closed its doors in late 1997, Japanese bank shares actually did become almost worthless and UBS took a bath. More fundamentally, it appears that the UBS traders had the final word on valuations, much as Nick Leeson did at Barings. He who does not learn from history is doomed to repeat it.

Derivatives are just tools. Used properly by competent professionals, they can greatly improve portfolio liquidity, reduce trading costs and funding mismatches, and smooth out volatility. But they are tricky instruments and can open a company to catastrophic risks when they are used by amateurs, especially in a company with sloppy operations and poor position control. Compounding derivative positions, moreover, quickly introduces unmanageable complexity, even with the enormous improvements in portfolio mathematics and desktop computing power in recent years. At the margin, there are still cases where the standard math is just wrong, usually because of simplifying assumptions (normal distributions, smooth curves) in order to make the calculations manageable. And as Conrad Voldstad, cohead of Global Debt Markets at Merrill Lynch, pointed out, "Some people *choose* to speculate," and derivatives allow clever operators to take much larger risks than otherwise would be available to them.

Consider the following hypothetical example: a newly formed hedge fund* headed by an expert trader who's raised $1,000,000 in equity. As a first step, he uses his $1,000,000 as collateral for a yen loan of $5,000,000 because the interest rate on yen loans is virtually zero. He then uses the $5,000,000 as a margin deposit for a short sale (selling securities he doesn't own) of $25,000,000 of "on-the-run" U.S. treasury bonds. (The most recent issue of a specific maturity bond is "on-the-run," whereas previous issues are "off-the-run." On-

---

*There is no standard definition of a hedge fund, and most of the funds going by the name don't do much hedging. The term is applied to limited partnerships, most of them operating offshore, and with fewer than 100 investors, all of them extremely wealthy individuals and institutions, so they are beyond the effective reach of American regulation. Surveys suggest that there are about 3,000 hedge funds, disposing of about $200 billion in equity capital. The investment example here was inspired by Long Term Capital Management, who apparently invested in roughly similar ways. Most hedge funds, however, actually invest quite traditionally, and tend to be quite conservative in the use of leverage. About 30 percent of the funds use no leverage at all, while 55 percent use roughly the same degree of leverage that is available to most individual investors. Only about 15 percent of the funds had leverage ratios of more than 2:1; the extremely high leverage employed by LTCM was very unusual.

the-run issues tend to trade temporarily at slightly higher values than off-the-run issues because there is more trading activity. That gap will close as the new issues are absorbed into the market, creating an opportunity for an arbitrage.) The trader uses the $25,000,000 proceeds from the short sale to buy $25,000,000 in off-the-run bonds, betting that the price of the two issues will move closer together.

At this point, the trader's made two separate bets: that the yen won't appreciate, otherwise he'll lose money when it's time to pay back his yen loan; and that the bonds he's sold short will fall in value relative to the bonds that he's bought. But in the meantime, he's got $25,000,000 in bonds sitting in his portfolio, so he uses them as collateral for a repo with an investment bank, exchanging them for, say, $125 million in cash, a conservative margin level among professionals. He's obligated to return the cash plus accumulated money-market interest rates at a specified date, and he will have to increase the collateral if the value of the bonds he deposited falls. But he uses the $125 million to buy floating rate notes that pay a higher interest rate than the rate he has to pay on his repo, so he's covered there. He can then repo those notes with a second securities firm in exchange for cash, although he'll keep collecting the floating rate interest. At this point, he's converted his initial $1,000,000 in equity into $125,000,000 in free cash that he can invest however he wants. Now it's time for serious investing—even a rookie with that much cash could quickly build options and futures positions in billions worth of securities. Of course, if any of the positions go sour, the trader will have to stump up more margin; margin calls on hundreds of millions, or billions of derivatives positions could eat up his little bit of capital in an eyeblink, and the whole structure would come crashing down. Something like that happened in real life in August and September 1998.

Ooops!

Long Term Capital Management, the $100 billion–plus hedge fund that was rescued in a coordinated effort led by the Federal

Reserve in September 1998, had perhaps the most glittering array of partners of any investment vehicle in history. It was founded by John Meriwether, formerly the star trader at Salomon Brothers, and the general partners included the Nobelists Myron Scholes and Robert Merton of Black-Scholes fame, and David Mullins, a former vice-chairman of the Fed with long experience in capital markets. Meriwether was the key figure, while "names" like Scholes and Merton were used mostly to impress potential investors and, one presumes, to discuss broader strategic issues. (There is no reason to expect Nobel prize-winning finance professors to be good traders.)

LTCM's investors included the dozen or so most senior executives at Merrill, top executives from Bear Stearns and Paine Webber, and a long list of financial institutions, including UBS of Switzerland, Sumitomo Bank, the central bank of Italy, and similarly experienced other players. If the lesson of Orange County, Barings, and Gibson was that financial novices shouldn't play with dangerous weapons, LTCM demonstrated that top pros can get in very serious trouble too.

Meriwether was a "relative value" trader. He sought out positions in related instruments that appeared to be mispriced relative to each other, like the on-the-run and off-the-run treasuries described above. Profitable arbitrages were easy to find in the unsettled debt environment of the 1980s, but have been relatively scarce in the more stable markets of recent years, and usually involve constructing very complex positions involving multiple instruments in multiple currencies. One of the simpler bets that LTCM made, for instance, was that with the advent of the euro in 1999, rates on Italian government debt and German government debt would move closer together (i.e., Italian debt would be worth more in terms of German debt). If you were long on Italian debt and short on German debt, you would make money if that happened.

In efficient markets, arbitrage opportunities are small and fleeting, so it usually requires considerable leverage to make decent profits. LTCM was usually leveraged in the 20–25:1 range (investing $20–$25 of borrowed money for every dollar of invested equity), which is not especially high for Wall Street trading operations. By using options and futures, however, they could take notional positions in the billions. Nobody was worried about their leverage. Because of the stellar reputation of Meriwether and the LTCM partners, they had no difficulty obtaining almost whatever amounts of equity or credit they pleased. Investors were being turned away, and banks and securities firms were happy to lend with only the sketchiest of documentation. Chase even syndicated an unsecured loan of about $600 million.

In the four years that LTCM operated, its returns were good—20 percent, 41 percent, 43 percent, and 17 percent—but not so high as to knock your socks off. Investors in Microsoft, for instance, averaged about 60 percent annual returns over those same years without any leverage at all, and the unleveraged S&P 500 beat LTCM's return in 1997. After its disappointing 1997 returns, LTCM returned about $2.3 billion of investors' money on the grounds that it lacked sufficient profitable investment opportunities.

Throughout 1998, almost all of LTCM's bets proceeded to turn sour. World financial markets were especially disturbed in the summer. The Asian currency crises of 1997 had seemed to abate in the spring but suddenly erupted with increased ferocity and spread quickly to Latin America. Brazil, Argentina, Mexico, and even previously stable Chile appeared to be on the brink of major crises, and prices fell on almost all risky debt instruments. The worries about safety caused the price of U.S. treasuries to *rise,* as investors from around the globe flocked to U.S. treasuries as the safest port in a storm. The crisis intensified in late August when Russia defaulted on its bonds. Investors, who had come to expect IMF or other friendly-government bailouts of major country debt, were shocked that no one stepped forward to stop the Russian meltdown, and bond prices plummeted sharply everywhere—again, except in the U.S. treasury market, where prices were pushed up even faster by the flood of money fleeing for safety.

Since LTCM was heavily invested in risky debt instruments, it sustained enormous losses. The spread between Italian and German debt, for instance, widened rather than converged, since German debt suddenly seemed a much safer choice. In addition, when LTCM hedged its positions, it apparently used U.S. treasuries as the hedging instrument of choice, as most traders do. If you have found a bond that seems to be a good investment, but would like to hedge against a general rate increase, you can do so by shorting some other bond. Traders usually hedge with treasuries because they're so readily available. Although your bond and treasuries may not be perfectly correlated, a general rate increase will usually affect them both. In that case, the gains on the short position should offset, at least in part, the losses on your portfolio bonds. But if treasuries *rise* when all other bonds in the world fall, as happened in the summer of 1998, you will lose on *both* sides of the hedge—and that seems to have happened at LTCM.

LTCM started the year with about $4.8 billion in equity; through July, it had lost about $500 million, and it lost another $2.1 billion in August. Almost all of its lenders were fully collateralized, or nearly so, with the collateral marked to market daily. As the value of LTCM's portfolio plummeted, it was met by a flood of margin calls, and by mid-September, it was drawing heavily on the Chase unsecured loan, and its equity had shrunk to $600 million. (The very high leverage ratios of 100:1 or even more often reported for LTCM date from this period. Obviously, as your equity base shrinks, your leverage ratio increases proportionally.)

Word had been circulating on the Street for some weeks that LTCM was in serious trouble, and the fund informed the New York Fed of its difficulties in early September. A couple of weeks later, under pressure from its creditors, it made a full report of its position, and the Fed, working through Goldman, Merrill and the Morgan bank, put together the rescue operation. The fifteen members of the consortium stumped up the cash to keep LTCM's positions alive in return for 90 percent of the firm's equity. Meriwether continued on the job to wind down the fund's position, but under the supervision of the consortium's oversight committee.

Although the rescue was much criticized in Congress and the press, it was not a bailout in the usual sense of the term. No government money was involved, and the investors and partners in the fund lost practically all of their $4.8 billion investment, which should be enough to give anyone pause. Some of the partners had borrowed heavily to finance their positions and were reportedly facing personal bankruptcy. UBS of Switzerland, one of the biggest investors, lost more than $700 million, its second loss of that size in two years, and several senior executives were forced to resign. By the end of the year, it appeared that LTCM's lenders would get all their money back; and since debt markets stabilized in the wake of the rescue announcement, the consortium expected to make a profit on its $3.5 billion equity stake. Paying back creditors while letting equity investors take their lumps is what rescues are supposed to do.

More important, the rescue averted near-certain financial chaos that could have persisted for weeks, and possibly for months. At bottom, the only collateral LTCM's creditors owned were the instruments in the fund. Since LTCM could no longer meet margin calls, there would have been a mad scramble to sell the collateral, dumping $100 billion or so of relatively illiquid securities on the markets. Prices would have plummeted on all risky debt instruments, generating huge mark-to-market writedowns at all securities firms, and yet another cycle of margin calls, more forced sales, and more writedowns. A number of firms may have been pushed into insolvency, and crippled financial markets would have spread disruption and hardship everywhere. It's difficult to see that the Fed had any choice but to move in.

In the postmortems of the LTCM crisis, some bankers have pointed out that its risk models were surprisingly out of date, considering the pedigree of the firm. But that seems beside the point. No model would have predicted the Russian default sufficiently in advance, and other experienced investors, like George Soros, took a bath in Russia at the same time. The year before the LTCM crisis, another Merrill executive, speaking on the limits of models, said: "The mathematicians tell you that a one-day 20 percent drop in equities happens, how often—once every fifty years? And what about a $150 billion loss in S&Ls, or overnight yields of 1,000 percent in European currencies [which happened in 1992], or a collapse in a major market like junk bonds? How often can those happen? Well, we've seen them all within just a few years. And if you're hedging Italian equities, what do you do when the market suddenly decides to close for five days, so there's no way of knowing what values are?"

The problem is one that statisticians call "leptokurtosis": at its outer limits, the tail of a bell curve may be fatter than we think; extremely unlikely events *do* happen. Meriwether, one must assume, was well aware of his risks. The convergence bets he was making at LTCM probably would have paid off 80 to 90 percent of the time; but the chances of all his bets going bad at the same time must have seemed infinitesimally small.

In efficient markets, in short, above-average returns come with above-average risks. Exceptional traders like Meriwether may be able to beat the markets most of the time, so investors stop asking questions and give them large amounts of money to play with. Clever derivatives traders can parley large amounts of money into truly colossal positions, and can trigger a deluge when they roll snake-eyes.

Chapter Eight

MORTGAGE MAYHEM

"Collateralized Mortgage Obligation," or "CMO," is not nearly as catchy a term as "junk bond," and CMOs weren't associated with flashy takeover deals the way junk bonds were. But when the junk-bond market went down in flames in 1990, the total volume of high-yield bonds outstanding was only about $200 billion, and the market's paper losses were in the $22 billion range. The much-less-publicized CMO market was five times as large, growing from a standing start in 1983 to nearly $1 trillion in just ten years; in 1993 alone, Wall Street issued more than $350 billion in new CMOs. But when CMOs suffered through their own crash in 1994, the public hardly noticed, although investor losses were more than twice as high as in the junk-bond debacle. Just as junk bonds brought down Drexel, Burnham, turmoil in the CMO market spelled the end for Kidder, Peabody, one of the most blue-blooded of Wall Street firms, with Boston roots and more than a century of investment banking history.

In the slightly longer run, just like junk bonds, CMOs proved far too valuable an innovation to be consigned to the rag-and-bone shop of bad ideas. After the coronary thrombosis of 1994, the market remained comatose through most of 1995 and 1996, but had almost fully recovered by 1998—although CMO structures are simpler, buyers are smarter, and much of the razzle-dazzle that so delighted Wall Street's rocket scientists is gone. The whole experience perfectly illustrates the recurring cycle of financial innovation. Technological, demographic, or industrial change creates an essentially new financial demand. After a few false starts, some new invention—an instrument, a trading methodology—brilliantly meets the challenge. An exuberant development period follows, as more and more firms pile in to take advantage of the sudden opportunity. Exuberance quickly becomes gross excess, precipitating a crisis. The subsequent crash burns off the excesses, buyers and sellers adjust their expectations, regulators update their rules and alarm systems, and yesterday's brilliant innovation becomes just another of the industry's workaday departments.

Financial Innovation and Liquidity

Finance is mostly about liquidity. The more readily one kind of asset can be converted into other kinds of assets, the easier it is to assemble pools of investment capital and the quicker the pace of commercial activity. Until Arab and Indian merchants invented the bill of exchange, trade in the ancient Mediterranean was largely a matter of barter. But when a piece of paper embodying the promise of a distant merchant became acceptable payment, and bills could pass freely from hand to hand, trade accelerated dramatically. An Eastern merchant could sell his load of spices for bills and then trade the bills for silks, or more spices, or a bigger palace—goods of all kinds had become more liquid. Jay Gould financed his railroads by selling claims on the roads' future earnings, but in the absence of clear rules governing the rights and duties of a corporation and its stakeholders, railroad stocks and bonds were relatively illiquid—it was hard to convert a railroad share into next month's groceries. Morgan's great contribution in the 1890s was to regularize the positions of claimants and establish a system for monitoring risk so traders could buy and sell with reasonable confidence in the underlying value of a security. The new liquidity of American stocks and bonds undammed a great flood of capital and triggered two decades of stupendous industrial growth.

Through most of American history, the obligations of the federal government have represented the greatest volume of financial instruments, and have been the most liquid. The government has been careful to maintain their liquidity by guarding their high reputation for creditworthiness, by issuing them in a variety of maturities and denominations to match the needs of investors, and by ensuring an active dealing and trading market. As Alexander Hamilton foresaw, safe and liquid American government debt became the foundation investment for any well-run financial institution—not just in the United States but eventually in most of the rest of the world as well.

Measured by volume, the second most important American financial instrument over the past half century, by a wide margin, has been the lowly residential mortgage. In 1996, the outstanding value of residential mortgages was about $3.8 trillion, a number not much less than the value of federal debt in the hands of the public, and some two and half times bigger than the value of outstanding corporate bonds. But in contrast to treasury paper, mortgages have always been relatively illiquid instruments—gnarly, unpleasant things, with special features that make them awkward to hold and difficult to trade. Illiquidity has real economic consequences. If fund managers fear getting stuck with illiquid investments, they will demand higher returns. In the case of mortgages, that extra interest worked its way though the economy as higher financing costs for home buyers, fewer home sales, and less construction activity. Eliminating frictional costs like these is what the financial industry is for, and the effort to inject greater liquidity into the market for mortgages is a saga that stretches over twenty-five years, culminating in the creation of the CMO and the crash and recovery of 1994–96.

The Evolution of CMOs

CREATING AN INDUSTRY   Restarting the home building industry and encouraging family home ownership was a special object of the New Deal, and federal tax and banking policy has been pro–home buyer ever since. The federally chartered and federally insured savings and loan industry dates from 1934, as does the standard form of the modern American home mortgage—a long-term (up to thirty years), fixed-rate, level-payment instrument with monthly coupons that consist mostly of interest payments in the early years and gradually shift to principal payments as the mortgage ages. New Deal housing experts also understood that unless S&Ls could sell off their mortgages, lending would grind to a halt as soon as they had lent up to the limit of their current deposits. So they created the Federal National Mortgage Association, or "Fannie Mae," a federally chartered agency whose mission was to create a secondary market in mortgages—buying up mortgages from S&Ls to replenish their cash and let them carry on lending. (The S&Ls would continue to collect monthly payments as before— "servicing" the mortgage—and remit the money to Fannie Mae.)

The very success of the nation's housing policy, however, meant that demand for new housing usually outran the industry's financing capabilities. When mortgage growth slowed sharply in the 1960s, despite a booming national prosperity, Congress stepped in in 1970 with legislation that rechartered Fannie Mae and created a new Government National Mortgage Association, or "Ginnie Mae," and a third organization, the Federal Home Loan Mortgage Corporation, or "Freddie Mac." Ginnie Mae is a government agency authorized to create a secondary market in FHA- and VA-insured mortgages. Freddie Mae and the new Fannie Mae are private corporations, although they operate under government supervision. They are authorized to buy up high-quality conventional (non–federally insured) mortgages with principal amounts geared to middle-income home buyers. All three agencies are authorized to raise financing on the private markets. Only Ginnie Mae's obligations actually carry a government guarantee, although investors usually treat Fannie Mae and Freddie Mac paper as if it were guaranteed, on the theory that Congress would never allow federally chartered housing agencies to default on their debts.

THE BIRTH OF MORTGAGE-BACKEDS In the first year of its existence, Ginnie Mae issued the first "mortgage-backed security," a debt obligation that was not itself a mortgage but was secured by a *pool* of mortgages. The first mortgage-backeds were based on a pool of federally insured thirty-year mortgages, all paying the same interest rate and all with a maturity date within a month of one another. In return for their money, investors received "pass-through certificates" entitling them to receive a pro rata share of the interest and principal paid to the pool, precisely as the pool received it. "Ginnie Maes," as the pass-throughs quickly became known, were a great success. In effect, long-term investors like insurance companies and pension funds could buy long-term government-guaranteed paper paying considerably higher interest rates than treasury notes and bonds. And because homeowners paid such high rates for mortgages, there was enough left over for Ginnie Mae to pocket a slim arbitrage profit on the deal. Fannie Mae and Freddie Mac quickly produced their own versions of mortgage-backeds, and by the end of the decade, investment banks, led by Salomon Brothers, were packaging up so-called jumbo mortgages—with face values outside the Fannie Mae and Freddie Mac limits—into mortgage-backeds of their own. The value of new mortgage-backed issuance jumped from just under $3 billion in 1972 to more than $20 billion in 1980, and almost $90 billion in 1983, all of which represented new capital for housing. Despite the economic turmoil of the 1970s and 1980s, the rate of growth in mortgages outstanding maintained double-digit levels in all but two serious recession years.

The volume of mortgage-backed trading, however, was still a disappointment to Wall Street. Salomon Brothers had built an impressive mortgage-backed trading capability under Lewis Rainieri—the story is told with great verve in Michael Lewis's *Liar's Poker*—but the operation was reportedly hemorrhaging money because of low volumes. The 1982 Garn–St. Germain S&L legislation was actually a bailout for Salomon as well as for the S&L industry. Sharply rising interest rates in the late 1970s and early 1980s had devastated the market value of mortgages in S&L portfolios, but because of the peculiarities of S&L accounting, portfolio losses did not have to be recognized on the books until the mortgages were sold. So S&Ls naturally stopped selling, which meant that there was no cash for new lending, and no mortgages for Salomon to trade. Garn–St. Germain allowed S&Ls to spread their loss recognition over forty years, which unblocked the secondary market. But the new volumes still fell short of the hopes of mortgage-backed enthusiasts, because of certain fundamental problems that mortgages present for secondary market investors.

PREPAYMENT RISK   Compared with standard bond-type instruments, mortgage-backed securities are unusually cantankerous animals. The monthly coupons on mortgages, to begin with, are a nuisance for investors used to the semiannual coupons on treasuries and corporates. In addition, treasury and corporate bonds are almost always "bullets"—principal is not paid until maturity—so the monthly amortization of principal on mortgage-backeds usually required big adjustments in investor bookkeeping. But the biggest problem is *prepayment risk*. Like a treasury bond, a mortgage-backed is a long-term instrument, so its value can be dramatically affected by changes in interest rates. A modest increase in interest rates will cause the value of a long-term treasury to drop substantially, and investors can calculate the change in value quite precisely from the initial yield, the maturity, and other terms of the bond. In the case of a mortgage, however, there is no way of knowing what its real maturity *is,* for homeowners have the right to pay off their mortgages whenever they please—in effect, homeowners own an "embedded option" to prepay or not. Pass-through certificates channel principal and interest payments to investors exactly as they occur, without any guarantee on their timing, so all the underlying uncertainty is also passed through to investors.

In a market as big as mortgages, there are naturally some definite patterns. Prepayment behavior is quite seasonal—most homes are sold in the spring and summer—and almost no one pays off a mortgage in the first three years of its life. From that point, prepayments occur at a fairly predictable clip, following the rhythm of relocation, death, and divorce. About half of all thirty-year mortgages are prepaid by about the twelfth year, and after fifteen years or so, prepayments drop off sharply—the "burnout" factor: People who have stayed put that long, it seems, tend to stay put forever.

If that were all, the risk would be relatively manageable. But prepayment behavior also varies with interest rates. A period of high rates means expensive mortgages and fewer home sales, so mortgage prepayments will slow dramatically. The opposite happens when rates fall, because then homeowners rush to refinance their mortgages whether they are moving or not, so the rate of prepayment will accelerate. From the standpoint of a pension fund manager, this is the worst of all possible worlds. Bond values vary with both the term of the bond and the prevailing rate of interest. When rates rise, bond values fall, and the longer-term bonds fall the most. In the case of mortgage-backeds, however, when rates rise, the mortgage-backed's value falls just like a bond, *and the term gets longer* because of slower prepayments, so the value falls even more. The risk is not symmetrical. When rates fall, bond values rise, and the pension fund manager can book healthy mark-to-market profits. But in the case of mortgage-backeds, when rates fall, homeowners *prepay,* so the fund manager finds herself holding an unexpected slug of cash that she has to reinvest in a low-return environment.*

MOTORCYCLES TO TRICYCLES The economic turmoil of the 1970s was a harsh training ground for professional investors and consumers alike in the risks and opportunities of fluctuating interest rates. Investors became much more wary about the pitfalls lurking in long-term fixed-rate instruments, while consumers discovered the thrills of, say, using a second mortgage to invest in high-return money market funds. In particular, investors learned

---

*It's even worse than that, for prepayment risk also creates *negative convexity,* a chronic disease as nasty as it sounds. When interest rates are low, a small increase in rates will cause the price of standard bonds to fall more than when rates are high. (A change from 3 percent to 3.1 percent has more impact than a change from 12 percent to 12.1 percent.) If one charts the value of a treasury bond on a graph (price on the vertical axis; interest rates on the horizontal axis), the resulting curve is therefore convex to the origin, falling steeply at low interest rates, with the rate of decline leveling out at higher rates. Mortgage-backeds, however, exhibit the opposite behavior. At low rates, the influx of principal repayments offsets the normal price drop, while at high rates, the suspension of principal payments makes prices fall even more sharply. The resulting curve is therefore *concave* to the origin, or "negatively convex." Negative convexity wreaked havoc with fund managers who, as they were accustomed to do with other bonds, tried to hedge positions in mortgage-backeds by taking offsetting positions in treasuries. When crises hit, they discovered that their "hedges" actually just increased their losses.

to become much more cautious about mortgage-backeds, as they realized that prepayment behavior was not a simple function of maturity and interest rates, especially as consumers became more sophisticated about refinancings. Investors loved the high returns of mortgage-backeds, and all big portfolios had some, but the growing appreciation of interest rate and prepayment risk was a distinct curb on appetites.

Freddie Mac addressed the problem in the late 1970s with the introduction of Guaranteed Mortgage Certificates, or Freddie Mac "MCs," which Wall Street instantly dubbed "Motorcycles." Freddie Mac not only guaranteed the principal and interest of its Motorcycles, but it also guaranteed the timing of the *cash flow,* which made prepayment risk moot. Investors naturally loved them; the first tranches sold out quickly, and the Street was clamoring for more. But the problem with the Motorcycles was that the more risk Freddie Mac removed from investors, the more it was taking on itself. If consumers stopped refinancing mortgages because of high rates, for example, the loss of expected cash flows might make it impossible both to service the Motorcycles' cash flow guarantees and to meet its other obligations.

In late 1982, Lee Bresland, Freddie Mac's senior financial executive, and the current CEO, turned for advice to Larry Fink's mortgage-backed team at First Boston. After studying the problem, First Boston recommended a new mortgage-backed structure consisting of three different tranches—a "fast pay," a "medium pay," and a "slow pay." The new instrument would pay out all the principal and interest from a pool of mortgages, as before, but without a Motorcycle-type cash-flow guarantee. Instead, all of the proceeds from the pool would be dedicated to the fast-pay tranche first, and only then to the medium-pay tranche, and last of all to the slow-pay tranche. With a huge pool of mortgages behind it, there was almost no possibility that the fast-pay tranche, which had a maturity of only three years, would deviate significantly from the expected cash flows. In effect, the Street would get paper with a maturity and payment predictability more like those associated with shorter-term treasury notes, with at least an implied government guarantee, and paying better returns. The medium-pay tranche would have more prepayment risk than the fast-pays, but still less than the normal mortgage-backed, while all the residual risk would be borne by the slow pays.

The great advantage of the structure was that the interest rate paid on each tranche could be tuned so it was consistent with the prepayment risk. So although most of the prepayment risk was off-loaded on the slow pays, they paid much higher returns than the other two, so were still a good investment for institutions willing to accept some instability in capital values in exchange for high current returns. In addition, because principal repayments were dedicated first to the earlier tranches, slow-pay buyers were protected against a surge of early prepayments. The simple trick of sequencing the cash flows made it at least theoretically possible to slice and dice the principal and interest from standard mortgage pools to meet almost any investment need. For example, banks had never been mortgage-backed buyers, because they could not take long-maturity risks with a short-term deposit base, but they were likely to be enthusiastic buyers of the short-term fast-pays. "Lee asked me how much we thought we could do," Fink recalls, "and I said, 'A hundred million.' So Lee said, 'Well, let's try for a billion,' and I said, 'Sure,' although of course I had no idea if we could do it. But he did insist that we bring in Salomon as a comanager because Lewie had built up that big mortgage-backed trading desk, which was fine with us." The new instruments were naturally called Tricycles, because of the three-stage payment sequence.

There was a hiccup. Fink and Freddie Mac thought they had IRS clearance for the accounting treatment of the instruments, but just a couple of days before Freddie Mac and the First Boston–Salomon team were planning a full-dress announcement at the annual Mortgage Bankers' Association dinner, they got a call from the Treasury quashing the deal—"the worst day of my life," says Fink. But the team regrouped and came up with another formula with the same basic structure, which someone—Fink can't remember who—called collateralized mortgage obligations, or CMOs. The CMO was a smash hit, one of the all-time runaway financial successes. The initial billion-dollar issue sold out almost instantly, and investor demand was such that Freddie Mac could

retain an 80-basis-point (.8 percent) spread on the deal, representing the difference between the CMO rates investors demanded
and the actual returns on the underlying mortgage pool. "That's an
$8 million overnight profit for Freddie Mac," Fink said. "It's a
pure arbitrage profit, and is the best measure of how inefficient the
mortgage market still was."*

The Capital Markets Take Over

The mortgage market got much more efficient in a hurry. First
Boston did two more CMOs that year, and Salomon did one of its
own, for a total of $5 billion in CMO issuances in 1983. By 1987,
new CMO issuance surpassed $100 billion, and it reached its peak
of about $350 billion in 1993, with nearly $900 billion in outstandings. By the early 1990s, about two-thirds of all mortgages were
being securitized and resold, about half of them as CMOs. Wall
Street made a lot of money, but home buyers reaped huge savings as
well. Prior to CMOs, mortgage pass-throughs typically traded at a
spread of about 250 basis points (2.5 percent) over treasuries of
comparable maturity, a spread far higher than is warranted by the inherent credit and prepayment risk. Most of the penalty reflected the
frictional costs of investing in pass-throughs. They were simply
clumsy instruments that matched up poorly against institutional investment needs, so investors demanded an extra-high price for buying them. Once the CMO format allowed investment banks to turn
mortgage pools into designer instruments, the price premium exacted by investors dropped dramatically. The academic consensus is
that by about 1987, the average mortgage interest rate spread over
comparable-maturity treasuries had dropped by about 100 basis
points (1 percent), and that the narrowed spreads have been main-

---

*In 1986, the government authorized REMICs (or real estate mortgage investment con-
duits), which are essentially the original Fink design. Most CMOs are now actually
REMICs, but they look alike to investors, and statistical sources usually lump REMICs
and CMOs together. In this chapter, "CMO" will be used to refer to any structured security, as distinct from a simple pass-through, supported by mortgage-pool cash flows. A
fuller description of the CMO/REMIC distinction is in the Notes (page 270).

tained ever since. By the mid-1990s, the annual savings to home owners was estimated at about $17 billion a year.

The efficiencies introduced by the CMO demonstrate the pervasive impact the capital markets can have on an industry. A generation ago, the lion's share of mortgages were originated by S&Ls. The local S&L gathered up local savings deposits and reinvested them in local mortgages, along the way performing all the functions associated with creating and maintaining a mortgage—confirming the credit of the home buyer and the value of the house, properly accounting for the mortgage on its balance sheet, collecting the monthly coupons, and following through on late payments or defaults. S&Ls usually retained most of the mortgages they issued, but whenever mortgage growth outran its financing capability, the S&L could sell off some of its portfolio to Fannie Mae and generate free cash for more lending.

Today's market is radically different. In the first place, most mortgages are now originated by "mortgage bankers" rather than by S&Ls or commercial banks. A mortgage bank does not look like a traditional bank—it does not take deposits, has no wood paneling or marble counters, often has no consumer offices at all, and certainly has no ATM machines. Instead, it gathers mortgages through networks of mortgage brokers, who get paid for putting home buyers in touch with the lowest-cost sources of financing; or through home builders, who frequently include financing as part of the new-home package; or through condo developers; or through companies that manufacture housing. Sometimes the mortgage banker will service the loans itself, but more frequently, the servicing will be contracted out to specialist servicing companies, highly computerized operations that can manage mortgage billing and accounting operations at rock-bottom prices and razor-thin margins. Instead of funding its mortgages with savings deposits, the mortgage bank uses them as collateral for CMOs, pass-through certificates, or other forms of securities, which are sold through Wall Street investment banks.

Dynex Financial, for example, is a medium-sized but highly successful mortgage banker based in Richmond, Virginia. With fewer than 120 employees, it developed multiple mortgage sourcing networks of brokers, developers, and builders (although it has recently sold off much of its residential business to focus on other lines). As of the end of 1996, it had almost $4 billion in assets, about $3 billion of which was held as collateral for CMOs. The pools were conservatively collateralized so the paper got top ratings. Of the remaining $1 billion, about $750 million were adjustable-rate mortgages that the company was holding for investment—picking up the spread between the mortgage rates and its own cost of funds—while the remainder were new mortgages waiting to be securitized. Net 1996 income was almost $75 million, or more than $600,000 per employee, far higher than in most industries.

The entire business is intensely competitive, sans loyalties, driven almost entirely by price. Home buyers never heard of Dynex, and Dynex got their business only because it offered the best mortgage rates to a broker. Competition for servicing business is fierce, and the servicing companies squeeze out their profits from fractions of percentage points. The investment banks that underwrite CMOs are constantly calling on mortgage banks for more "product" that they can sell off to investors. The tension between the low-ball mortgage rates needed to build up product volumes, the high returns demanded by CMO investors, and the necessity for the underwriter, the mortgage banker, and servicer all to make a profit constantly drives to lower costs and greater efficiency. This is planets removed from the old S&L "3-6-3" world—where executives gathered 3 percent savings deposits, lent them at 6 percent, and were on the golf course by three.

A major theme of the recent cycle of financial revolution has been the absorption of institutional turf by the capital markets and the consequent "unbundling" of basic financial functions. Consumers now put their savings where they think they can get the highest return—money market mutual funds, equity funds, whatever. Mortgage bankers compete hard for "product," while professional fund managers and traders, who measure their profits in the hundredths of a percent, buy the mortgage bankers' CMOs and other securities. The old notion of a full-service S&L seems almost quaint.

Much the same process has been at work in commercial banking. Providing working-capital loans to corporations, for example, was always a bread-and-butter banking business. Corporations paid standardized interest rates and fees, and were expected to keep hefty checking account balances besides. Company treasurers usually spread their business around two or three of the bigger banks, and the ties were cemented on the golf course. It was called "relationship banking," a comfortable, networked world that mirrored on a bigger scale the cozy old-boy ties of the Jimmie Stewart–era neighborhood S&L. By the late 1970s, however, many banks had lower credit ratings than their blue-ribbon customers, because of bad foreign loans, oil loans, and real estate loans. Why borrow from a bank, Street firms asked their clients—you have to pay their high funding cost plus a profit besides. So the commercial-paper market was born. Instead of borrowing working capital from banks, all of America's biggest companies now sell short-term paper to institutional investors through Wall Street at low interest and razor-thin fees.

Most of the rest of traditional banking functions have been attacked by Wall Street in the same way, and chopped up, functionalized, unbundled, or put into separate subsidiaries—foreign-exchange trading, investing of surplus cash flows, syndicating loans, buying and selling trade paper. A similar phenomenon is under way in the life insurance industry. The traditional "whole life" insurance product paid a guaranteed death benefit and included a savings buildup, at miserable interest rates, that could be borrowed against (at punitive rates), or converted into a lump-sum payment or annuity at the policy's maturity. Almost all the bigger brokerage houses and mutual funds now offer a range of insurance-type products, in which the death-benefit cost is clearly separated from the savings flows and the consumer typically directs the investments himself. And just like the commercial banks, life insurance companies are struggling to reinvent themselves and become more like stock brokerages and investment banks.

The absorption of financial businesses by the capital markets almost always conduces to lower costs and greater liquidity, if only because of the savage competitiveness of Wall Street firms. But the temporary loss of institutional tethers usually means a transition marked by wild excesses, which was resoundingly demonstrated by the short history of CMOs.

The tendency to excess, in CMOs as with many other 1980s innovations, was vastly enhanced by the spread of powerful desktop computers. Young PC spreadsheet jockeys added an upbeat tempo to the 1980s junk-bond and takeover markets, but they didn't create anything fundamentally new. J. P. Morgan and Jay Gould employed semi-legendary human calculators who turned out the same kind of spreadsheets as the Lotus kids at Drexel did; it just took a bit longer. CMOs were different. Even Fink's first three-tranche structure—beguilingly simple as it looks now—required a mainframe computer to run all the possible variations. Later-generation CMOs would have been impossible even to imagine without cheap and very powerful personal computers and workstations at the financial engineers' fingertips.

Excess

Primitive societies frequently engage in pointless invention out of sheer creative exuberance. Some inventive exercises become art, but many—like lip ornaments, ear stretchers, and elaborate tattoos—are bizarre and dangerous. The late-stage elaborations of CMOs are in the ear-stretcher category.

All the inventions were customer-driven. Fink's simple three-tranche structure was still too unpredictable for many big investors. Even a "fast-pay" tranche, the most predictable of all, would perform as expected only within an interest-rate band: if rates moved up or down a lot, say by a full percentage point or so, all bets were off. The medium-pay and slow-pay tranches would be even more unpredictable, and none of the tranches was completely protected against prepayment risk.

Investment banks quickly figured out that they could make tranches almost as predictable as they pleased if they divided each tranche into a planned amortization class (PAC) bond and a Companion. Within a very wide interest rate band, the cash flows could be directed to the PAC in precisely the sequence the customer had bargained for, while shortfalls or excesses were absorbed by the Companion. The predictability of an individual bond, or at least some of them, could also be improved by multiplying the number of tranches. Even better, it helped to add on a Z-bond at the end of the sequence—a zero-coupon instrument (hence the "Z") that accrued interest but received no cash flows at all for many years or until all the other instruments had been paid out. An amusing wrinkle was "jump" Z-bonds—upon some occurrence, the Z-bond would jump to the head of the class. The prospects for titillating speculators were almost endless.

The vast majority of residential mortgages are fixed-rate, but investors often prefer floating-rate instruments—as rates go up, so do the returns from their investments. No problem for the clever CMO designer—simply create a bond with an interest rate that adjusts according to some index, and direct cash flows to satisfying those interest payments first. Then have a Companion bond that is an *inverse* floater. If rates rise, the floater will absorb a disproportionate share of the cash flows, so the interest available for the Companion will fall. And vice versa: if rates fall, returns to the floater will fall with them, but payments to the inverse floater will rise. (And often quite sharply. Because floaters were easier to sell, the Street would usually create two or three floaters per inverse-floater Companion. Relatively small changes in the rates would therefore have disproportionate impact on the Companions.) It was hailed as the perfect investment hedge.

The elaborations flowed on. Since the mid-1980s, the Street had been "stripping" pass-throughs like GNMAs, so an investor could buy just the interest coupons (interest-onlys, or IOs) or just the principal repayments (POs). POs are the ideal bull-market instrument. When rates are falling—a bull market for bonds—principal prepayments accelerate. An investor who bought a PO at a price that assumed that cash returns would start in, say, seven years might be pleasantly surprised to be paid off in five. Falling rates, on the other hand, are death for IOs—early prepayments of principal mean the end of interest payments, so the value of the IOs drops to zero. (IO buyers took big losses during the benign rate environment of 1997 and 1998.) Stripping CMO tranches, especially *Companion* tranches, offered real excitement—if a Companion was volatile, think of the possibilities of Companion *strips,* or better, *inverse floating* Companion IOs!

It was more than a little insane. Investment banks were converting perfectly ordinary pools of mortgages into ramshackle pyramids of financial instruments as heavily ornamented as a Gothic cathedral. By the early 1990s, mortgage pools were being routinely cut up into sixty different CMO tranches, often with three or four classes of Z-bonds at the bottom of the structure and a wild profusion of floaters, strips, Companions, sticky-jump Zs— a whole new race of financial gargoyles. Traders still reminisce fondly about truly heroic 125+-tranche structures.

But mortgage pools are closed systems. The only money that can be paid out to service CMO bonds is the interest and principal collected by the pool. The more one tranche is protected against volatility, the more volatile some other tranche necessarily becomes. And when the slicing and dicing is carried to extremes, spinning out dozens of different kinds of CMO bonds, the interaction between the various bonds can become so complex that it swamps the computing power of even the most powerful machines. A buyer of a PO with an expected effective maturity of two years might wake up to discover that a small shift in interest rates had moved the effective maturity out to fifty or sixty years. Anecdotal evidence suggests that a great volume of the most volatile instruments—the "toxic waste," in Street parlance—was offloaded to unsophisticated investors chasing yield: doctors' pension funds, municipal treasurers, S&Ls, Indian tribes. It was an easy sell. These were, after all, instruments fully secured by pools of federal agency mortgages, and salesmen could say without a twinge of conscience that the risk of default on principal and interest was negligible or nonexistent. It was the *when* and *how long* the payments would be made that was at issue, of course, but those were details buried in the fine print.

The Brief Rise of Kidder, Peabody

Although it got off to a late start, by the late 1980s Kidder, Peabody dominated the CMO business much as Drexel had junk bonds. The presiding genius over the Kidder CMO empire was Michael Vranos, barely thirty years old in 1990. Vranos had joined Kidder in 1981 out of the undergraduate math program at Harvard. (For Vranos, the choice of Kidder was easy—it was the only firm that offered him a job.) Mortgage-backeds and CMOs appealed to his mathematical instincts, and he became a superb trader and designer of new instruments. Vranos's aptitude for CMOs coincided with Kidder's need to refocus its business after being tarnished by the 1980s insider trading scandals, and top management essentially gave him a free hand. Within a very short time, Kidder was managing more than a third of all new issues and running by far the biggest and most sophisticated trading desk. Real estate professionals looking for creative mortgage financing beat a path to Kidder's door—deals could be done in a matter of days. The developer would close his deal with Kidder financing, and the resulting mortgages would be chopped up and distributed through the Kidder network within hours.

But it took more than trading smarts to build a CMO colossus. It was easy to distribute clean CMO bonds, with well-protected cash flows. The problem was the toxic waste. The more attractive the CMO engineer tried to make the PACs and other vanilla-basic bonds, the more highly volatile by-products he produced. Since there were limits to what even the most enterprising sales force could stuff into doctors' pension funds and S&Ls, winning deals in a fiercely competitive market often meant that the bankers swallowed the toxic waste themselves. Kidder's great advantage was that it was owned by General Electric, one of the world's biggest companies, with an ocean-sized balance sheet. As long as the CMO business was highly profitable, Vranos could tap virtually limitless capital to keep it growing. By the early 1990s, Kidder's inventory of CMOs was in the $10 billion range, far bigger than any other firm's, which gave them enormous originating and trading power. One of the next biggest players was Daiwa Securities, which had the deep pockets of its Japanese parent behind it. "It shows what you can do with dumb equity," says Fink.

The growing risk in CMOs was masked by an unusually benign interest rate environment. By the late 1980s it was clear that many commercial and investment banks were badly overextended, a fact forcefully underlined by the crisis in S&Ls. To cushion the banking system through a difficult transition, the Federal Reserve began pushing interest rates down in late 1989, a policy that it continued through the recession of 1990–91 and the Gulf War. Falling rates generated an unprecedented wave of mortgage refinancings, and some CMO investors were hit very hard—IOs, for example, lose value quickly when rates fall. But fixed-rate instruments as a group did very well, so most investors were flush with profits and willing to take chances with CMOs. CMO issuance zoomed to one new record after another, and almost subconsciously, investors shifted their portfolios to anticipate continuously falling interest rates. The stage was therefore set for a full-blown crisis, which was finally triggered in 1994 by a little-known firm named Askin Capital Management. When it failed, it brought the whole CMO market down with it, and spelled the doom of Kidder.

Askin's Disease

David Askin was a refugee from Drexel, where he had acquired some fifteen years' experience in mortgages, had risen to head of fixed-income (bond) research, and had become one of the more acclaimed of Wall Street's "rocket scientists." In its last years, Drexel had made a profitable side business selling Askin's computerized techniques for analyzing complex bond portfolios. After Drexel's demise, Askin formed his own management company and took over a small group of fixed-income funds. Earning terrific returns almost entirely from CMOs, he increased his assets under management sixfold, to $610 million, in just two years, with most of his investments coming from big insurance companies and pension funds. Askin made no secret that he was investing in the most exotic of all CMO instruments, but he claimed that his investing technology made his portfolios immune to interest rate movements. "We're in weird stuff," he bragged, "but we're very confident with the structure and prepayment risk even in a 69-tranche deal, because we do this all day long."

Askin's appetite for buying the most toxic of CMO byproducts naturally endeared him to the Wall Street firms pumping out new bonds, and they were delighted to finance his funds. By the end of

1993, Askin had used margin accounts at Kidder, Bear Stearns, Merrill Lynch, and others to parlay his $610 million in assets into a $2 billion–plus position in "weird stuff." Kidder even had a special account, the Special Account Facility Pool, set up solely to finance Askin's purchases, which were often scheduled months in advance. Margin accounts, however, like all leverage, have a nasty way of biting investors at the worst times. When a brokerage firm finances an investor's security purchases, they hold the securities as collateral for the loan. Collateral is adjusted each day; if the value of the securities falls, the investor must stump up cash to cover the difference between the new value of the securities and the amount of the loan. If the investor fails to come up with the cash—meet the "margin call"—the brokerage firm is entitled to sell the securities and proceed against the investor for the difference.

For David Askin, Armageddon happened on February 4, 1994. In a major policy reversal that took most of Wall Street by surprise, the Federal Reserve raised the discount rate by a half percent and made it plain that it intended to tighten monetary policy for the foreseeable future. Market rates jumped sharply—the yield on the ten-year bond, the one most closely related to mortgages, was up more than 120 basis points by April—and Wall Street was treated to yet another demonstration of the terrible price of leverage when things go wrong.

The Fed's rate surprise underlined two very scary facts about CMOs. The first is that it's almost impossible to forecast the risk of the more exotic instruments. Askin's portfolio was simply not as market-neutral as he thought. According to an analyst for the eventual bankruptcy trustee, he was heavily weighted toward instruments like inverse floater IOs, which "drop off a cliff" when rates rise. More important, the rate shock showed how illiquid the CMO market really was, despite its huge size. Instruments like treasuries, or IBM shares, are deeply traded—there are always crowds of buyers and sellers, and a number of Wall Street firms "make a market" in the instruments, actively buying and selling for their own account in a way that ensures that prices move in an orderly fashion. But the very nature of CMOs, especially the more exotic tranches, is that they are designer instruments, hard to understand by anyone but the original producer and a small coterie of customers. In times of strain, the only reliable buyers are the firms that created them in the first place. But in the turbulent rate environment, they were experiencing the same balance sheet strains as everyone else, and had no interest in burdening their books with more of their own toxic waste.

With no buyers, as Askin discovered to his grief, the most authoritative pricing sources on CMOs were the firms he had bought them from. Ominously enough, they were the same firms who held Askin's CMOs as collateral against his margin loans, so whatever price they set would determine the size of his margin calls—he was at their mercy. Bear, Stearns was reputedly the first to move. On March 2, they made a $63 million margin call, which Askin negotiated down to about $40 million. Over the next week, they made two more margin calls, which Askin paid. Then, with most of his funds down by 20 to 28 percent, Kidder and the other firms, alarmed that there would be nothing left for them, came barreling in with margin calls of their own. It was over almost in the blink of an eye, although a few of Askin's clients futilely tried to stem the tide by meeting margin calls with their own cash. By the time Askin filed for bankruptcy protection in April, his investors had lost every dime of their $600 million. (As of this writing, Askin was still in litigation with the firms who bankrolled him, alleging that they seized his collateral at prejudicially low prices and subsequently resold it at substantial profits.)

Askin's disaster coincided, almost to the week, with the revelation of the Joseph Jett trading scandal at Kidder (see Chapter 7). Ironically enough, the two catastrophes came in the same month that the firm was the subject of an admiring profile in *Institutional Investor,* an industry bible, that praised it as one of the crown jewels in the General Electric diadem, especially singling out its "advanced financial control systems." Two disasters in one month was enough for GE. Management realized that it was in a business that it did not understand, and it simply shut Kidder down. Most of the brokerage operations were sold off to Paine Webber, and Larry Fink, who by then headed his own firm, Blackrock Investments, was brought in to work off the huge mortgage-backed portfolio. Closing down the most important CMO market maker and trader inevitably traumatized the entire market. Investors great and small suffered the same 25+ percent price declines that Askin did. The Shoshone Indians lost half of a $5 million investment in just four months. Glaxo Pharmaceuticals lost about $140 million. The Bank of Montreal dropped $51 million. A number of so-called short-term government income mutual funds turned out to be full of CMOs and suffered huge losses—although in most cases, the sponsors made up investor losses. At Paine Webber, the cost was $180 million. By most estimates, total market losses—the clean CMOs and the toxic waste together—was about 6 percent, or some $55 billion.

By the end of the year, it was almost oxymoronic to speak of a CMO "market." New underwritings, which were running in excess of $1 billion a *day* in the first quarter of 1994, dropped off to almost zero. Traditional mortgage-backeds were also down from their peak but not nearly as much, as investors clearly expressed a preference for instruments that were easier to understand. The total volume of new agency-backed CMOs issued in 1995 was only $23 billion, but volumes crept back up to $65 billion in 1996, and by 1997 the market had made a substantial recovery. New volume exceeded $175 billion, or a bit more than half 1994's volume, and CMOs outperformed all other investment-grade fixed-income instruments. Like junk bonds, CMOs got battered in the market turbulence following the Long Term Capital Management rescue, but had recovered strongly by the end of the year.

Newer CMOs are much simpler and cleaner than in the market's glory days, although 30-tranche structures (down from an average of 60 in 1993) are still common. But as Fink says, "Investors are lot smarter now, and they scrutinize CMOs much more carefully than they used to." His own business places much less emphasis on CMOs and mortgages than it once did. "They've gotten pretty dull," he said. "You don't see smart people going into CMOs or fixed-income any more." Dullness is the surest sign of a cycle of invention coming to a close.

———————————————

Chapter Nine

MR. ZEDILLO AND MR.
SUHARTO MEET MR. GOULD

The S&L crisis of the late 1980s is by far the largest in recent American financial history. The losses in the 1987 market crash were theoretically higher, but they were just paper losses. The S&L losses represented real costs; the government had to go to the capital markets, raise $150 billion, and pay it out to depositors and other claimants. But measured against the string of financial crises elsewhere in the world over the past twenty years or so, the S&L crisis looks like small potatoes. S&L losses amounted to about 3 percent of annual GDP. But a prolonged financial crisis in Spain (1977–85) cost almost 17 percent of GDP; one in Finland (1991–93), 8 percent of GDP; in Sweden (1991), 6 percent of GDP; and in Norway (1987–89), 4 percent of GDP. Crises in the developing world tend to be even more expensive. One widely cited analysis lists a dozen financial crises costing 10 percent of GDP or more. In the 1980s, crises in Argentina, Chile, and the Ivory Coast all cost more than 25 percent of local GDP, and more recently, problems in Venezuela and Mexico cost some 18 percent and 12 to 15 percent of GDP respectively. Russian GDP is collapsing at the rate of 10 percent a year. Some experts insist that the scale and frequency of the recent crises are unprecedented.

There may not, in fact, be much going on that is really new. Crises may indeed happen more frequently, if one simply counts countries getting into trouble, but there are now many more countries participating in the capital markets. The breakup of the Soviet Union alone introduced more than a dozen new players, most of which quickly found themselves in deep water. Two of the most dramatic of the recent crises, if only because they seemed to catch the markets so unaware, are the Mexican peso crisis of 1994–95 and the Asian currency crisis of 1997–98, which is still evolving as this is written. In gross outline, however, they track reasonably closely with nineteenth-century financial crises in America. Development economics may not have changed that much.

Development Crises in America: 1873 and 1893–95

The Civil War catapulted America into the industrial age and forced a government with a long tradition of fiscal conservatism to come to grips with high finance. Throughout most of the 1850s, the federal budget hovered in the $50 to $60 million range, with relatively little growth in debt. The government started to run $10 million–plus deficits toward the end of the decade as both North and South girded for war, and total debt stood at a bit over $90 million on the eve of Fort Sumter. Annual federal (Union) spending then ballooned to $1.3 *billion* by 1865, partly financed by a new income tax but mostly by borrowing. The 1865 federal deficit was $964 million, or 74 percent of the total budget, and by the war's end, the public debt had jumped to $2.7 billion.

Smart money in Europe doubted that the Union could be held together, so the North was forced to finance its war almost entirely from internal resources. Total foreign liabilities increased by only about $185 million during the war, and in most years the Union actually had a trade surplus. Borrowing was mostly in the form of 10- to 20-year bonds that were sold for greenbacks but were redeemable in gold; a bond buyer was therefore betting both that the federal government would survive and that within a decade or so would be sitting atop a big enough gold pile to pay off its borrowings. Although some banks and government suppliers took bonds under duress, most of the bonds met a receptive market. More than $360 million in bonds was placed just by Jay Cooke's retail sales operations.

Victory brought a half decade of financial euphoria. The war had required huge forced-draft investments in factories, roads, logistics, and a rudimentary network of railroads. The Union Pacific had been authorized in 1862, and at war's end, its promoters were anxious to push it through to completion. European yield chasers, aware that they had missed out on the war bonds, tripped over one another in the rush to buy into American industrialization. Between 1866 and 1873, $1.1 billion in new net investment poured into the country, and in 1872 America ran a $123 million trade deficit, or about 23 percent of its exports—both in percentage and in dollar terms the biggest trade deficit from the founding of the republic until 1935.

The surge in imports was caused partly by the need for capital goods—steel rails, locomotives, machine tools, and the like. But this was also the dawn of America's Gilded Age, when the likes of Jay Gould, Jim Fisk, and Cornelius Vanderbilt were building mansions in New York and Newport; when America's new rich were ransacking Europe for old master paintings and using ancient sculptures for hatracks; when men sported solid-gold cigar cutters, and ladies got diamond bracelets as dinner party favors. It was a whole new standard of monied vulgarity, at least until interest payments started falling due and a string of railroad defaults burst the bubble in 1873.

Today's news is filled with stories about "hot money," and how frighteningly fast investors can cut and run in computerized markets. But in 1873, relative to the speed of information—it could still take a month for a ship to cross the ocean—investors reacted about as quickly. Foreign investment dropped from $242 million in 1872 to zero by 1875, and then completely reversed between 1876 and 1879, when America was forced to ship almost $400 million in capital back to Europe. Europeans were dumping everything they had, taking huge portfolio losses in the process. American merchandise exports continued to grow steadily, but imports dropped by a third. By 1878, America's trade surplus was 40 percent of exports. During the sixty years after the mid-1870s, America ran a trade deficit only once.

The crash of 1873 reinforced the conservative instincts of the central government, which immediately set about mopping up excess greenbacks, taxing state bank note issues to reduce credit, and getting its fiscal house in order, despite much kicking and screaming in Congress. Renewed growth pushed up federal excise revenues, but spending was held flat from 1875 to 1890; in 1882, a third of federal revenues went for debt retirement. To grasp the scale of the shift, imagine President Bill Clinton defending a trillion-dollar budget surplus. Tight credit worked through the economy in the form of steadily falling prices in the latter half of the 1870s. With the supply of greenbacks under control, the government announced full greenback-gold convertibility for international transactions in 1879. From that point till the end of the century, inflation was essentially zero. Europeans hesitated for about two years—was America *really* going to pay off those Civil War bonds in gold? Then capital came pouring back in, at a rate of $150 million a year for ten years, on top of the very large earnings from American trade surpluses. Having played the role of Europe's Mexico, America would now try its hand as a proto-1980s Asia.

For the entire decade of the 1880s and into the 1890s, America was a model of fiscal rectitude, ignoring a substantial overlay of public corruption. The economy grew strongly the entire time, and—after the fierce deflation of the 1870s—the money supply grew rapidly, partly because of the inflow of capital from Europe and partly because of the monetization of silver in 1890. But there was still no inflation, and few signs of an asset bubble. The availability of free land in the West probably capped real estate prices outside of a few major cities, while the perennial unprofitability of railroads prevented a stock market boom—stock prices were basically flat from 1880 to 1900. Savings were very high, and excess liquid capital disappeared into mattresses. The stock of tangible assets almost tripled in twenty years, and there were massive investments in public infrastructure and amenities during the entire period—street cars, roads, water systems, public schools, hospitals, parks, and police forces.

A series of economic reverses in the 1890s briefly called America's commitment to the straight-and-narrow into question. Currency speculators made a run at the greenback in 1895 and almost succeeded in knocking America off her gold perch. The precipitating event, however, was a crash in railroad securities in 1893 that scorched many naive European investors—shades of 1873—and Europeans were net repatriators of capital in 1894. The fundamental problem was that America was grossly overinvested in railroads. None of the lines was running at a profit, and it would be decades before economic activity could fully utilize all the capacity. But periodic railroad crises seem to have had little effect on the real economy. The lines kept running, while the never-ending price wars kept rates down. The main losers were British merchant-aristocrats who got stiffed on their interest payments, and besides J. P. Morgan, who cared about them?

More worrisome was the Populist flirtation with bimetalism, pushed hard by western silver mining interests and farmers. Farms are inherently leveraged enterprises, so farmers like cheap money. Part of the farmers' complaints sprang from money illusion: yes, farm prices were flat, but so were the prices of everything else. They had some real grievances, however. Wholesale prices had fallen faster than retail prices, probably reflecting the growing market power of big companies, so the terms of trade were turning against the little guy. And Morgan's restructuring of the railroads temporarily pushed up freight rates after many years of below-cost services. The Silver Act of 1890 mandated a minimum level of silver coinage at a silver/dollar rate that was slightly cheaper than gold, so arbitrageurs snapped up gold, shipping much of it overseas. The banking lobby won the Silver Act's repeal in 1893, but the reputational damage had been done. America had backed up its commitment to greenback-gold stability by maintaining a massive $100 million gold reserve, but the gold mountain melted away so fast—as much as $9 million a day was fleeing the country—that the George Soroses of the nineteenth century sniffed a devaluation.

Pierpont Morgan thereupon made one of his grand stage entrances—not for the last time using his personal prestige in the global financial community to supply the lack of an American central bank. Along with August Belmont of the British house of Rothschild, Morgan rhinocerosed his way into a White House meeting where President Grover Cleveland and his Cabinet were hashing out the crisis. (Cleveland was a friend but anxious not to appear in thrall to Morgan.) Morgan sat silently and restlessly through the Cabinet's prolonged dithering, then announced that there was $9 million left in the reserve, and he had in his office a $10 million gold draft from Europe. The game was up—were the gentlemen prepared to listen? They were. Within a few days he engineered a huge American gold bond issue to purchase 3.5 million ounces of gold, stopping the speculators in their tracks. When the bonds were distributed two weeks later, they sold off at such a premium that the underwriters made enormous profits, bringing a storm of Populist recriminations upon the head of Morgan and his "Jewish" friends.

Pressures eased after 1896, although Populist political successes kept the bankers jittery. A European wheat famine pushed farm prices up, and big Yukon gold strikes made money more plentiful. From that point, the cause of bimetalism was just a nostalgic rallying cry. The 1895 speculative currency strike against America, in fact, is probably best understood as the last spasmodic kick from the *ancien régime*. Capital started flooding out from America again in 1897, but this time the outflow was caused not by Europeans pulling out their money but by Americans investing overseas. Although it was beyond the comprehension of the anglophilic Morgan, the world's financial map had been turned on its head, and New York was replacing London as the world's financial capital. For the next seventy years, the huge trove of American savings would be the financial engine for the rest of the world, Europe included.

The Peso Crisis: Mexico, 1994–95

David Hale, the chief economist for Zurich-Kemper Financial Services, calls the Mexican peso crisis "the first great liquidity crisis to result in part from the rise of mutual funds as important global financial intermediaries." Hale is right, of course, because there were no mutual funds in 1873, but the "hot money" reaction of nineteenth-century European bondholders and 1995 American mutual fund managers have a great deal in common.

Mexico's introduction to global capital markets was one of the shooting stars of the 1970s petrodollar follies. In the midst of the 1970s oil price shocks, the Carter administration turned on the monetary pumps in the hope of inflating away the real value of oil. Suddenly awash with funds, American banks prowled the world looking for sovereign borrowers who could swallow great gulps of money without the tedium of credit checks. Mexico's huge oil reserves and expectations that oil was heading for $60 a barrel made it a favorite target of the pin-striped set, who shoveled in upward of $100 billion in loans, mostly for grandiose state-company projects. Paul Volcker's 1979–81 clampdown on American credit and the decontrol of American oil prices put paid to Mexican illusions, and the country defaulted in 1982. There followed a long period of capital flight and depression. Between 1983 and 1988, Mexico sent, on average, about 6 percent of its GDP overseas, mostly to service old debts.

The painful petrodollar saga was finally wrapped up in 1988–90. Representatives of Mexican business, agricultural workers, and trade unions signed a Pact of Economic Solidarity to cut inflation, restrain costs and wages, eliminate fiscal and trade deficits, and put the economy on a free-enterprise footing. The major American banks finally wrote off their uncollectible petrodollar-era loans, and the new "Brady bond" program* allowed Mexico and other Latin American debtors to place most of their external debt on a manageable long-term footing.

For the first few years of the 1990s, Mexico's performance was spectacular. Inflation was cut from an annual rate of nearly 160 percent in 1987 to only 7 percent in 1994. Big state industries were privatized, government deficits were eliminated, and GDP growth jumped from near zero to about 4 percent from 1989 through mid-1991. The entire experiment in liberalization was crowned by the signing of the North American Free Trade Agreement (NAFTA) in 1993. Growth in Mexico came amid a mild American recession and very low American short-term interest rates. Portfolio man-

---

*The bonds, named after Bush administration Treasury Secretary Nicholas Brady, were created from assemblages of deeply discounted defaulted Latin American bank loans. Most of them are long-term with the principal secured at maturity by zero-coupon U.S. treasuries. Since long-term zeros sell at only a small fraction of their final value, the scheme allowed the selling countries to give buyers a dollar-based security at a very low cost. (There is no American guarantee.) The Brady bonds were an elegant way for all parties to recognize their losses once and for all and get off to a fresh start. Brady bonds have since become one of the most widely traded of emerging-market instruments, and several exchanges have introduced Brady bond futures and options.

agers in the United States were chasing yield, and "global diversification" became the buzzword at mutual fund companies.

The Mexican recovery strategy was built around a strong peso. A strong currency lowers the price of imports, and so acts to curb inflation and keep competitive pressure on local companies. In the case of a capital-poor developing country, it signals to outsiders that the value of their investments will not be eroded away by devaluations. The other side of the coin is that the strong-currency country has to run a very tight ship. If local productivity *doesn't* keep pace with foreign competition, local industry will be destroyed by imports. Strict monetary and fiscal discipline are needed to ensure a high savings rate and to channel available capital into productivity-enhancing investment instead of consumption.

Mexico's strategy was coming unstuck as early as 1992. To begin with, the inrush of foreign investment forced the currency higher than even the government wanted. (To invest in a foreign country, you must first buy the local currency, so large-scale dollar investments in Mexico naturally bid up the peso-dollar exchange rate.) At one point, the Mexican central bank was selling pesos to drive down the exchange rate, which is an absurd position for an emerging-market country. Local costs, moreover, could not keep pace with the exchange rate, so Mexican exports were quickly priced out of the market. Growth slowed to a crawl, and the trade account flipped back into deficit, although the inflow of capital was more than sufficient to finance it.

Classical economics gives a government two choices at this point: either devalue, or really tighten up on credit to force local costs down. (Economists disagree violently on which choice would have been right for Mexico.) Facing an election, however, the government chose the worst of all possible policies—it *loosened* internal credit controls *and* still tried to maintain the high external value of the peso. Mexican bank credits grew at a compound rate of 26 percent from 1990 through 1994. Predictably, the trade deficit soared to 29 percent of exports, much of it because of a surge of luxury and consumer goods imports. At this point, Mexico was in much the same position as the United States in 1872: yield-crazed investors were flooding the country with money, so currency reserves were actually growing even as the trade account ran amok. Just as America was at the mercy of British bondholders, Mexico was utterly dependent on the continued flow of money from American mutual funds and pension funds. But unlike even the petrodollar banks in the 1980s, fund managers had no permanent ties to the country—they just liked the yields.

The game was up when the Federal Reserve raised American interest rates in February 1994—the same fateful rate increase that brought down the CMO market. Miraculously, there was no immediate capital flight from Mexico, despite rising political tensions, including a festering rebellion in the South, the assassination of the ruling party's presidential candidate, and a trail of murder and corruption that led to the family of the Mexican president, Carlos Salinas de Gortari. Part of the reason was that Salinas and his finance minister, Ernesto Zedillo, who succeeded Salinas as president, had excellent relations with American institutional investors and swore, again and again, that there would be no devaluation. More important, Mexico quietly offered to exchange peso-denominated bonds for a new instrument called the tesobono, a short-term note indexed to the dollar—in effect, a promise to protect investors against devaluation. During 1994, external debt denominated as tesobonos grew from $2 billion to $29 billion, while peso-denominated government bonds dropped from $20 billion to $3 billion. No alarms were sounded by the American treasury. In fact, in the wake of the NAFTA passage, the Clinton administration was proudly trumpeting America's burgeoning trade surplus with Mexico.

The tesobonos temporarily prevented a capital flight, but no new funds were coming in, and Mexico, a country with a GDP not much bigger than that of Los Angeles, was running an $18 billion trade deficit, which could be financed only by drawing down reserves. The Mexican elite, with longer memories than fund managers fresh from business school, were the first to move. Mexico had always devalued in a crisis—about every six years since 1976—so rich Mexicans started moving their money overseas. By December, official reserves had dropped to barely a third of the level of the outstanding tesobonos; currency speculators smelled default and started dumping pesos. On December 16, the government announced a peso devaluation of 15 percent. Instead of calming the markets, it started a headlong rush for the exits, as investors and fund managers—many of whom felt "deceived"—dumped everything with the name "Mexico" on it. Within just a few days, the government gave up defending the peso and let it float freely; in a short time, it fell to roughly half its pre-December value, where it was still hovering in early 1998.

The consensus estimate is that foreign investors suffered about a $30 billion mark-to-market loss in the December–January meltdown. The IMF cobbled together a $16 billion rescue package in early January, but the announcement only accelerated the capital flight. Because of the shift to tesobonos over the previous year, almost all Mexican external debt was short-term and dollar-indexed, so principal amounts had risen sharply in peso terms. With some $50 billion falling due in 1995 alone, the IMF package was clearly not enough to stave off default. By this point, investors' herd instinct was threatening economic stability in Argentina and Brazil, and the Clinton administration stepped in with a proposed $40 billion American rescue package. When that failed to win sufficient support in Congress, Clinton and his treasury secretary, Robert Rubin, announced that they would use $20 billion from an "exchange stabilization reserve fund" under presidential control as the core of a multinational aid program to reschedule the short-term debt.

With the immediate crisis under control, Mexico's apparent turnaround was quite rapid, again much like the United States in 1873. The initial shock stopped the economy dead in its tracks— real GDP dropped by 7 percent in 1995. But a more competitive peso turned the trade account around very quickly. Exports jumped 31 percent in 1995, while imports fell; the net trade surplus of $7.4 billion represented a $25 billion swing in just one year. By 1997, the government was still sticking to the 1988 privatization and economic liberalization program, all the American loans had been repaid, and the trade account was still in surplus. Mexico was badly battered by the backwash of the crises in Asia, Russia, and Brazil throughout 1997 and 1998, but by year-end 1998, there was reason to hope that it had weathered the storms. Inflation hovered in the 15 percent range for most of 1997 and 1998, which is good performance for Mexico, and GDP growth was a solid 7 percent in 1997 and 4.6 percent in 1998, much better than the Latin American average. The trade balance was also positive in 1997 and turned negative only with the very sharp fall in the price of oil exports in the summer of 1998, but the government was cautiously tightening spending to avoid fueling another luxury-goods import binge.

Postmortems on the Mexican crisis have tended to focus on the speed of the reaction. In an era of globalized, computer-driven, derivative-enhanced trading, "gypsy capital" can flee a country at the flick of a computer key. More interesting, perhaps, is how long the money *stayed*. The investment cycle leading up to America's crash in 1873 lasted for about six years, and by 1871 or so there were ample signs that the money was being misused. It took till 1873 for that realization to sink in, and another year or two for Europeans to disinvest. In the case of Mexico, although the disinvestment process was very rapid, it took about as long for investors to realize that something was seriously wrong. The tardiness of nineteenth-century investors in reacting to bad news is understandable: Communications were very slow, and much of the basic data analysts now take for granted, like monthly trade-balance reports and balance-of-payments tables, either didn't exist or were grossly deficient. But Mexico had relatively good numbers. Throughout 1993 and 1994, investors could watch the ballooning trade deficit on their Reuters and Bloomberg screens, see how rapidly the maturity of government debt was shortening, chart the slide in international reserves, and observe the growing gap between reserves and dollar-indexed commitments like tesobonos. Some economists made quite explicit warnings. And yet traders sat there until there was a crisis, and then screamed that they had been "deceived." Where is the information revolution when you need it?

Crisis in Asia: 1997–98

Premonitory rumbles of difficulties in Asia grew in volume in 1996, mostly emanating from Thailand, one of the newer generation of the "Little Tiger" developing countries. Heavy investment from Japan and booming export sales to America had fueled one of the region's fastest growth rates, and the country's relatively weak institutional infrastructure was having trouble keeping pace. The baht, the Thai currency, was tightly tied to the dollar, and the dollar's strong rise in 1996 undercut exports, coincident with sharp drops in the overheated Thai property and stock markets. Currency speculators made several runs at the baht in 1996 but were beaten back by central bank intervention. Pressures increased in early 1997 and became heavy and sustained in May. The central bank fought back grimly until, its foreign exchange reserves exhausted, it threw in the towel on July 2 and allowed the baht to float.

The collapse of the baht was not much of a surprise, just another case of wolves thinning out the herd. The shock was how fast the currency attacks spread throughout the region, for a brief time threatening to engulf almost all the world's developing economies. Within days of the Thai capitulation, there were speculative runs against the Philippines, Malaysia, and Indonesia, all of which offered only token resistance before devaluing. Pressures spread to Hong Kong in October, precipitating a one-day 23 percent drop in the Hang Seng index that led directly to the October mini-crash in America. Hong Kong held off the speculators but at the cost of a sharp recession. Korea capitulated in November, with up to $100 billion in foreign-currency loans on the brink of default. For a brief time the pressures spread to Mexico, Argentina, and Brazil, and on to Eastern Europe, especially Hungary and the Czech and Slovak Republics. Most of the countries beat back the speculators, sometimes with token devaluations but always at great cost to local economic growth. When the smoke cleared in early 1998, the clear losers were Thailand, Malaysia, Indonesia, and Korea.

Asia's "Little Tiger" economies—Thailand, Malaysia, Indonesia, Singapore, Taiwan, Hong Kong, Korea—had all won macroeconomic gold stars throughout the 1980s and early 1990s. Like the United States a century before, they had balanced budgets, high savings rates, beehive economies, strong growth, and strong currencies. Just as the United States tied its greenbacks tightly to gold, most of the Pacific Rim economies pegged their currency to the dollar, the world's most important trading currency. Public corruption was rife in many of the Asian countries, just as in nineteenth-century America, and like America, the Little Tigers usually ran current account deficits as the result of large overseas investment flows and the import of capital equipment.* And like nineteenth-century America, they were powerful magnets for industrial capital seeking higher returns.

America's financial crisis of 1893–95 ensued when British investors realized that American railroad cash flows could not possibly support their grossly inflated debt structures. Speculators reasoned that railroad defaults and the inevitable flight of overseas capital would create a credit crunch in America that would be an irresistible temptation to inflation and a devalued greenback. The flirtation with silver only confirmed inflationist fears, so speculators starting converting their greenbacks into gold and shipping bullion back home, until they were defeated by Morgan's gold pool and the clear American determination not to inflate.

Without pressing the parallels too far, the Asian crises evolved in a broadly similar manner. With interest rates falling throughout the industrialized world, yield-chasers were drawn to the fast-growing Little Tigers. The primary investment intermediaries were global banks, especially German and Japanese banks. (American bank exposure was only about a fourth as great as Japan's.) Just as in 1880s America, the capital inflows were far greater than could be employed profitably. The Little Tiger economies absorbed about half of all developing-country bank lending in the 1990s, and gross domestic investment averaged 35 to 42 percent of GDP in 1996 and 1997, or about triple the rate in the big industrialized countries.

In Indonesia, Thailand, and Malaysia, excess investment worked through primarily in the form of stock market and real estate bubbles, exemplified by the Malaysian-Indonesian competi-

---

*Unlike the United States in the 1890s, most of the Asian countries also ran trade deficits, but they were driven by capital-goods imports rather than by consumption goods as in Mexico. Industrializing Asian countries do not have nineteenth-century America's cushion of raw material exports.

tion to build the world's tallest office towers. Stock market capitalization jumped from 113 percent of GDP in Malaysia in 1990 to 315 percent in 1996. (United States stock market capitalization was only 109 percent of GDP in 1996.) Equity capitalization increases over the same period in Indonesia and Thailand were of similar magnitude, but starting from much lower levels—from 7 percent to 42 percent of GDP in Indonesia and from 28 percent to 54 percent of GDP in Thailand. A tightly knit political and business elite, and engrained traditions of public corruption, especially in Indonesia, only added to the overall wastefulness of investment. The Korean experience was different only in the details. Excess cash inflows were directed through the banking system to favored industrial conglomerates, the *chaebol,* to finance unprofitable ventures in semiconductors, automobile factories, and steel and chemical plants.

The unique feature of the Asian currency crises is that they originated in the banking system rather than in loose government fiscal and monetary policy—which, as in Mexico in 1994, is the more usual case. In all four countries, local banks plumped up their balance sheets by borrowing short-term yen, marks, and dollars at low interest rates and relending long-term in local currencies at much higher interest rates. (About 70 percent of East Asian foreign-currency loans were due in a year or less.) Like American S&Ls in the 1980s, they were running a mismatched book—borrowing short and lending long—with the added fillip that they were mismatched in currencies as well. In effect, they were making a double bet that the returns from their baht, won, or ringgit loans would be sufficient to fund continued rollovers of the foreign currency loans *and* that local currency exchange rates would be stable over the long term.

Foreign investors were also making a double bet. The first was that loans to Asian banks were implicitly guaranteed by their governments, and the second was that the host governments would always have the foreign exchange to make good on the guarantee. The foreigners were probably right that Asian governments were willing to underwrite the debts of their private banks, but as a consequence, they paid little attention to what the banks were doing with the money. Even though all the Asian governments had strong foreign-reserve positions, it wasn't enough to pay off their banks' foreign-currency debts when the local loans went sour. In that respect, the German and Japanese banks were repeating the earlier mistakes of American banks in Latin America. The Latin American petrodollar loans were usually explicitly guaranteed by local governments, but the guarantees were worthless when central banks ran out of foreign exchange.

Although it is true that the 1997 crises swept through developing countries like a prairie fire, it actually took a long time for the conflagration to build. The Thai crisis percolated for more than a year, as speculators repeatedly tested the resources of the central bank, and for overseas investors, it was an object lesson in Asian realities.

Modern currency crises tend to be worked through in the forward markets, because transaction costs are so low. A speculator betting against the baht will sell baht for dollars in the forward market, hoping that the baht/dollar rate will have fallen by the time he must cover his contract. Such speculation is not without risk. The forward sales will tend to push forward rates below the spot rates, so if the target country manages to maintain the spot rate, the speculator will take a loss when he is forced to cover his contract. (For example, assume the dollar:local currency spot rate is 1:100. As a run develops, forward selling pressure may push forward rates down to 1:102. But if the government maintains the spot rate, on the contract date the speculator will have to buy local currency at 1:100 in the spot market and deliver them for dollars at 1:102.) Since currency positions are usually highly leveraged, tiny losses on the contracts quickly compound into very serious money.

The speculators' forward sales also require a counterparty willing to assume the future obligation of delivering dollars for baht. The standard counterparties in currency markets are commercial banks, but bank currency trading desks like to run a balanced book of business, and will accommodate the speculators only as long as they can find other counterparties wanting to buy baht forward. During a currency run, they will not find such counterparties and will have to lay off their positions with the central bank, if it is willing. If it is not, the commercial banks will be forced to square up their books by entering the spot markets and covering their forward obligations by selling baht for dollars, which will drive down the baht spot price. Unless the central bank intervenes at that point to maintain the spot rate by buying baht with dollars, the speculators will have won. Speculators betting on a devaluation are therefore constantly testing the central bank's resolve, maintaining the selling pressure, and watching the level of foreign-exchange reserves. That's what happened in Thailand throughout 1996 and early 1997.

But when speculators start probing, a feisty central bank will try to bloody their noses and scare them off. In early 1997, when forward selling pressure built dramatically in Thailand, the central bank retaliated by prohibiting banks from selling baht to currency speculators. (Baht could be sold only in connection with documented trade transactions.) When speculators needed baht to cover their short positions, therefore, they were forced to buy in offshore markets, where baht were scarce. In mid-June, the one-month offshore baht borrowing rate shot up to an annualized 300 percent, and the central bank briefly seemed to have the upper hand. Speculators were hemorrhaging money, while the government still claimed very large dollar reserves.

Unfortunately for Thailand, the reserves turned out to be a fiction. The central bank was reporting the gross money in its vaults, $32 billion, correctly, but all but $3 billion had long since been committed to forward contracts. (The Thai central bank reportedly misrepresented its reserves even to the country's finance minister.) Once the truth about the reserves leaked out, it was over in two weeks. The government devalued, the baht fell steadily until it had lost about half its value, and the speculators made their killing.

For foreign-currency traders, the experience was an eye opener. It appeared: (a) that at least some Asian governments would lie about their foreign-exchange reserves; (b) that Asian commercial banks could handle very little pressure without turning to their governments; so (c) the banks were probably making very little money on their local business; which meant that, (d) all the buzzing economic activity and spectacular office towers might be the last illusory blowout before a crash. Time to sell.

It is in the nature of currency markets that pressures build very quickly. Speculating against a currency is not costless, as the Thai experience shows. Because of leveraging, covering forward sales at losses of even a few tenths of a percent can be very painful, but on the other hand, the gains from a 10 percent or 20 percent devaluation are enormous. Betting against a government trying to maintain a fixed exchange rate is therefore something of a one-way option, in which the potential losses are much smaller than the potential gains. Once selling pressure builds, moreover, pricing in the forward markets quickly adjusts to reflect the possibility of a windfall, so only first-movers make the biggest profits. In short, the risks of jumping in early are much less than the profits lost by coming in late. Almost the instant a devaluation becomes plausible, therefore, the markets react with a rush. Markets also reacted quickly in the nineteenth century, although higher transaction costs—shipping bullion was expensive—allowed governments greater leeway to stray. But once the threshold was breached, currency runs still developed quite rapidly.

In that light, the prairie-fire currency attacks throughout the late summer and fall of 1997 make perfect sense. Any country whose accounts were as opaque as Thailand's, whose development had proceeded at a comparable speed, or that exhibited any of the same symptoms of cronyism, or politically directed investments, was likely to be sitting on the same problems. The quickest way to find out was to attack, and attacks were cheap. Hong Kong, Taiwan, the Philippines, Argentina, and Brazil all stood up under the assaults, although at significant economic cost. Indonesia and Korea proved to be possibly in even worse shape than Thailand, and Korea had lied about its reserves as egregiously. In both cases the problems were so deep-seated that it is hard to imagine that they would have been better off left alone. Malaysia was something of a middle case.

A study by the economist Jeffrey Sachs and his colleagues examined twenty-two developing countries that suffered currency attacks in the wake of the Mexican crisis, and concluded that the process was not as mindless as it sometimes appeared. None of the target countries was a true innocent. All had indulged in some degree of economic misbehavior—loose monetary or fiscal policy, allowing reserves to run down relative to the country's commitments, politically directed investment, encouraging real estate or stock market bubbles. In most countries, the speculative attacks imposed real economic costs, but a year later, the authors could find few lingering negative effects, while the attacks had served as a sharp reminder to stay on the straight path. The market's winnowing process may be brutal and expensive, but there may not be readily available alternatives. Finally, it bears mentioning that the "hedge funds," of which George Soros's is the most famous, had little to do with either the Mexican or Asian currency crises. They were big traders throughout both crises, but as often as not were on the wrong side of the trades. Soros's funds took a huge loss by making large purchases of the Indonesian rupiah just before it went into free fall.

Summer 1998

Hopes that emerging markets were stabilizing in the early months of 1998 were dashed by economic turmoil in Russia throughout the summer. When Russia defaulted on its obligations in August, there was another wave of panic selling of all risky instruments, triggering a full-blown financial crisis that persisted well into the fall.

RUSSIA   Since the fall of communism a decade ago, Russia has been something of a special case for international investors. Its long-standing role as a major power supported the illusion that it is a first-world economy, while its possession of nuclear weapons lulled investors into a belief that the West would tolerate any degree of outrageous behavior on the part of the country's managers.

Seventy years of communist rule, however, left only a shattered hulk of a state, run by former Soviet oligarchs and a newly rising criminal class, and possessing none of the institutions or traditions that underpin successful free-market economies. As the country's primitive economic machinery ground to a virtual halt in the late 1990s, successive governments flooded the country with worthless paper money and swallowed huge amounts of Western aid and loans, much of which ended up in the oligarchs' overseas bank accounts. Investors surely knew this, but, with short-term ruble-denominated loans carrying interest of 90 percent in the summer (and 450 percent in September), were willing to invest in the prospect of continued bailouts. Consortia of American and European investment banks floated $5 billion in long-term dollar-denominated Russian bonds in June (a substantial portion of which was used to repay loans from those same investment banks) at yields of only about 10 percent.

By the end of the summer, however, with Russia facing a heavy volume of overseas debt repayments, the IMF finally declined to supply additional loans, and the government "restructured" its obligations. The ruble was sharply devalued, and has since continued to fall; a moratorium was placed on the payment of external private debts; holders of ruble instruments were stiffed; and negotiations were opened with the holders of the eurodollar bonds, which, only a couple of months after their issuance, lost about 90 percent of their face value. As of the end of the year, discussions with external debt holders were still in progress, and there was some expectation that the country might permanently repudiate its Soviet-era debts.

FALLOUT   The Russian default led to a sharp spike in yields of all risky instruments and an all-out flight to the issues of the most stable industrial countries, like the United States and Germany. The flight to safety was exacerbated by the forced deleveraging of major trading houses throughout the world. Anyone who owned junk bonds, CMOs, or emerging market instruments of any kind was hit with margin calls as the value of collateral plummeted, causing a wave of duress selling to raise margin cash or unwind positions. The collapse of Long Term Capital Management was only the most spectacular example of rapid deleveraging; almost all major banks and securities firms suffered through very difficult third quarters. The turmoil persisted for about two months, until markets were brought back to a semblance of normalcy through a combination of monetary easing in the United States and Europe and symbolic actions like the LTCM rescue.

The disruptions touched off another round of speculative probes by international currency traders. Almost all Latin American currencies came under pressure, although Brazil may have been the hardest hit. Brazil's position in mid-1998 was in many ways similar to Mexico's in 1995. It had built a good record of partial reforms, like reducing inflation a thousandfold, and had become the darling of international investment managers. But by 1997, poor fiscal management—large budget deficits, absurd public-sector pensions, and a grossly overstaffed government sector—was spilling over into a growing trade deficit that was funded by short-term "hot money" flowing into the country in pursuit of yield. When the hot money fled home after the Russian default, about half of Brazil's international reserves melted away in a matter of weeks. A major devaluation was staved off only by a massive $42 billion support package orchestrated by the IMF and the Clinton administration. By the end of the year, Brazil's financial system had again reached a shaky stability, and the Cardoso government was at least halfheartedly attempting to hack away at the most egregious state subsidies.

All East Asian currencies came under selling pressure and spreads on dollar-denominated government debt widened dramatically, almost tripling on Indonesian paper; spreads were still high at the end of the year but were returning to more normal levels. Markets were further spooked by the imposition of capital controls in Malaysia and by strong government market intervention in Hong Kong, both of which warrant special comment.

Finance purists mistrust capital controls because they distort market signals; but markets do not work perfectly, and sand-in-the-wheels interventions, like trading halts on Wall Street, have often proved their usefulness. Chile, which has been known for its straight-and-narrow finances, has long imposed an implicit tax on short-term money movements. (You can't collect interest until your money has been in the country for a year.) The rules are easy to circumvent through offshore swaps, but still act to deter hot-money capital flows. A common thread running through recent crises in Mexico, Brazil, and East Asia has been the financing of trade deficits and other long-term obligations with short-term investment inflows—in other words, running a mismatched book, just like the S&Ls did—which automatically sets the stage for a crisis when the short-term inflows dry up. In principle, international financiers and local central banks should know better than to allow such mismatches to develop. In practice, the chance to make a quick buck overrules common sense, so sand-in-the-wheels limitations on capital flows may be a good idea. The test of a system is whether the government also attempts to maintain a reasonably valued currency and transparent accounts or merely uses the controls to mask economic irresponsibility. As of this writing, the jury was still out on the Malaysian system.

The Hong Kong intervention was quite different, for it came after the government claimed that large offshore hedge funds were attempting to work a "double play"—shorting the HK dollar and the Hong Kong stock market at the same time. Since the government was strongly committed to maintaining the value of the HK dollar, the speculators reasoned that selling pressure would force it to raise interest rates. (Higher interest rates usually trigger foreign buying of a currency.) The higher interest rates would then depress the value of Hong Kong stocks and presumably generate big winnings on the stock market short. The government intervened very forcefully, clamping down on currency transactions and buying heavily in the stock market, with a total cash infusion of about 6 percent of the market's capitalization. World market conditions began to ease a few weeks after the intervention and the speculators, if such there were, would have taken heavy losses. Hong Kong's interventions ceased in the fall, and a private company was created to manage down its stock positions in an orderly way. The government has warned that it reserves the right to strike at any future suspected speculations. The Hong Kong incident, if the government's allegations are true, would be one of the very few recent cases of foreign speculators actually attempting to manipulate markets. In almost all other instances, as in Brazil, the root problem has been unsustainable economic imbalances, foolish investors, and feckless government policies, not marauding speculators.

Picking Up The Pieces

The American treasury played the lead role in supervising the 1994–95 Mexican crisis, and the International Monetary Fund is coordinating the rescues of the Asian economies and Brazil. Russia may well be allowed to sink by itself. The rescues are not subsidies, but medium- to long-term loans of scarce foreign currencies at market interest rates. The Mexican loan was quickly repaid, and the IMF also has a good record of collecting on its loans (although the American Congress tends to think of IMF appropriations as grants). The loans are freighted with a host of conditions aimed at changing the more objectionable practices in the distressed economies.

It is remarkable how little the prescriptions have changed since the nineteenth century. The economic programs agreed in Korea, Thailand, and Brazil, for example, are very much in the spirit of J. P. Morgan's restructuring of American railroads in the 1890s. The primary goal is to eliminate the flim-flam: to generate truthful statements of international reserves, to make banks comply with capital standards, to close down insolvent companies and banks, to write off uncollectible debts, to end the subsidies to favored businesses or elites, and, perhaps most of all, to insist on honest accounting and reporting, both by the government and companies. In short, as countries emerge from third-world to first-world status, they have to build first-world institutions to go along with it.

Economists disagree strongly on the details of rescue plans: Should you devalue immediately or try to defend the currency? Can you ease out of a subsidy regime or should you quit cold turkey? Can a small country maintain completely open capital markets and still fend off hot-money investors? There are no "right" answers to any of these questions.

If anything, the recurrent crises expose the poverty of the

economists' view of the world. In the real world, countries have "thick" institutional systems—cultural reflexes and habits, unwritten rules of behavior, shared social expectations, attitudes that inform expectations in almost every daily transaction. But those are omitted from the "thin" models favored by economists. The embourgeoisement of the West is one of the most fundamental of social revolutions, but it stretched over the entire period since the crumbling of the feudal system. Russia lacks more than good accounting systems; as its commercial dealings have demonstrated, it seems barely to appreciate basic concepts, like the sanctity of contract, that were inculcated in the West over hundreds of years. When the warlords take the money home, like czars or medieval kings, mathematical models are beside the point.

Much of the financial commentary on the Asian crisis has focused on the new dangers of a global economy, the changes wrought by computers and telecommunications, as if the financial world were sailing on uncharted seas. In truth, there is not much new. The core problem in Asia had nothing to do with technology; it was simply dumb bank lending. The problems in Mexico and Brazil stemmed from foolish governments riding a wave of hot-money yield-chasers. Those are the same mistakes the British managed to perpetrate in America in the 1870s, and the North Americans in Latin America in the 1970s and 1980s, in both cases without the help of computers. Currency crises run their courses faster than they used to, but measured by previous crises, there is no evidence that the degree of punishment is any worse. Whether more damage is done by a quick swipe of the executioner's ax or by torture that stretches over months or years seems a moot point.

Complex crises do not lend themselves to clean solutions. In the wake of the early 1980s petrodollar crises, the world finally muddled its way to a rough-justice set of solutions. The banks took heavy losses, and the stock prices of banks like Citibank and Chase Manhattan were hit very hard. Some of the bad debts were socialized. All the offending countries suffered severe economic pain. The remaining written-down defaulted debts were extended and rescheduled so the debt-service burden became reasonable. But the process took years, imposing immense suffering on developing countries. One hopes that, with the strong spirit of enterprise in Asia, and the greater experience and sophistication of Latin American governments, this time around we can do better than that.

——————————————— ■ ———————————————

Chapter Ten

REFLECTIONS ON
REGULATION

A Future Financial Crisis

Fast-forward a few years from now to a high-tech life insurance underwriter. At the trading desk, the traders are hunched in front of their computer screens, keying in bids on broker policy offers. The traders have their own arcane jargon: "100" is a life policy on a thirty-five-year-old married nonsmoking white woman of average weight and no unusual health risk factors living in a specified set of zip codes; it accrues interest at a fixed rate equal to the current treasury bill rate, and has an annuity option at age sixty-five. Punch in the actual variables to any number of proprietary models to price any specific policy to four decimal places. A number under 75 is considered "junk," but some firms have created profitable junk-based sidelines. Substantial intellectual property is tied up in underwriter pricing models, but cheap software alternatives are eroding their advantage; some old-line traders still don't trust the models, and they price by feel. Big underwriters once maintained their own networks of brokers, but with the advent of the nationwide Insurnet trading system, it became impossible to prevent the sharpest brokers from surreptitiously offering their best product to the highest bidders.

Underwriters rarely keep product on their books for more than a few weeks; they either trade it or package it up into CIPs (collateralized insurance pools), which Wall Street firms sell off to institutional investors. Only five years after a thirty-two-year-old math whiz—let's call him Lucas Lizard—stunned the financial markets with the first original-issue billion-dollar interval-reset CIP, total CIP outstandings are already approaching the trillion-dollar mark. Almost single-handedly, Lizard has propelled Hadley and Baxendale, once a vaguely disreputable penny-stock brokerage, near to the very top of the underwriting league tables. Underwriters and CIP traders at other firms are known to fret about the grip that Lizard has achieved over the CIP market, but everyone concedes that his pricing and execution are superb, and no one complains for the record. Old-line, full-service insurers have either reinvented themselves as mutual fund companies or been bought up and dismembered by Wall Street firms interested in picking their bones for CIP product.

Retiring baby boomers have become extremely sophisticated insurance customers, and CIP returns depend on a complex interplay between interest rates, the range of payout options (various forms of annuity or lump sum distributions), and how consumers actually exercise their options. An active futures and options market permits CIP investors to simulate virtually any risk-return CIP profile and to hedge their redemption positions. (Traders call annuity-weighted derivatives annies and lump-sum-weighted derivatives lumpers.) Some analysts have expressed concern that the stable rate environment of the past several years has lulled the Street into building a big overhang of annies. Lizard scoffed at the pessimists at the annual CIP Brokers' Association dinner, pointing out that most positions are fully hedged by interval-reset puts, and that no CIP investor had ever incurred a principal loss. Readers know the rest of the story.

The question is, when the CIP market, or some other yet-to-be-invented financial market, crashes, why should we care? The answer is not quite as obvious as it may appear.

Consider, for example, the 1992 collapse in the price of IBM stock. Over the course of the year, IBM stock values fell by some $53 billion, dropping by $30 billion during just a few weeks in November and December. The losses at IBM dwarfed all the much-publicized losses in derivatives trading taken together. They were about twice as big as all the losses in junk bonds during their worst year, about the same size as the losses during the collapse of the trillion-dollar CMO market in 1994, and about a third as big as all the losses from the decade-long debacle in the nation's savings-and-loan industry. The junk-bond market, moreover, made a full recovery from its crash within a year or two, but it took almost five years for IBM shares to climb back to their 1992 highs, and they now pay much lower dividends. In the wake of the crash, some 200,000 IBMers lost their jobs, even more suffered serious impairment of their retirement nest eggs, and the housing market in IBM executive country still hasn't fully recovered. Finally, the IBM crash was a surprise. Almost all of Wall Street's IBM analysts, most of whom had grown fat licking cream from IBM teacups, had forecast at least decent IBM earnings until the very eve of the crash.

But the fall of IBM was never perceived as a crisis the way junk bonds, derivatives, CMOs, and S&Ls were, or as the inevitable CIP crash doubtless will be. The sudden collapse of such an important company was obviously a major event. There was much interest in how it could have happened, and much justified anger among employees and investors, who felt cheated or misled. But the attributes of a public crisis—the head-shaking editorials, the regulatory alarms, the flurries of legislative proposals, the staple jokes about junk bonds on late-night comedy shows—were all missing.

How to account for the difference? First, and possibly most important, the calamity at IBM, devastating as it was, did not violate standard assumptions about stock market investing. Stock prices fall. And once the smoke cleared, IBM's problems were ones that everyone could understand: the company had gotten top-heavy, its technology was stale, newer competitors were much nimbler. Contrast that with the perception of the stock market crash of 1987, when it seemed that mysterious new forces—program trading, index arbitrage, portfolio insurance—had made markets uncontrollable and unpredictable. Similarly, the problems in junk bonds and derivatives made it look as if Wall Street had been captured by a latter-day Prince of Darkness, aka Michael Milken, or by irresponsible computer wizards. People readily accept the risk of driving fast on a highway but are terrified at the prospect of unknown strangers leaping on them in the dark.

Secondly, the problems at IBM did not represent a systemic crisis. If anything, IBM's problems confirmed the vigor of the American computer industry. As grand a company as it had once been, not even an IBM was immune to the competitive onslaught from brash upstarts like Microsoft, Intel, Sun, and Oracle. A company was in trouble, but not the whole economy or the financial infrastructure. Unlike the collapse of Chrysler in the 1970s, which was taken to signal troubles in the entire American manufacturing sector, the IBM crisis was understood to be bounded from the very start.

And finally, no taxpayer money was involved. Because the financial sector is so intimately intertwined with the workings of the monetary system, major financial companies are often bailed out by the government, as with the Continental Illinois bank in 1984. The costs of rescuing the S&L industry were borne almost entirely by taxpayers. More subtly, although no one ever voted on it, the Federal Reserve may have shoveled as much as $5 billion a year of public money into the banking sector from 1991 through 1993 to help bind up the wounds from a decade's misadventures in real estate, foreign loans, and leveraged buyouts.*

The financial sector, in other words, is different. It is the economy's plumbing system. A company failure, even a big one like IBM's, is like a broken sink, but a failure in the financial sector threatens the entire water supply. The money involved in the Drys-

---

*For roughly three years, beginning in January 1991 and ending in February 1994, the Fed was very aggressive in pushing down short-term interest rates. The spread between the rate at which the Fed lent money to banks overnight and the rate on 10-year treasuries widened from 1.18 percent in early 1991 to 3.85 percent by the end of 1992. Although the Fed justified its rate policies as a way to increase lending to business, business lending actually was flat over the period. Instead, banks increased their holdings of treasuries by more than $200 billion by the end of 1992, representing all their asset growth. In effect, they could borrow cheap from the Fed—usually at about 3 percent—and then lend the money right back at 6 to 7 percent. The difference was pure profit—no need for loan offices, lending staff, or credit checks. The consequent increases in capital were a major factor in helping American banks comply with the new "Basle Accord" international standards for bank capital. The $5 billion calculation assumes that the whole spread increase was subsidy, which may be aggressive, but it does not include the huge trading profits that Wall Street made from rate arbitrage, so the estimate is probably low. The CMO crisis happened as soon as the Fed reversed its policy in 1994, which suggests how dependent the financial sector had become on Fed interest policy.

dale episode was relatively trivial, for example, but it placed the whole overnight-financing system at risk. The derivatives crises, even ones as big as Barings', usually involved relatively small amounts of money. They were scary because they implied, with much truth, that the captains of finance did not know what they were about, that their ships were steaming at record speeds through unknown seas.

It is therefore with good reason that finance is among the most regulated of all businesses. The American system of regulation can appear a bit of a patchwork—the Federal Reserve, the FDIC, and state banking authorities; the SEC, the CFTC and various other state and federal bodies for securities sales and trading; insurance commissions; and many others. But it is the most successful in the world, fostering the deepest, most liquid, most flexible, most creative of all financial markets. More kinds and sizes of businesses can raise capital more easily in the United States than anywhere else, and no other markets have such a degree of household participation.

The ramshackle American institutional structure works because of considerable intellectual consensus on purposes and methods, much of which was first embodied in New Deal securities legislation, one of the period's most enduring achievements. The first presumption is that in a state of complete information, markets should rule. Absent fraud, one should, at least in principle, be able to sell any kind of security to anyone, but only if the risks have been completely disclosed. Mere pretense of disclosure won't do. If you're Charles Keating, you can't sell junk bonds to people who think they are making S&L deposits, no matter how thick a prospectus you hand them. Prudential had to pay back $1 billion to customers who suffered losses on investment partnerships they could not possibly have understood. On the other hand, if you're rich enough to pay for lawyers and accountants, especially if you're a corporation or a financial institution, you shouldn't expect the government to look out for you. That's what made the Bankers Trust derivatives cases so interesting.

The second presumption is that firms in the financial sector must have sufficient capital to suffer major reverses before failing or falling back on government insurance reserves. The corollary is that firms that run through their capital must be allowed to fail. That principle has been occasionally violated at enormous cost. The 1982 coverup of the disaster in the S&L industry is the most dramatic example, but not the only one. In 1984, the government bailed out Continental Illinois's depositors, regardless of whether they were covered by deposit insurance, on the "too-big-to-fail" theory, although the bank itself ceased operations. The beneficiaries of the government largesse were customers, primarily corporations, with deposits in excess of the $100,000 insurance limit. Conceivably, if big corporate depositors had taken their lumps, they would have paid much greater attention to what banks were doing with their money, and the banking sector might have tightened up on unwise lending much sooner than it did, especially in financing the more ludicrous late-1980s LBOs.

Treasury Secretary Robert Rubin has recently voiced the same concern about currency market bailouts—investor behavior will never improve if the government always pays off their dumb bets. The Russian experience may be a useful antidote to that complacency. It also bears repeating that the rescue of Long Term Capital Management was not a bailout in the Continental Illinois sense. Government regulators coordinated the rescue, but the original equity investors lost almost their entire stake. The operation is best understood as a reorganization in bankruptcy, but without the delays of the bankruptcy courts. The creditors protected their positions, but had to put up $3.6 billion in equity to do it.

As a practical matter, the two primary principles—that markets should rule and that losses should fall where they may—are hemmed in with a host of minor restrictions and practical compromises. So we have circuit-breaker rules, margin requirements, uptick short-sale rules, and the like. Academics often bemoan such interventions, because they interfere with the purity of the market's price signals. But the practical consensus seems to be most of the "sand-in-the-wheels"-type restrictions are sensible and useful. Despite continued grumbling over this or that aspect of the circuit-breaker rules introduced after the 1987 crash, for example, they seem on the whole to have worked reasonably well. Similarly, it makes good sense for governments and international agencies to intervene, as in Mexico in 1995 and Korea in 1997–98, to stop a currency crisis from running its full brutal course. Protecting the innocent usually entails protecting a few of the guilty as well.

The relative smoothness with which the American regulatory system has absorbed twenty-five years of extraordinarily rapid financial change and development demonstrates its fundamental strengths. There have been rafts of new instruments and trading methodologies, a huge increase in scale, massive democratization of the investment markets, a top-to-bottom restructuring of the pension industry, and much more, but the basic institutions and operating assumptions are intact, and for the most part working well. At the same time, the great depth and enormous liquidity of the American markets, coupled with generally intelligent and market-sensitive regulatory policies, have allowed them to navigate sectoral crises—like CMOs, junk bonds, and the Barings collapse—with little lasting damage. In the 1920s, agricultural crises in Europe may well have triggered the Great Depression; merely contrast that experience with the ease with which the financial markets shrugged off the 1997 Asian currency crises. To be sure, Asian problems will impose a penalty on near-term American growth, and almost certainly portend growing trade deficits, but there is no reason to expect a 1920s-style economic paralysis.

Healthy as the markets are, a generation of financial revolution has also created great strains. There have been many forced adjustments and realignments, and there is still much catching up to do. There is certainly no regulatory crisis, but that may be all the more reason to seize the opportunity for an unpressured rethinking of purposes, institutions, and structures.

Because of the great complexities of virtually every regulatory question, the remainder of the chapter concentrates primarily on identifying issues, rather than making specific recommendations. The discussion is organized under the headings of Institutions, Disclosure, Systems, and Globalization.

Institutions

The fable of Lucas Lizard is far from a fantasy. When the home-finance industry was attacked by the capital markets in the 1980s, it was quickly divvied up among specialists—risk evaluation is performed by mortgage bankers, billing and collection by servicing companies, and mortgages are funded by chopping them up into a variety of securities that match investors' portfolio needs. The present-day insurance industry is at least as top-heavy and inefficient as the old home-finance business, and it is hard to believe that the capital markets can't find at least the same 100 basis points of fat that it squeezed out of mortgages. In modern markets, 100 basis points attracts the brilliant, the ambitious, and the greedy the way a carcass attracts blowflies, and Wall Street has been quietly circling around insurance for some time.

Investors Guaranty Fund, for example, is a Bermuda corporation offering a patented securitized insurance product that is tailored to meet difficult-to-insure corporate risks, like catastrophic utility infrastructure storm losses. IGF sources product through specialist risk-assessors/underwriters and parcels out the insured risks into tranched securities, which are not unlike CMOs. Different classes of securities will have sequenced claims on premium flows and commensurately sequenced liabilities when an insured event occurs, while hedging technology will be used to protect against worst-case events. IGF is hardly alone. Catastrophe insurance options, linked to claim-service reports, have been trading on the Chicago Board of Options since 1995, and several firms are beginning to make markets in Catastrophe, or CAT, bonds, sure signs that securitization is proceeding apace. Extending the concept to other classes of insurance is an easy step.

From a regulatory perspective, IGF, CAT bonds, and Lucas Lizard all demonstrate the tendency of the capital markets to commoditize risk and colonize the rest of financial services. In one way or another, any transaction involving an exchange of cash flows, however contingent, can be packaged up as a capital-market instrument—a fixed-income bond, a floating-rate note, a future, an option, or some combination thereof. The shift of business from specialized financial channels to commoditized market instruments usually lowers transaction costs and increases liquidity, so systemic risk is probably reduced, at least in the long run. But the process inevitably pressures prevailing regulatory assumptions.

In the not-so-distant past, regulatory organizations lined up rather neatly against types of financial enterprises—banks, thrifts, insurance companies, securities firms, commodities traders, and the like. Now securities firms mediate the greatest portion of mortgage financing by underwriting mortgage-backed instruments; they also mediate an increasing share of bank credit by underwriting asset-backed securities of all kinds, from credit card receivables to ordinary bank loans, and as the IGF example suggests, they may someday mediate a substantial share of insurance risk. At the same time, of course, banks and insurance companies are deriving an ever greater portion of their revenues from investment banking and securities and mutual fund sales. The fact that innovations in financial services so often involve a reshuffling of regulatory responsibilities may itself be a contributor to the short-term crises that seem to be the inescapable price of progress.

The same blurring of regulatory responsibilities involves security types as well as institutions. Robert Merton recently listed some fifteen different ways to take a position in the stock market—holding a portfolio of cash and stock index options, for example—only a few of which involved actually buying stocks or securities regulated by the SEC. When the CFTC was created in 1974—in response to a Ponzi-type options scam that bilked investors of some $70 million—it was given "exclusive" jurisdiction over commodity futures and certain commodity options, although a last-minute Treasury amendment exempted bank currency forwards (and later swaps) from CFTC jurisdiction. The legislation, however, left considerable ambiguity as to what a "commodity" was; indeed, the law seems to define almost *anything* as a commodity. Since the SEC had more or less equivalent jurisdiction over "securities," there ensued a fifteen-year catfight over whether, say, GNMA futures and options were commodities or securities. An early-1980s truce achieved an approximate sorting out of jurisdictions, establishing, for example, that stock index futures were the CFTC's responsibility while individual stock options belonged to the SEC—although disputes still crop up from time to time.

The basic problem, of course, is that modern hybrid instruments aren't easily classifiable one way or the other. One judge deciding an SEC-CFTC clash over futures-like stock "index participations" likened it to deciding "whether tetrahedrons belong in square or round holes." Consider, say, a zero-coupon structured note that accrues interest at a fixed rate but has the additional fillip that the principal at maturity is partly dependent on the price of oil or some other commodity. Since the early 1990s, the practice has been to apply standard options-pricing math to separately value the "commodity-dependent" and the "commodity-independent" components of the note, irrespective of how they are labeled. If the structured note's oil futures component is the most valuable, jurisdiction lies with the CFTC, otherwise with the SEC. Rough-and-ready rules of decision like these are inelegant, but they may be more practical than intellectually satisfying grand realignments.

Steven Wallman, a former SEC commissioner, has recently proposed a broad "goal-oriented" restructuring of regulatory responsibilities. He suggests, for example, that the Federal Reserve might exercise oversight over all financial activities that pose "systemic" risk; that an SEC-like organization might be responsible for all consumer protection and fraud issues; that an FDIC-like organization could look after solvency and insurance questions; while some new entity crafted from pieces of existing agencies would supervise markets and exchanges. Wallman's taxonomy of objectives is useful and ingenious, but such a comprehensive rejiggering of responsibilities would be almost inconceivably complicated, and if the history of jockeying between the SEC and CFTC is any guide, probably quite impracticable.

A more important question than *who* should regulate is *what* should be regulated. Several years ago, for instance, Lowell Bryan, the head of the financial institutions consulting practice at McKinsey, proposed dividing the banking system into regulated and (relatively) unregulated segments. "Basic" banks would take insured deposits at low rates of interest and provide checking and other transactional monetary services, operating under strict and detailed regulations to assure the smooth functioning of the country's monetary system. All other bank businesses would be hived off into broadly gauged financial services companies, much like full-service investment banks, subject only to the SEC, CFTC, exchange, and other regulations that normally apply. Their depositors would get higher interest rates, but without the protection of insurance. Given the popularity of money-market mutual funds with check-writing privileges, one could argue that the industry has been quietly restructuring along these lines anyway, although regulatory structures lag considerably behind.

There has also been a strong recent push for further deregulation of derivatives. The vast majority of derivative transactions are already substantially unregulated. They are executed in the OTC (off-exchange, "over-the-counter") market, usually with commercial or investment banks as counterparties, and are subject neither to exchange rules nor to CFTC or SEC oversight. Bills have been introduced in the Congress that would, in their stronger versions, greatly expand the class of exempt transactions by deregulating most commodity trading between "professional persons," and also streamline or eliminate CFTC approval of new futures contracts. According to the CFTC, which is strongly opposed to the bills, they would exempt up to 90 percent of currently regulated trading. The legislation has received strong support from major trade groups, like the Futures Industries Association, and the major commodities exchanges.

The contrasting industry and CFTC arguments are illuminating. The CFTC tends to wave the consumer protection flag. Deregulation, it argues, would mean abolishing, for most trading, "registration, fitness standards, risk disclosure to customers, recordkeeping and sales practice standards . . . [and standards relating to] segregation of customer funds, net capital requirements, financial reporting, margining of accounts, and special bankruptcy protections." The industry responds, essentially, that the markets have professionalized so fast that consumer protection is a side issue. In his Congressional testimony, the chairman of the Chicago Mercantile Exchange emphasized the explosive growth in OTC markets compared with the relative stagnation of CFTC-regulated exchange-based trading, and stated, "The argument that the CFTC's style of minute regulation strengthens markets by increasing the confidence of market users is a regulator's fantasy. No market or market user believes it. Has any segment of the OTC derivatives market been heard to demand the right to operate under the aegis of the CFTC in order to inspire customer confidence? Has the swap market been stunted by the lack of federal oversight?" The deregulation push is ironic, for only a decade ago, in the wake of the market crash, Congress was teeming with proposals to *tighten* trading regulation.

As of early 1998, the deregulation legislation is not likely to pass in any of its current forms, but it poses difficult questions that apply to every market. When regulated and unregulated markets exist side by side, as is the case with exchange-traded and OTC derivatives, the regulated markets are inevitably at a cost disadvantage. Burgeoning offshore markets only exacerbate the problem. But at the same time, unregulated markets feed off the stability of the regulated portion of the industry—the OTC derivatives markets rely on the availability of highly liquid, standardized, exchange-traded contracts for the raw material to construct their own highly customized instruments. The CFTC, in fact, has been trying to reduce its regulatory intrusiveness, although obviously too hesitantly to satisfy its industry. In much the same way, over the past decade or so the SEC has steadily broadened its exemptions for transactions between professional investors and traders and various classes of "qualified" individuals, on the sensible principle that people well able to look after themselves should do so.

Abstracting from all these developments, there are some clear trends:

- The long-term regulatory tendency will be toward a more sharply tiered system of oversight, based not on institution type but on the financial function being performed, the presence of systemic risk, and the relative competence and power of the parties to a transaction.
- The protective function of regulation will focus on transac-

tions where the customers are households and small businesses. Transactions between institutions will continue to be deregulated, subject to after-the-fact interventions in instances of fraud or sharp practices. Bankers Trust, for example, had a free field to sell whatever it wanted to Gibson Greetings or Procter & Gamble, who should have known better. But the CFTC and the SEC still had the authority to discipline the traders who were shown to have engaged in sharp practices, and the companies recovered much of their losses in court.

- Standards of capital adequacy will gradually substitute for prescriptive operating regulations. Since the institution of the Basle Accords in 1988, capital-to-asset ratios in the banking system have more than doubled, and market forces are pushing toward stronger capital bases for most financial institutions. Sophisticated swaps customers closely scrutinize the capital adequacy of their counterparties. The recent wave of mergers among investment banks and brokerages is driven primarily by the necessity for improving the efficiency of capital deployment. Controversies will center on the degree to which capital standards should be codified in regulations or left to the judgment of markets. The "right" answers will be different in different markets and different businesses at different times.

- The locus of domestic financial regulation will continue to migrate away from states to the federal government. Competition between state and federal thrift regulators was a source of mischief in the 1980s S&L crisis, and with the steady securitization and demutualization of the insurance industry, the current state-based insurance regulatory system, with its quirky accounting and capital standards, is becoming an expensive and troublesome anomaly. Local regulation undoubtedly permits more fine tuning in pursuit of local objectives than is possible in a unitary national system. Mortgage bankers who source through brokers, for example, are subject to federal antidiscrimination regulations, but if they don't open local offices, they escape local antiredlining rules. Banking and insurance, however, are no longer local businesses, and for all their occasional virtues, antiquated state regulatory systems are too often just snug little political sinecures that have long outlived their usefulness.

Finally, a word about hedge funds. The crisis at Long Term Capital Management has led to a chorus of demands for regulation of hedge funds, as also happens after each emerging-market currency crisis. Not much will come of it. Most hedge funds, in any case, are registered offshore so they can't be forced into detailed disclosures by American regulators. Further, the wealthy and sophisticated investors in hedge funds don't need the government to look after them. Who cares if John Meriwether, Myron Scholes, or UBS of Switzerland loses a bundle in a hedge fund? The SEC monitors the net capital levels of major securities firms, but none of the firms that sustained equity losses at LTCM was even remotely close to endangering its capital adequacy.

The core problem disclosed by the LTCM fiasco was that banks and securities firms were too lenient in their lending. Because of the reputation of the LTCM principals, few of the lending institutions made any inquiries at all regarding the degree of leverage the fund was employing, or the liquidity of its portfolio. While the loans were usually fully collateralized with liquid instruments, the banks were not nearly so protected as they thought. The firm's core portfolio comprised highly illiquid instruments with highly volatile capital values. If LTCM had tried to sell off its portfolio to meet margin calls in the August–September crisis, its portfolio value would have plummeted, and the banks would have found their collateral tied up in a bramble of crisscrossing repo agreements and other claims.

There is no denying that the crisis at LTCM posed a systemic risk, but that was true only because the principals had been allowed to play with so much money. Dumb lending is usually at the heart of any financial crisis. Normally, funds employing LTCM's strategies would have been required to post substantial excess collateral to cushion against rapid market movements, which would have the further effect of reducing their leverage. Both the Federal Reserve and the Comptroller of the Currency have tightened up their oversight in the wake of the LTCM incident (they monitor lending procedures, not individual loans) and, without much prodding, banks and securities firms have called in their lines to hedge funds that look at all risky. Indeed, some of the sharp yen-dollar movements in the fall of 1998 may have related to the rapid deleveraging of speculative securities positions at hedge funds and trading firms. (Ultra-low-interest yen loans are usually at the base of current leveraging strategies.)

Officials and regulators will always be confronted with dilemmas when dumb decisions threaten the viability of apparently critical institutions. But the very arguments for deregulation—that unfettered markets improve system flexibility and liquidity—imply that the financial system will be able to absorb business failures more readily. At the end of the day, the LTCM crisis was managed quite smoothly, and the failure of Barings amounted to hardly a hiccup. Contrast that with the worldwide chaos unleashed by the failure of the Creditanstalt, a mid-sized Austrian bank, in 1931. Occasions will still arise when the cost of prolonging a crisis seems clearly to outweigh the value of the salutary lessons to be learned from allowing it to run its course. Sometimes governments will have to step in, as was deemed wise in the recent cases of Mexico and Korea. Officials can only follow the dictates of common sense as circumstances dictate.

If it is true, however, that the overall trend is toward greater deregulation, at least among professionals, then standards of disclosure become commensurately more important. But in the recent past, controversies over disclosure issues have been at least as fierce as those over deregulation.

Disclosure

It wasn't the size of the early 1990s string of major-company derivatives losses that was so scary, but that they appeared out of the clear blue sky. Diligent analysts, who thought they understood a company's strategy and competitive position, found earnings expectations shattered as if by some malign genie. Simply outlawing derivatives, as many clamored, would be foolish, since they are such valuable adjuncts to financial management. The proper response, clearly, is to *disclose*—to set out a company's derivatives position in such a way that investors can tell how much risk a company has taken on. Would that it were so easy.

The responsibility for establishing financial disclosure standards, and opining on difficult questions, rests with an independent, private organization, the Financial Accounting Standards Board, or "Faz-bee." FASB is directed by a board of prestigious senior accountants, academics, and former company CFOs. Both the SEC and the American Institute of CPAs treat the board's rulings as authoritative, so they are effectively binding on any business that publishes financial results. American accounting standards may be the strictest and most complete in the world, as foreign companies hoping to trade on American exchanges often discover to their grief. In 1993, for instance, when Daimler-Benz registered its securities in America, six-month results that had been reported as a gain of DM168 million in Germany were converted to a loss of almost a billion marks under American rules. The great depth and liquidity of American financial markets is at least partly due to the generally high quality and integrity of American financial reporting.

FASB rulings are often controversial, however. The rule-making process is public, so financial executives are free to lobby, and sometimes they succeed in beating back FASB initiatives. There was a storm of protest when FASB insisted that companies report retiree health-benefit liabilities in 1990. One writer said that the change "would cripple the competitiveness of thousands of American companies, put untold billions of dollars of business loans into default, send stock prices skidding, and deprive many workers of health care benefits after retirement." But FASB managed to make the rule stick, even though GM, for example, saw its reported net worth shrink from $27 billion to $6 billion overnight. It's no accident that the corporate drive to control health care benefits dates from the time companies were forced to own up to their true costs.

FASB was less successful with a 1993 proposal to require companies to report the "fair value" of employee stock options. Most stock-option plans grant a future right to buy the company's stock at the market price at the time of the grant. Standard practice was to value such options at their "intrinsic value," which was held to be zero, since at the time of the grant the stock price and exercise price were the same. But it is clearly absurd to treat stock options as if they are valueless, since they are among the most eagerly sought after of all benefits. Reasonably enough, therefore, FASB proposed pricing the options at their fair value at the time of the grant, using Black-Scholes or other standard models, and expensing them as a cost of compensation.

The proposal was greeted with such shock and horror by financial executives that one could never have guessed that you can calculate option values on a standard hand calculator. In the event, FASB backed down: While strongly encouraging fair-value option costing, it still permits intrinsic-value accounting. It's hard to understand what all the shouting was about. Microsoft may be the most avid user of employee stock options of all big companies, but when it applied the fair-value methodology to its 1997 financials, reported earnings were reduced from $2.63 a share to $2.42. Not trivial, but hardly worth going to the wall over, and the disclosure probably increased the company's credibility with investors. A Harvard Business School study suggested that the most vociferous protesters were companies whose CEOs had very large option packages, and *Business Week* speculated that the protests were "just a smoke screen to avoid publicizing bosses' high pay."

But the stock-option battle pales against the storm that broke over FASB's efforts to upgrade derivative accounting. The American Bankers' Association was particularly active in organizing opposition, and there were proposals in Congress to reduce FASB's power or eliminate the organization altogether. The Financial Executives' Institute, an association of company CFOs, suggested cutting off its funding, and even Federal Reserve Chairman Alan Greenspan weighed in on the bankers' side. The opposition grew to such a pitch that it prompted several alarmed speeches by Arthur Levitt, chairman of the SEC, who warned against jeopardizing the delicate public–private partnership that the FASB-SEC arrangement represents. The new standards were finally adopted in 1998 after years of delay, and will start to take effect in 1999. The SEC plans to adopt parallel requirements effective in 2000. So far, at least, the sky has not fallen, and the banks have enthusiastically carried on their newly accustomed business of buying and selling one another.

In principle, it's not hard to value derivatives. The fair value of a derivatives contract is the price you could sell it for, or would have to pay someone to take it off your hands. There are, to be sure, problems valuing highly customized contracts, but widely accepted modeling techniques generate approximate results. Even flawed valuations would be more informative than currently prevailing historical-cost accounting, which tells investors very little. Under current rules, a very risky swap—say, receive fixed and pay some LIBOR-squared formula on a large notional principal— might not appear in the financial statements at all if no cash changed hands at contract time. If the swap then goes badly wrong, the cash outlays would be recorded on the income statement as they occur, or might even be hidden in the balance sheet. FASB's proposals would make the company carry the full present value of the swap on its balance sheet and then, as rates move, show changes in the value of the swap as a profit or loss. Most well-run financial companies already present such information in their financial footnotes.

But apparently straightforward accounting questions have a way of getting very gnarly. Suppose your company has borrowed money through a fixed-rate noncallable bond. Later, you become unhappy with your fixed-rate commitment because you think rates might fall, so you enter into a receive-fixed/pay-floating swap. But you guessed wrong and rates rise, so you have to record a loss on your pay-floating liability. Fair enough, you say, but there were *two* sides to this transaction. Now that rates have risen, your obligation on the fixed-rate bond looks much more palatable—in fact, other borrowers would pay a premium to borrow at that rate. So you should be able to post a *gain* on your pay-fixed bond to offset the loss on your pay-floating liability. Marking to market in this way, however, is usually reserved for securities in trading accounts, while normal debt outstanding is just listed at its historical amount. But still, it would be misleading to record gains and losses from just one side of a hedged position, and it could discourage sensible hedging activities, so FASB agreed that both sides of a hedge could be fair-valued, even if one of the legs is an instrument that otherwise would not ordinarily be treated that way.

But that creates a new problem: how do you tell what's a hedge? A treasurer who has taken a big loss on a dumb derivatives contract could scurry around at the end of a reporting period looking for offsetting instruments that he could revalue to cover up his losses. And what if a hedge is effective only over time? You might take losses on one leg of a position this quarter, but offset them with gains on the other leg in the next. What if you're hedging a contract you haven't entered into yet? Or creating a hedge against the interest portion of a contract but not the credit portion? And so on. FASB seems to have worked diligently to come up with reasonable answers for all these cases, but as might be imagined, the process stretched through hundreds of hearings and generated thousands of pages of testimony and FASB drafts and commentary, and a book-length FASB research report exploring the underlying issues.

The truth is, any solution will be messy. Some of a company's outstanding bonds will be carried at fair value while others are carried at historical value, depending on whether or not they're hedged. The matching rules will miss some offsetting legs of some hedges. For instance, some banks hedge their deposit liabilities, but deposits are hard to mark to market because their true cost includes branch overhead and other customer services. So for the moment, at least, FASB won't permit fair-valuing deposits—which the banking industry tried to inflate into an argument for dropping the proposals altogether. A much more conceptually elegant approach would be to require that companies carry *all* financial assets and liabilities at fair value, whether they're hedged or not. Most accounting-standards bodies, in fact, think that's the way to go, but the complexities are daunting, and companies who do not normally engage in hedging activities are understandably skeptical. Much of the groundswell against the FASB plan came from smaller banks, who do not make extensive use of derivatives, but who feared that the proposals were just the first step on the road to full fair-value accounting.

The complexities of derivatives accounting aren't FASB's fault, however. Over the past generation, financial managers have accumulated a vast and complex armory of risk-management tools that can't be captured by simple accounting statements; simplicity, in this case, amounts to concealment. There are a few cases where the FASB rules will probably make earnings look more volatile than they really are—as in the case of a bank-deposit hedge, where only one side of the position is fair-valued. But the old rules erred in the opposite direction, and allowed potentially huge sources of earnings volatility to go unreported altogether. Concepts and formulas that seemed hopelessly arcane just ten or fifteen years ago are now part of everyday financial parlance. It may take another ten years for investors and accountants to catch up, but the sooner started the better.

Systems

Charlie Hallac and, until the fall of 1998, Dan Napoli* headed up risk management at Blackrock Investments and Merrill Lynch respectively, and their approaches to their jobs illustrate the promise and the limitations of systems as a risk-management tool.

Blackrock is an investment management firm with about $100 billion of assets under management at the end of 1997. All its clients are large institutional investors—pension funds, insurance

---

*Napoli was reassigned following the LTCM fiasco in the fall of 1998. To an outsider, the move looked like scapegoating. LTCM directly violated the tenets of the "anti-star" system that was fundamental to Napoli's risk-management program (see below). But the credits to LTCM, and presumably the decision not to require normal documentation, were approved at the very highest levels of Merrill, and the company's top dozen or so executives were investors in the fund. The lesson of LTCM in all likelihood is not that the internal risk management system was faulty in itself, but that senior management circumvented it. Merrill was extremely cooperative in providing material and interviews for this book, but as of this writing was not talking about LTCM.

companies, and the like. The company's founder and CEO is Larry Fink, the primary inventor of CMOs; the firm got its start in the mid-1980s selling closed-end mortgage-backed funds but has since expanded into virtually every major class of security. CMOs and other mortgage-backeds present unusually complex risk-management and computational issues (see Chapter 8), so Blackrock placed heavy emphasis on systems and risk control from its inception, and was distinguished as one of the few major mortgage-backed players to come through the 1994 CMO crisis relatively unscathed.

From a risk manager's perspective, Hallac is triply blessed. In addition to his hat as risk manager, he is in charge of Blackrock's systems, and has had the luxury of building them from scratch, using modern languages and modern client-server and database technologies. All the firm's securities are in a single database that drives all the trading, accounting, and other auxiliary systems—a trader cannot make a trade that the accounting system does not know about, or which is outside the trader's transaction authority, or which violates the firm's risk-management parameters, because those controls are built into a unitary processing stream. Maintaining that discipline requires that no product be introduced unless all the system elements are in place. "There's inevitably pressure to cut corners rather than miss the market on a hot new product opportunity," Hallac says, "but Larry's always held the line, because risk management and systems are such an important part of our reputation."

Napoli's approach at Merrill Lynch was necessarily different. The firm's worldwide assets under management are approaching $1 trillion, and it trades nearly $100 billion in securities for its own account. His department was created in the wake of Merrill's 1987 mortgage-backed trading fiasco (see Chapter 7), after an internal postmortem made it plain that Merrill had no comprehensive picture of its exposures. Merrill is an aggressive technology investor, but the firm has a vast range of businesses operating in locations throughout the world and has no choice but to depend on huge, batch-oriented "legacy" systems for key accounting and portfolio-management functions. There is no practical possibility of its constructing a Blackrock-style single-database securities-management system within the foreseeable future. Merrill has at its disposal all the same analytic technologies as Blackrock and engages in extremely sophisticated exposure modeling, but it can never be absolutely sure that it has caught every trade or every important term in a derivatives contract. So Napoli paid equal attention to creating checks and balances and layers of reviews to ensure that a disinterested human judgment is superimposed on all critical transactions.

The precise design of a risk management system is probably less important than the attitude. At Merrill, the checks and balances were built in by having Napoli and his staff report directly to the very top of the company, outside of the normal operating channels. Ticket clerks no longer work for the traders, as they did in 1987. Now they report up a separate line to operations and accounting, and they can't go home unless every trade is fully accounted for. A "twists and wrinkles" committee looks at anything that appears out of the ordinary, even if it's making money— *especially* if it's making money. Napoli preached skepticism of easy profits, and "stars" were to be regarded with suspicion. "The star system was the root of the problem in 1987," he said. "Now, if a trader starts making a lot of money, I tell my staff to *assume* he's cutting corners somewhere, and we'll look extra hard at the risks he's undertaking. For example, some of our older systems probably have the same accounting anomalies that Joe Jett took advantage of at Kidder. But I like to think we would have been all over him as soon as he started booking such big profits, and would have caught it pretty quickly."

Both Hallac and Napoli are relatively young men, but their careers span a revolution in financial technology. "In the mid-1980s," Hallac said, "if you wanted to do a comparatively simple 5 to 10 tranche CMO, you had to run it overnight or on a weekend. I show the kids on our trading desk the mortgage yield books we used in the seventies and early eighties. They think it's hilarious that we actually looked up yields in a table. Computing really shaped the industry's development. Ten years ago there was no point even thinking about most of things we just take for granted now."

The same systems that helped create the bewildering variety of new instruments and trading technologies also offer unprecedented tools for understanding and managing risk. It's fairly routine now to display for a fixed-income portfolio, in addition to the maturity and yield of each instrument, its duration (the volatility of yield with respect to rate changes), its convexity (the volatility of the volatility of yield), the volatility of the instrument's spread over treasuries, and so on down the analytic ladder. At Blackrock, Hallac's system monitors portfolio volatility with respect to the entire treasury yield curve—what happens to the whole portfolio when the two-year rate changes but not the five-year, and vice versa. (Since any portfolio can be decomposed and reconstructed out of other instruments, everything is relevant.) There is much greater precision in identifying and calculating the impact of embedded options. Even a plain vanilla instrument like a treasury future embodies options—there is a time window for settling a contract, a choice among conforming instruments, and so forth, all of which create opportunities for profits and losses.

Huge leaps in processing power mean there is less need to rely on simplistic models that, for example, assume bell-shaped outcomes when empirical evidence shows that they are sharply skewed, or which place arbitrary limitations on external variables to keep the calculations manageable. Portfolio managers now run "lattices," like the decision trees of a chess-playing computer. Simulate a long series of events, like rate changes or nonparallel shifts in the yield curve, on a complex portfolio, and the interaction of securities can produce surprising results that conventional models would have missed. Stress testing of portfolios is now standard practice—assume some outrageous external event that wreaks havoc in the markets and see what happens to your portfolio.

But no one pretends that computers are the whole answer. Even the best chess-playing computers can test only so many moves ahead. At some point, the analyst must fall back on simplifying models or give up the game, and sometimes—less often than formerly, but still sometimes—the models are just wrong. Both Hallac and Napoli are skeptical of "value at risk" calculations that model the effects of, say, the craziest week in the past ten years on current portfolios, because they easily miss lurking long-dated options, and no models factor in events like a Russian default.

Gains on one side of the ledger are often offset by risks on the other. The recent spate of mergers among large financial firms, like Travellers' combination of Smith Barney and Salomon, and Citicorp and Travellers, will allow cost-savings and operational efficiencies that should improve the ratio of capital allocated against each business, which is to the good. But the mergers will inevitably increase systems risk, at least in the short term. Few legacy systems are completely documented—as the difficulties in fixing the "Year 2000 Problem" demonstrate—so there almost certainly will be hiccups as the companies press toward system mergers. The reports of managerial chaos at the Citicorp/Travellers "Citigroup" elevates concerns. Although the SEC issues systems-policy guidance memoranda and inspects for compliance, it does not have the capacity to conduct full-blown audits of systems and risk-management capabilities. Perhaps it should.

American regulatory jurisdiction applies primarily to American securities and securities firms, but the buzzword of the 1980s and 1990s has been "globalization," which introduces a different set of questions.

Globalization

The globalization of high finance is a centuries-old phenomenon, and the basic issues have changed little over the years. Can investors get good information from a foreign country? As the recent experiences of Thailand, Indonesia, and Korea demonstrate, it's not much easier now than it was a hundred years ago. Can investors rely on foreign governments not to interfere with their profits by mucking with exchange rates or capital flows? The answer, as always, is—not always.

Diversification, in academic theory, reduces volatility, and therefore risk, and so academics argue that the wise investor allocates a portion of her portfolio to foreign securities. Whether the academics are right is not clear; the added risk from currency adjustments may well offset any diversification gains, as has certainly been the case in the latter half of the 1990s. Most of the time, however, investors send their money overseas not in pursuit of a theoretically ideal portfolio but because they are chasing *yield*. Investors who take risks with their eyes open have nothing to complain about, but mutual fund yield chasing stung many small investors during the European currency convulsions of the early 1990s. What could sound safer than a "short-term government income fund"? It took gimlet-eyed investors with a taste for fine print to figure out that those high yields came from *foreign* money market instruments and leveraged positions in foreign-currency derivatives. Disclosure standards, however, have been steadily tightened over the past several years.

Informing domestic investors that they are actually buying foreign securities is the easy part. The more difficult challenge is to achieve sufficiently common standards of disclosure, capital adequacy, and trading procedures throughout the world such that that investment can safely flow to the most productive channels regardless of national boundaries. At first blush, since there is no regulatory agency with the authority to insist on international standards, the task might appear hopeless, but voluntary initiatives have managed to make quite impressive progress in recent years. While the current situation is far from ideal, the recent track record suggests the possibility of continued progress.

The 1988 Basle Accords for capital adequacy in international banks is the most striking example of international regulatory cooperation. The banking authorities of the "Group of Ten" industrial countries adopted uniform rules for measuring banking capital and assigning capital requirements against various classes of assets. The rules had real bite: the Accords set a standard bank capital ratio of 8 percent of weighted assets, half of which had to be "Tier One" capital—essentially primary equity or unrestricted cash reserves. Most American banks had to double their capital base to meet the standard, and in Japan and some European countries, the required capital increases were by a factor of four or five or more. Severe discounts were also applied to the "hidden equity" that Japanese and continental banks frequently use to manipulate their balance sheets. All of the major G-10 country banks achieved the Basle standards by about 1995. Maintenance of compliance has become virtually a Good Housekeeping Seal for participation in quality international transactions; noncompliant banks are usually unacceptable as OTC derivatives counterparties or must pay a heavy financial penalty to participate. Of major recent concern is the failure of Japanese authorities to recognize the full extent of the bad loans on their banking sector's balance sheet, and the resort to gimmicky expedients, like market write-ups of equity holdings, to maintain Accords compliance. Regulatory pusillanimity in Japan could threaten the consensus behind the Accords, or more probably, merely further reduce the competitiveness of Japanese banks in international transactions.

The standards are far from perfect, and contain a residue of politics—for example, all OECD government debt is treated as if it were of equivalent creditworthiness, which is ridiculous. The Basle Committee on Banking Supervision has published a number of extensions and amendments to the basic Accords to keep up with market developments, and has also adopted uniform regulatory standards, including standards regarding derivatives reporting, most of which have been adopted by the participating countries. As of early 1998, the Committee was publishing draft proposals for innovative market-oriented risk-measurement rules that would allow institutions considerable leeway in adopting home-grown risk-measurement methodologies, as long as the techniques meet Committee standards of adequacy. Economists are hopeful that model-based risk measures, since they would implicitly allow the differential treatment of government debt, may offer a quiet way to strengthen the system without provoking embarrassing nationalistic arguments.

Regulation coordination in securities is not nearly as advanced as it is in banking, but there has been considerable coordinative activity over the past several years. Following the 1995

Barings crisis, the futures-trading regulators of the United States, the U.K., Japan, Hong Kong, and Singapore agreed to strengthen procedures to prevent default and to protect customer funds. The initial agreements were expanded into cooperative arrangements involving twenty-three countries, and active work is under way on developing international best practice and disclosure standards. The SEC and its counterparts in most of the developed countries have also formed several joint working groups with the Basle Committee to strengthen in-country regulation of multinational entities.

The American insistence on open markets and full disclosure is often viewed as a ploy to facilitate the colonization of foreign financial sectors by powerful American firms. It probably is. Irritatingly enough for non-Americans, amid the shattered wreckage of the "Asian system" of secretive, "relationship-based" corporate financial and business networks, it is hard to think of an alternative. For the foreseeable future, as long as the capital base and global reach of American financial services firms outstrip those of any conceivable national competitors, the international financial regulatory environment is likely to acquire an increasingly American look.

The question remains: How can the government anticipate the crash of Lucas Lizard's CIP empire? One constant in all the crises reviewed throughout this book is that the regulatory responses come only *after* a crisis hits its peak. The United States began to standardize disclosure and accounting standards for securities offerings only after the massive fraud of the 1920s and the ensuing market crash. It took the S&L crisis of the 1980s to bring honest accounting for thrifts, and it wasn't until the banking sector suffered huge losses in real estate and foreign loans that regulators began to enforce stringent capital standards. The junk-bond market was already collapsing when the Federal Reserve tightened up on LBO lending in the late 1980s, and it was only after the implosions at Drexel and Kidder that federal auditors began to look more closely at the real risks of the paper firms were carrying on their balance sheets. Regulators had recommended separating accounting and trading functions for decades, but Merrill Lynch didn't take the advice seriously until it was hit with big mortgage-backed losses, and no one really applied the pressure until after the fiasco at Barings. It took a long string of losses in derivatives trading before banking authorities, securities regulators, and accounting standards boards began to address in a concentrated way the difficult issues of risk analysis and reporting. International investors have relied on foreign central bank reports for many decades, but it is only now, perhaps, after a long string of currency crises, that bond buyers and international monetary authorities seem determined to insist that they mean something.

That regulators should be always in the position of sweeping up broken glass after the event is hardly surprising, given the cycle of innovation and crisis described in the previous chapters. In almost every case, the financial system responds spontaneously to new demographic, economic, or technological developments. The improvisation brilliantly solves the immediate problem and earns big profits for the innovators. Imitators come pouring in, push the new solution to its limits, and precipitate a crisis. The crisis works its course, latecomers take big losses, academics and regulators figure out what happened, and then institutions—regulatory systems, accounting procedures, disclosure rules, capital standards—catch up.

It may never be possible for authorities to anticipate all, or probably even very many, of the changes afoot in the financial system. Such wisdom and efficiency is not to be achieved in this world. But it may be possible to catch some. The trick is to tap into the innovations in their early stages. Herewith a modest proposal: Regulators should ask the dozen or so top financial services firms to fill out a simple questionnaire at the end of each year that shows what their most recent crop of top business school hires are working on—not just their general assignments but precisely what they're doing. In the early and mid-1980s, the brightest kids were going into junk bonds and LBOs. A few years later, the rocket scientists were taking over, and the emphasis was derivatives, CMOs, and exotic portfolio strategies. Emerging-market equities were hot in the early 1990s. Eastern European markets may be drawing the best graduates now.

Two decades is a short sample, but it does suggest that crises follow the talent with a lag of about three years. Plenty of time to set up SWAT teams and shore up systems for when the deluges break—as they always do and inevitably will.

NOTES

Introduction

The Law and Bubble anecdotes are from Charles Mackay, *Extraordinary Popular Delusions and the Madness of Crowds* (New York: Harmony, 1980). The book was originally published in 1841. The quotes are from pp. 62–63.

ONE Boom and Bust in Early America

Bray Hammond, *Banks and Politics in America from the Revolution to the Civil War* (Princeton: Princeton University Press, 1991), an update of a book originally published in 1957, is still the *locus classicus* for nineteenth-century American finance. For wildcat banking, see pp. 600–626. The "furioso" quote is on p. 601. For American conditions in the first twenty years of the decade, see Henry Adams's famous accounts in his *History of the United States During the Administrations of Thomas Jefferson* (New York: Library of the Americas, 1996), pp. 5–121, and *History of the United States During the Administrations of James Madison* (New York: Library of the Americas, 1996), pp. 1287–1300. Population data are from the U.S. Dept. of Commerce, Bureau of the Census, *Historical Statistics of the United States: Colonial Times to 1970* (Washington, D.C.: U.S. Government Printing Office, 1975). For the chronic American capital shortage, see Frederick G. Jensen, *Capital Growth in Early America* (New York: Vantage Press, 1965). The Adams quote is from his *Jefferson,* p. 43. For the development of modern trade regimes, see Fernand Braudel, *Civilization and Capitalism, 15th–18th Century: Vol. 3, The Perspective of the World* (New York: Harper & Row, 1984).

The "key weapon" and Amsterdam quotes are from pp. 66 and 245, respectively. For Biddle and the Second Bank of the United States, besides Hammond, Thomas Payne Govan, *Nicholas Biddle: Nationalist and Public Banker, 1786–1844,* offers an extremely detailed account of the Bank's operations. And for the interplay between Biddle and the Barings, besides Govan, see Ralph Hidry, *The House of Baring in American Trade and Finance: English Merchant Bankers at Work, 1763–1861* (Cambridge: Harvard University Press, 1949). Govan and Hidry cover almost all the same episodes in roughly the same detail, but Govan with an American spin, and Hidry with a British one. The Viner quote and Biddle's "It is difficult" are from Hammond, pp. 32 and 307–8, respectively. Baring's "Now just observe" is from Hidry, p. 114; the "gets in all" and Bates's "more straightforward" are from ibid., p. 113.; "the central banking" is in Hammond, p. 441.

The account of Jackson's veto mostly follows Hammond, supplemented by Robert Remini, *Andrew Jackson and the Course of American Democracy, Vol. 3, 1833–1845* (New York: Harper & Row, 1984). The Gouge and Calhoun quotes are from Hammond, pp. 608, 609, and 607; "dressing up" is from 443. Hammond points out that by paying off the national debt, Jackson was simply substituting one set of liabilities for another. The argument is that a funded national debt would have provided a base for creating an indigenous system of credit that could be expanded as the national productivity grew; without that capital base, credit was provided by foreigners.

For Jacob Barker, the most complete available account of the takeover episode is his own defense, consisting mostly of his lawyer's speeches in various courts and newspaper clippings. See Jacob Barker, *The Conspiracy Trials of 1826 and 1827: A Chapter in the Life of Jacob Barker* (Philadelphia: George Childs, 1864). Remini presents Biddle's postveto behavior in the worst possible light, accusing him of engineering a "murderous squeeze" (p. 111) on the economy in order to force a reversal of the veto, but even Remini concedes that Jackson had no idea of the importance of the Bank to the economy; nor did Jackson appreciate the financial self-interest of many of his advisers in the demise of the Bank.

For Ward and the Barings, I follow Hidry. Ward's "is my knowing" and his quotes on individuals, Bates's "The system of," and Ward's credit classifications are from pp. 158, 133, and 296, respectively. There is also a collection of useful essays on this period in Robert Fogel and Stanley

Engerman, *The Reinterpretation of American Economic History* (New York: Harper & Row, 1971).

TWO Fleecing the British

For the legend of Gould, see Matthew Josephson, *The Robber Barons: The Great American Capitalists, 1801–1901* (New York: Harvest Books, 1962), and Charles Francis Adams, Jr., and Henry Adams, *Chapters of Erie* (Ithaca, N.Y.: Cornell University Press, 1956). A thorough revisionist history is Maury Klein, *The Life and Legend of Jay Gould* (Baltimore, MD: John Hopkins University Press, 1986). The quote from Josephson is on p. 147; the Adams quote is from *Chapters,* p. 105; and the Drew quote from Klein, p. 3. In general, I follow Klein, although the Adamses have much colorful detail on the Erie wars.

The quote from Dickens is from his *The Life and Adventures of Nicholas Nickleby* (New York: Penguin Books, 1978, p. 76). For the evolution of corporate law in America, I relied on Lawrence M. Friedman, *A History of American Law* (New York: Touchstone, 1985). Robert Higgs, *The Transformation of the American Economy, 1865–1914, an Essay in Interpretation* (New York: John Wiley, 1971), stresses the criticality of a modern system of property and commercial law to an industrial transformation. The Adams quote on corporations is from *Chapters,* pp. 96–97.

The quotes from Trollope's *The Way We Live Now* (New York: Oxford University Press, 1941) are on pp. 324, 325, and 327. For the Union Pacific and Credit Mobilier, besides his *Life,* I used mostly Maury Klein, *Union Pacific,* vol. 1 (Garden City, NY: Doubleday, 1989). For the development of the rail industry, I also used Robert Fogel, *Railroads and American Economic Growth: An Essay in Econometric Interpretation* (Baltimore, MD: Johns Hopkins University Press, 1964); Robert Fogel and Stanley Engerman, *Reinterpretation*; Alfred D. Chandler, *The Railroads, the Nation's First Big Business* (New York: Harcourt, Brace, 1965), and *Scale and Scope: The Dynamics of Industrial Capitalism* (Cambridge, Mass.: Harvard University Press, 1990).

The statistics on American economic growth are all drawn from *Historical Statistics.* For postwar price trends and capital inflows, see also James Kindahl, "Economic Factors in Specie Resumption: the U.S., 1865–1879," in Fogel and Engerman, *Reinterpretation,* pp. 468–79. A good general history of the period is Sean Dennis Cashman, *America in the Gilded Age, From the Death of Lincoln to the Rise of Theodore Roo-*

sevelt (New York: New York University Press, 1993). The Nevins quote is from his *John D. Rockefeller: The Heroic Age of American Enterprise* (New York: Scribners, 1940), vol. 1, p. 444. For comparative American-European income data, see David Landes, *The Wealth and Poverty of Nations* (New York: Norton, 1998), pp. 232 and 294–309, plus Landes's skeptical discussion of the sources in the chapter notes.

Morgan's restructuring of the railroads mostly follows the accounts in Ron Chernow, *The House of Morgan: An American Banking Dynasty and the Rise of Modern Finance* (New York: Atlantic Monthly Press, 1990), and in Higgs, *Transformation.* The details of the 1901–7 merger movement are from Ralph L. Nelson, *Merger Movements in American Industry* (Princeton, N.J.: Princeton University Press, 1959).

THREE Fleecing the Middle Classes

For Andrew Carnegie, Joseph F. Wall, *Andrew Carnegie* (Pittsburgh, Pa.: University of Pittsburgh Press, 1989), is the most recent of many biographies; for Morgan, Ron Chernow, *The House of Morgan: An American Banking Dynasty and the Rise of Modern Finance* (New York: Atlantic Monthly Press, 1990). The "Anabaptist" quote is in Wall, p. 784. In current dollars, the creation of U.S. Steel was the largest leveraged buyout in history until the 1989 RJRNabisco deal.

Carnegie's testimony is reprinted in William S. Stevens, ed. *Industrial Combinations and Trusts* (New York: Macmillan, 1914), a fascinating compilation (pp. 112, 116–117). For Standard Oil, see Ron Chernow, *Titan: The Life of John D. Rockefeller, Sr.* (New York: Random House, 1998), which supersedes Allan Nevins, *John D. Rockefeller: The Heroic Age of American Enterprise,* 2 vols. (New York: Scribners, 1940), although Nevins has rather more detail on the high-quality internal administration of Standard Oil. Chernow documents Rockefeller's reliance on political corruption, which Nevins omitted, although he apparently had the evidence. Rockefeller would presumably have justified the bribery by arguing, with considerable truth, that the country's primitive political and legal institutions did not contemplate an organization like his. Politicians therefore lined up to be paid so he could go about his business. (Without excusing all of John D.'s methods, it is something of an anachronism to read modern concepts of monopoly and common-carrier obligations, relative to railroads and pipelines, back into the 1870s and 1880s.) The "astonished" is from Nevins, vol. 1, p. 476; Rockefeller on Morgan, Chernow, p. 390. Gary on Gary dinners is from Stevens, pp. 387 and 392. For Charles Schwab, see Robert Hessen, *Steel Titan, the Life of Charles M. Schwab* (New York: Oxford University Press, 1975). The quote from Taylor is from p. 167. For wartime investment banking, see besides Chernow, Vincent Carossa, *Investment Banking in America: A History* (Cambridge, Mass.: Harvard University Press, 1970). The Warburg quote and that from the "later scholar," Edwin Gay, are on p. 238.

The history of the Pecora investigations follows Carossa and Chernow. The quote from Allen is in John Kenneth Galbraith, *The Great Crash, 1929* (Boston: Houghton, Mifflin, 1961), p. 82. The exchange with Dillon is in Carossa, p. 346. For Insull, see Forrest McDonald, *Insull* (Chicago: University of Chicago Press, 1962), especially pp. 237–301.

FOUR   White-Collar Willie Suttons

A great many books have been written on the S&L disaster. The ones I found most useful were Martin Mayer, *The Greatest Ever Bank Robbery* (New York: Scribners, 1990); John R. Barth, *The Great S&L Debacle (Special Analysis 91-1),* (Washington, DC: AEI Press, 1991), which has many useful compilations of data; and Lawrence J. White, *The S&L Debacle: Public Policy Lessons for Bank and Thrift Regulation* (New York: Oxford University Press, 1990). White is a finance professor who was a member of the Bank Board during the height of the S&L disaster. While his book is a bit defensive, it offers an illuminating view of how apparently reasonable steps by intelligent people could compound to catastrophe.

Various committees of both the Senate and the House also conducted numerous hearings. See the useful chronology and illuminating testimony of Herbert Sandler, a successful, and conservative, California S&L operator, in "The Savings and Loan Crisis," in *Field Hearings Before the Committee on Banking, Finance, and Urban Affairs,* House of Representatives, 101st Congress, First Session, Jan. 12–13, 1989. The legislative and regulatory events are generally well covered in the *Congressional Quarterly* and the *Congressional Quarterly Almanac,* while many articles in *American Banker* cover developments from an industry perspective. I also benefited greatly from an extended interview with Dick Bianco, a former investment banker turned S&L operator, who is CEO of Ambase, Inc. All of the numbers on taxpayer costs and losses from individual institutions are, unfortunately, approximations drawn primarily from the contemporary financial press. FDIC staff—who appeared to be trying to be helpful—say that the confusion of shutting down the old Bank Board and FSLIC, and absorbing them into the FDIC, left a considerable snarl of records; in addition, the problem S&Ls have long since been merged out of existence (some through multiple mergers), so it is almost impossible to track losses to any particular operation.

The St. Germain quote and the "knock you" quote are from the *Congressional Alamanc*'s annual S&L issue reviews in the 1982 and 1989 editions, respectively. The "much more sophisticated" quote is from my Bianco interview. The Mayer quote is from p. 74 of *Bank Robbery*, while the Greenspan quote is from a letter reproduced in ibid., pp. 334–36.

FIVE Mephistopheles

For the colorful story of Milken and junk bonds, emphasis on the color, see James R. Stewart, *Den of Thieves* (New York: Touchstone, 1962), and Connie Bruck, *The Predators' Ball: The Inside Story of Drexel Burnham and the Rise of the Junk Bond Raiders* (New York: Penguin, 1989). Stewart headed the *Wall Street Journal* team that covered the insider-trading and junk-bond scandals; his book was a runaway bestseller, and has become the standard account. His condemnations of Milken seem much stronger than his own evidence supports, however, and as he concedes in the notes, he follows Boesky's highly prejudicial, and probably prejudiced, account of Milken's dealings throughout. (Boesky's plea deal depended heavily on his delivering Milken.) Daniel Fischel, *Payback: The Conspiracy to Destroy Michael Milken and His Financial Revolution* (New York: HarperBusiness, 1996), is an important corrective to Stewart's account, although Fischel probably goes overboard in the other direction. On the question of whether Milken actually committed serious crimes, as opposed to possibly numerous securities record-keeping violations, Fischel seems to have by far the stronger case. For a highly favorable view of junk bonds, see Glen Yago, *Junk Bonds: How High-Yield Securities Restructured Corporate America* (New York: Oxford, 1990). Yago is a bit of an apologist for the industry, but is more reflective of the academic consensus on the contribution of junk bonds than the scandal-flavored accounts of Stewart and Bruck.

During the mid-1980s, my primary occupation was as a valuation consultant for several LBO funds, so many details of buyout operations and procedures are drawn from that experience. Dick Omohundro, Joe Coté, and John Frebota, of Prospect Street Investment, headed Merrill Lynch's junk-bond operations during the 1980s, and were generous with their time and files. For data on high-yields and on the bond market generally, I used, e.g., *The High-Yield Annual Review,* published by Chase Securities, *The High-Yield Handbook,* published annually by First Boston, and a wealth of internal studies and academic papers furnished by Prospect Street, in addition to other standard market sources. Details on individual transactions are all available in the financial press and analysts' reports.

SIX   A Question of Scale

The account of the Drysdale episode is drawn primarily from SEC testimony provided under the Freedom of Information Act—*In the Matter of Drysdale Government Securities, Inc.,* File NY-5463, including testimony by Richard J. Higgerson, one of Chase's senior officers and Demmer's ultimate superior, June 23, 1982; Peter Demmer, June 21 and 22, 1982; and Thomas C. Melzer, head of Morgan Stanley's government trading desk, December 15, 1982. In their testimony, Drysdale principals Richard Taafee and David Heuwetter simply resorted to the Fifth Amendment. A detailed contemporaneous account is Chris Welles, "Drysdale: the Untold Story," *Institutional Investor,* September 1982, pp. 454–68, which is excellent for color and overview but not always reliable on details.

Heuwetter's employer was technically Drysdale Government Securities, a Drysdale subsidiary, but the subsidiary was created only in February 1982, and in any case proved an insufficient shield for the parent. In the text I report that the Chase law department "apparently assured" Demmer that he was only an agent. Their actual advice was not revealed because of lawyer-client privilege, but the whole course of the testimony makes it clear that Demmer was still confident that he was acting as an agent *after* he had been advised by the lawyers, except for the few instances in which Demmer or his staff had actually signed principal agreements. The "eventual loss" quote is from Demmer, pp. 363–64. Morgan's offsetting tactic is from Melzer, pp. 45–48, where he rather uncomfortably walks a tightrope of describing the offsets against Chase while denying that his firm knew that Drysdale was on the other side.

The most accessible history of modern portfolio theory is Peter L. Bernstein, *Capital Ideas: The Improbable Origins of Modern Wall Street* (New York: Free Press, 1992). My appreciation to Doug Love, founder of

Buck Pension Consultants, who for a number of years has been my primary resource for modern portfolio theory. The individual investor study "Why Do Investors Trade Too Much?," by Terrence Odean of the University of California at Davis, was reported in *The Wall Street Journal,* May 16, 1997.

Details on arbitrage are drawn mostly from the financial press, and on yield-curve arbitrage in part from Jay Borker, one of the early practitioners at Greenwich Capital. The quote on index arbitrage is from "A New Breed of Investor is Whipsawing Wall Street," *Business Week,* September 23, 1985. The futures-vs.-stock market transaction cost study is cited in Frank Fabozzi and Franco Modigliani, *Capital Markets: Institutions and Instruments,* 2nd ed. (Upper Saddle River, N.J.: Prentice Hall, 1996), p. 364. The 1990 index arbitrage study is George Sofinaos, "Index Arbitrage Profitability," *Journal of Derivatives* (Fall 1993).

The chronology of the 1987 market crash follows the hour-by-hour account in the Brady Commission Report, *Report of the Presidential Task Force on Market Mechanisms* (Washington, D.C., USGPO, January 1988). The quote in the text is from p. 69. There are a number of other major reports on the events, by the SEC, the CFTC, the GAO, and the London Stock Exchange, among others. Generous excerpts are conveniently collected in Robert J. Barro, et al., eds., *Black Monday and the Future of Financial Markets* (Homewood, Il: Dow Jones-Irwin, 1989), which amounts to an academic riposte.

The CFTC, which was anxious to fend off proposals for folding it into the SEC, commissioned three leading financial theorists—Merton Miller, Myron Scholes, and Burton Malkiel—plus a regulatory lawyer, John Hawkes, to conduct its study. Their conclusions also appeared as the article "Stock Index Futures and the Crash of '87," *Journal of Applied Corporate Finance,* Winter 1989, pp. 4–19. The academics argued that the role of portfolio insurance in the crash was usually overstated. Market values had risen some $600 billion between January and October 1987, so the $100 billion in insured assets were only a small percentage of the previous year's rise, hardly enough, they argued, to cause a crash. That argument, however, may not sufficiently recognize the effect of increased selling at the margin, particularly when basic systems are under strain— even modest amounts of abnormal selling pressure could trigger a system breakdown. They were on stronger ground respecting margin requirements: the daily cash settlement provisions in futures markets invalidate simple comparisons of margin percentages. Data on market performance during the 1997 downturn are from the NYSE and the CME. For a professional review of the post-crash regulatory changes, see "Black Monday, Ten Years Later," Remarks by Federal Reserve Governor Susan B. Philips, October 15, 1997; and Testimony of Brooksley Born, CFTC Chairperson before the Subcommittee on Securities of the Senate Banking, Housing, and Urban Affairs Committee, January 29, 1998.

SEVEN Black Magic

The description of the Rubin incident is based primarily on an interview with Dan Napoli, the senior risk-management executive at Merrill Lynch, supplemented by reports in the financial press. The details of the Orange County incident are primarily from *Report of an Investigation in the Matter of County of Orange, California, as It Relates to the Conduct of the Members of the Board of Supervisors,* U.S. Securities and Exchange Commission Release No. 36716, January 24, 1996; and *SEC Initiates Actions in Orange County Investigation,* U. S. Securities and Exchange Commission Litigation Release No. 14792, January 24, 1996. The Barings episode is based primarily on Judith H. Rawnsley, *Total Risk: Nick Leeson and the Fall of Barings* (New York: HarperBusiness, 1995), a precise account with a minimum of dramatics, supplemented by the financial press. The Jett incident is based on *In the Matter of Orlando Joseph Jett and Melvin Mullin,* U. S. Securities and Exchange Commission Administrative Proceeding, File No. 3-8919, May 20, 1996, supplemented by the financial press, especially an exceptionally detailed reconstruction in *The New York Times,* April 6, 1997.

There are many texts on derivatives-based trading and hedging. I found Atsuo Konishi and Ravi Dattatreya, eds., *A Handbook of Derivatives* (Chicago: Irwin, 1996), to be quite useful, as was an interview with Dattatreya. The prices in the 1992 IBM option example are from the weekly Value Line Options Survey. The Black-Scholes model was originally published in Fischer Black and Myron S. Scholes, "The Pricing of Options and Corporate Liabilities," *Journal of Political Economy,* May–June, 1973, pp. 637–54. The formula is:

$$C = SN(d_1) - Ee^{-RT}N(d_2), \text{ where}$$

$$d_1 = \frac{\ln(S/E) + [R + (1/2)\sigma^2]T}{\sigma T^{1/2}},$$

$$d_2 = d_1 - \sigma T^{1/2},$$

C = option price,
R = risk-free interest rate,
S = stock price,
Σ = volatility,
E = exercise price,
T = time to expiration of the option,
$N(d_1)$, $N(d_2)$ = probability values for d_1 and d_2.

The solution for d_1 also gives the "hedging ratio" for constructing a fully hedged portfolio. For a discussion of the model's unrealistic assumptions, see Fischer Black, "How to Use the Holes in Black-Scholes," *Journal of Applied Corporate Finance,* Winter 1989, pp. 78–83.

The discussion of the BancOne hedging strategy is from the bank's annual reports and 10ks; Ben Esty, Peter Tufano, and Jonathan Headley, "BancOne Corporation: Asset and Liability Management," *Journal of Applied Corporate Finance,* Fall 1994, pp. 33–56; and a discussion with John Russell, Jay Gould, and Steven Bloom from the bank's investor relations and treasury departments. All quotes are from the article except for that of Mr. Russell. One of the consequences of BancOne's hedges is that it enables them to simulate, e.g., positions in long-term CMOs, while avoiding the extra capital requirements normally associated with actual CMO holdings, which has the effect of enhancing the bank's apparent return on capital. In addition to counterparty risk, the swaps will generate unrealized gains and losses as interest rates fluctuate and the two legs of the swap are marked to market—if the swap is a perfect match, the changes should cancel out, but that is rarely the case in the real world. BancOne's total swap position, for instance, produced an unrealized gain of $47 million in 1995 and an unrealized loss of $38 million in 1996. If the gains and losses were brought into income, as the the new FASB rules will require, net income would have been approximately 1.5 percent higher in 1995 and 1.2 percent lower in 1996.

The referenced 1993- and 1994-vintage studies and statements include Federal Reserve Board, "Response to Questions Posed by Congressman

Leach," October 6, 1993; *Mutual Funds and Derivative Instruments,* U.S. Securities and Exchange Commission, Study Prepared for House Subcommittee on Telecommunications and Finance, September 26, 1994; *Financial Derivatives: Actions Needed to Protect the Financial System,* U.S. General Accounting Office, May 18, 1994; and Global Derivatives Study Group, *Derivatives: Practices and Principles,* Group of Thirty, Washington, D.C., July, 1993.

The details of the Bankers Trust/Gibson imbroglio are primarily from *In The Matter of Gibson Greetings, Inc., Ward A. Cavanaugh and James H. Johnson,* U.S. Securities and Exchange Commission Administrative Proceeding File No. 3-8866, October 11, 1995; and *In the Matter of Gary S. Missner,* U.S. Securities and Exchange Commission Administrative Proceeding File No. 3-9025, June 11, 1996. (Missner was a BT Securities employee who sold many of the derivatives to Gibson.) Generous selections from the tapes appeared in the financial press. See, for example, Kelley Holland, Linda Himmelstein, and Zachary Schiller, "The Bankers Trust Tapes," *Business Week,* October 16, 1995. The Metallgesellschaft episode is a greatly simplified version of the discussion in Christopher L. Culp and Merton H. Miller, "Metallgesellschaft and the Economics of Synthetic Storage," *Journal of Applied Corporate Finance,* Winter 1995, pp. 62–77. The CFTC inquiry into MGRM is Commodities Futures Trading Commission, *In the Matter of MG Refining and Marketing, Inc. and MG Futures, Inc.,* CFTC Docket No. 95-14, July 27, 1995. The quotes from Dattatreya and Voldstad are from interviews.

The LTCM story was extensively, almost interminably, covered in the financial press, although the principals were uniformly silent. A federal working group on hedge funds and over-the-counter swaps (of the kind that BancOne used) had been convened but had not yet reported when this chapter was completed. There are a number of official analyses of the LTCM events: See, for example, the statements of Julie L. Williams, acting Comptroller of the Currency; William J. McDonough, president of the Federal Reserve Bank of New York; and Richard R. Lindsey, director, Division of Market Regulation, Securities and Exchange Commission, all before the House Committee on Banking and Financial Services, on October 1, 1998.

EIGHT Mortgage Mayhem

My thanks to Larry Fink of Blackrock Investments, and to Tom Potts and Hance West, CEO and chief trader, respectively, of Dynex Financial

Corporation, for very helpful interviews. My primary source of statistics cited in this chapter is *The Mortgage Market Statistical Annual* (Washington, DC: Financial World Publications, 1996). Data on interest rates and mortgage spreads are from Federal Reserve series. I also found Frank Fabozzi, ed., *The Handbook of Mortgage-Backed Securities* (Chicago, Ill.: Probus Press, 1995), to be the most helpful of the many texts on the subject. My appreciation to Professor Kenneth Rosen of the UCal, Berkeley Economics Department and the staff at FNMA for clarifying issues related to the CMO influence on mortgage-treasury spreads.

Fink's original Tricycles were to be treated as clean sales of assets for tax and accounting purposes, which was consistent with the treatment of the Motorcycles. The Treasury put the kabosh on the sales treatment at the last minute, Fink believes, because the Reagan administration was working on a mortgage financing scheme of its own and didn't want Freddie Mac stealing their thunder. CMOs were treated like bonds and appear as debt on the issuer's balance sheet, hence the name. Freddie Mac decided they had the capital strength to carry the CMOs as debt and so went ahead with the program anyway. The REMIC legislation essentially permitted clean sale treatment for CMOs, which greatly increased the universe of possible issuers. Since the instruments are no longer obligations of the issuer, the designation "CMO" is anomalous, but no one seems to mind.

Among the many articles in the financial press on mortgage-backeds and CMOs, Michael Carroll and Alyssa A. Lappen, "Mortgage-Backed Mayhem," *Institutional Investor* (July 1994), pp. 81–96, is unusually complete. The Askin quotes are from this article. The official account of the failure of Askin Capital is in *In the Matter of Askin Capital Management, L.P., and David J. Askin,* U.S. Securities and Exchange Commission, Administrative Proceeding File No. 3-8710, May 23, 1995. The SEC memorandum details the sequence of margin calls, but without naming the firms making the calls; the identification of Bear, Stearns as the first mover is from the financial press. Because he is still involved in litigation, Askin declined to be interviewed for this chapter.

NINE   **Mr. Zedillo and Mr. Suharto Meet Mr. Gould**

The list of recent financial crises is from Morris Goldstein and Philip Turner, "Banking Crises in Emerging Economies: Origins and Policy Options," *Bank for International Settlements (BIS) Economic Paper,* October 1996. Data on American development crises are from the Commerce Department's *Historical Statistics,* and also see the sources cited in Chapters 2 and 3.

In general, data on recent currency crises were drawn from International Monetary Fund (IMF), *World Economic Outlook,* "Interim Assessment: Crisis in Asia, Regional and Global Implications," December 1997, and *World Economic Outlook,* May 1998, which offer a wealth of statistical data and analyses; IMF, *International Capital Markets: Developments, Prospects, and Key Policy Issues,* November 1997; BIS, *International Banking and Financial Markets Developments,* November 1997; and BIS, *Annual Report,* 1996 and 1997. Data on the Mexican economy are primarily from the series maintained by the Inter-American Development Bank; and for the Asian economies, by the Asian Development Bank. David Hale, the chief economist of Zurich-Kemper Financial Services, has published a number of insightful newsletters on both the Mexican and the Asian crisis.

For the Mexican peso crisis, the 1995 hearings before the Senate Banking, Housing, and Urban Affairs Committee contain an excellent collection of papers from many of the leading economists interested in the issue. Other papers I found helpful include Bradford DeLong, "The Mexican Peso Crisis: In Defense of American Policy Toward Mexico," *Foreign Affairs,* May–June, 1996 (longer version at http://econ161. berkeley.edu/Econ_Articles/); Nora Lustig, "The Mexican Peso Crisis: the Foreseeable and the Surprise," *A Brookings Working Paper,* The Brookings Institution, June 1995; Jeffrey Sachs, Aaron Tornell, and Andres Velasco, "The Real Story," *International Economy,* March–April, 1995; IMF, *Pamphlet Series No. 50,* "Lessons from Mexico for IMF Surveillance and Financing"; and the World Bank Group, "Mexico: Country Overview," in *Trends in Developing Economies, 1996.* The David Hale quote is from his letter, "Emerging Markets After the Mexican Crisis," January 17, 1995.

In addition to the sources cited above, I found the following sources helpful on the crises in Asia: Stanley Fischer, "The Asian Crisis: A View from the IMF," January 1998; Shigemitsu Sugisaki (Deputy Managing IMF Director), "Economic Crises in Asia," January 1998; Subir Lall, "Speculative Attacks, Forward Markets, and the Classic Bear Squeeze," *A Working Paper of the International Monetary Fund,* December 1997; and Paul Krugman, "Currency Crises" and "What Happened to Asia," both available from Krugman's web site, http://www.mit.edu/ krugman/. The IMF Country Stand-by Arrangements can be found on the IMF web site, http://www.imf.org. The 22-country study is Jeffrey

Sachs, Aaron Tornell, and Andres Velasco, "Financial Crises in Emerging Markets: The Lessons from 1995," Harvard University, Weatherland Center for International Affairs, WPS Paper No. 97–1.

TEN   Reflections on Regulation

Doug Love, IGF's CIO, provided much background material on the insurance industry, and we had a great deal of fun inventing the Lucas Lizard scenario. For a capsule history of the SEC-CFTC jurisdictional spat, see Wendy L. Gramm and Gerald D. Gay, "Scams, Scoundrels and Scapegoats: A Taxonomy of CEA Regulation over Derivative Instruments," *The Journal of Derivatives,* Spring 1994, pp. 7–24. The judge's quote is from the article. Steven Wallman's proposal is in his "Technology and the Securities Markets," *The Brookings Review,* Winter 1998, pp. 26–29. The competing quotes on commodities deregulation are from CFTC Chair Brooksley Born, "Caveat Emptor—Let the Buyer Beware," Remarks Before the End-users of Derivatives Association, April 11, 1997; and "The Dangers of Deregulation," Remarks to the Futures Industries Association, March 13, 1997; Testimony of John F. Sandner, CME Chair, before the Senate Committee on Agriculture, Nutrition, and Forestry, February 11, 1997, and before the House Committee on Agriculture, April 15, 1997. Robert Merton, "Financial Innovation and Economic Performance," *Journal of Applied Corporate Finance,* is a lucid overview of some issues relating to innovation and regulation.

Arthur Levitt, Chairman of the SEC, presents a thumbnail history of the FASB/SEC relationship, which includes the press quotes on the health-benefit and stock rulings, in "CPAs and CEOs: A Relationship at Risk," Remarks Before the The Economic Club of Detroit, May 19, 1997. On stock options, my thanks to Mark Neagle, FASB options project director for background information. Harold Bierman, L. Todd Johnson, and D. Scott Peterson, *Hedge Accounting: An Exploratory Study of the Underlying Issues* (Norwalk, Conn.: Financial Standards Accounting Board), is a thorough treatment. For current issues and controversies, I relied on, among other documents, the FASB Task Force Draft "Accounting for Derivative Instruments and for Hedging Activities," September 12, 1997, version (the most recent available), which contains many examples of the principles in practice, and in Appendix B, a detailed justification for the Board's decisions; submission and attachments of the American Bankers' Association to FASB (letter of Paul Salfi to

Timothy Lucas, October 14, 1997); letter of Edward Yingling, ABA Chair to Senator Phil Gramm, November 11, 1997; and letter of Alan Greenspan to Edmund L. Jenkins (FASB Chair), July 31, 1997. I also benefited from interviews with Bob Wilkins, FASB derivatives project director, and Salfi.

My appreciation to Dan Napoli and Charlie Hallac for extended interviews on systems and risk-management questions. The quotes are from the interviews. Frank Fabozzi, ed., *Advances in Fixed-Income Valuation, Modeling, and Risk Management* (New Hope, Pa.: Fabozzi Associates, 1997), surveys the current state of the art.

The "Basle Accords" are Bank for International Settlements, Basle Committee on Banking Supervision, "International Convergence of Capital Measures and Capital Adequacy" (July 1988). For reviews of current cooperative initiatives, see, for example, Brooksley Born, "The CFTC's International Initiatives in a Global Marketplace," Remarks Before the Exchequer Club, December 17, 1997; Federal Reserve Governor Susan D. Philips, "International Competition: Should We Harmonize Our National Regulatory Systems?," Remarks at Seminar on Banking Soundness, January 28, 1997; Deputy Treasury Secretary Lawrence H. Summers, "Building a Global Financial System for the 21st Century," Address to the Congressional Economic Leadership Council, August 12, 1997.

The placement office at Harvard Business School very kindly supplied Wall Street placement information for its last decade of graduates, but the information is not specific enough for the analysis suggested here.

INDEX

ABOUT THE AUTHOR

CHARLES R. MORRIS has many highly praised books to his credit, ranging from the fall of IBM (*Computer Wars*) to the rise of the American Catholic church (*American Catholic*). He has published his opinion pieces in *The New York Times*, *The Wall Street Journal*, *The Atlantic*, *The New Republic*, *Harvard Business Review*, and The *Los Angeles Times*. His wide-ranging career experiences include: managing partner of Devonshire Partners, a consulting firm; group executive at Chase Manhattan Bank; secretary of health and human services for the state of Washington, and assistant budget Director of New York City.